NATURAL MAN

A RECORD FROM BORNEO

The Author.

NATURAL MAN

A RECORD FROM BORNEO

BY
CHARLES HOSE, HON. SC.D. (CANTAB.)

MEMBER OF THE SARAWAK STATE ADVISORY COUNCIL
FORMERLY DIVISIONAL RESIDENT, AND MEMBER OF THE SUPREME
COUNCIL OF SARAWAK
AUTHOR OF "A DESCRIPTIVE ACCOUNT OF THE MAMMALS OF BORNEO,"
AND JOINT AUTHOR WITH PROFESSOR WILLIAM MCDOUGALL OF
"THE PAGAN TRIBES OF BORNEO"

WITH A PREFACE BY
PROFESSOR G. ELLIOT SMITH, F.R.S.

AND AN INTRODUCTION BY
BRIAN DURRANS

*WITH ILLUSTRATIONS AND A MAP SHOWING
THE DISTRIBUTION OF THE TRIBES*

SINGAPORE
OXFORD UNIVERSITY PRESS
OXFORD   NEW YORK
1988

Oxford University Press

Oxford   New York   Toronto
Delhi   Bombay   Calcutta   Madras   Karachi
Petaling Jaya   Singapore   Hong Kong   Tokyo
Nairobi   Dar es Salaam   Cape Town
Melbourne   Auckland
and associated companies in
Berlin   Ibadan

Oxford is a trade mark of Oxford University Press

Introduction © Oxford University Press 1988
First published by Macmillan and Co., Limited, London, 1926
First issued as an Oxford University Press paperback 1988

ISBN 0 19 588886 3

Printed in Malaysia by Peter Chong Printers Sdn. Bhd.
Published by Oxford University Press Pte. Ltd.,
Unit 221, Ubi Avenue 4, Singapore 1440

INTRODUCTION

This engaging book, which was first published in 1926 and has never been reprinted until now, did more than perhaps any other to dispel the stereotype of Bornean savagery from the public mind. Its author was one of the great figures in the history of colonial Sarawak, with a role and reputation to match his portly frame. In upriver longhouses, old people can still recall or relay stories about his physical size, how news of his imminent arrival sent young men scurrying into the forest for timber to reinforce the floors. Yet Hose and what he did are hardly as well known as they deserve to be. *Natural Man* is an uncosmetic portrait of the people behind the headhunting image and, despite its subtitle, was not just a 'record' of Borneo but an attempt to influence opinion. It cannot be fully appreciated, therefore, without a perspective on its author and his motives.

Charles Hose (1863–1929) was born in Hertfordshire, England, the second son of a clergyman of modest means and genteel connections. His childhood was split between rural Norfolk, where he showed an interest in natural history, and Felsted, a public school in Essex, where he was good at sports. His up-bringing fitted him for a respectable but uninspiring future, and when the young man entered his father's old Cambridge college in 1882 he probably had little idea of what to do with his life.

Then came a chance to change the whole course of his career. Through the intervention of his uncle, Bishop Hose of Singapore, Charles was offered an administrative cadetship in Sarawak under the second Rajah, Sir Charles Brooke. He seized the opportunity, abandoned his studies, and in 1884 left Liverpool for Kuching. He was not yet twenty-one, but his lack of formal qualifications and private means were offset by a good measure of self-confidence. The young Hose was now out to prove himself in a challenging career and to indulge his typically late-Victorian zeal for observing, classifying, and collecting the works of man and nature in the wonderful tropical environment that lay waiting for him. He had little to lose and a great deal to achieve.

Hose made rapid progress. After only four years of outstation apprenticeship, he was appointed Officer in Charge of the Baram District, becoming Resident (Second Class) three years later in 1891. The work gave great scope to his love of natural history and—as this book shows—to become familiar with the way of life of the various peoples in his charge.

For Hose, the indigenous people, animals, and plants were of compelling interest in their own right. Although his ethnographic studies were certainly pursued in fruitful collaboration with his administrative work, and therefore assisted the Brooke regime, one gets the impression that while he was in Borneo this practical application was only a supplementary excuse for how he preferred to spend his time. Later, however, a more developed argument emerged in some of his published writing, in which he explicitly justified studying local traditions as a means of enlightened colonial rule—the fullest statement of these views is given in Appendix B of his last book, *Fifty Years of Romance and Research* ... (1929). But essentially, and in the best sense, he was an enthusiastic amateur scientist for whom almost everything was worthy of attention.

Although always important to him, this side of his life eventually came to compensate for disappointment in his professional vocation. In the special conditions of colonial Sarawak, Hose seems to have been too successful an administrator for his own good. With his limitless fascination for the ethnography and natural history of the country, Hose was the ideal Resident in an area remote from the capital and other Europeans, and because he was unquestionably effective in maintaining order and handling local problems, the Rajah left him there longer than other officers would have tolerated. But if Hose's talents might have been even more productively harnessed in a higher post, the Rajah's loss was to benefit science. As he came to resent a lack of progress in his paid employment, Hose more than made up for it by building a reputation around observations and collections.

By 1904, when he was elevated to Resident (First Class) and given a lateral transfer to the Third Division at Sibu, Hose was a noted figure in Bornean studies. Then in his early forties, he got married, started a family, and three years later, doubtless with the future of his young son in mind, took early retirement on a pension, to which his long service now entitled him, of half his official salary. Punctuated by occasional visits abroad, the rest of his life was busy but largely spent in places that for an Englishman were unadventurous: he settled in due course in his childhood village of Roydon, spent most of World War I in King's Lynn in charge of a munitions factory, and ended his days in Surrey.

His retirement was an anticlimax, however, only in contrast with the exotic setting of his salaried career, for with the advantage of more spare time and fewer distractions, Hose now pursued his interests in the people and natural history of Sarawak as energetically through writing and lecturing as he had done through field observations and collecting while in the Rajah's service.

While he could not support his dependants exclusively on what he might earn from his knowledge of Borneo, writing became a minor means of supplementing his official pension and also fulfilled his main objective of consolidating a scientific reputation and disseminating what he saw as the wider lessons to be drawn from his experience of ethnography and colonial administration. Letters written to colleagues and friends shortly before his retirement suggest that at this time he was not well off. The causes are not hard to find. As if being the second son of a clergyman were not bad enough, his hospitality to foreign scientists and explorers visiting the Baram had drained his resources, and the Rajah refused to cushion his officers' salaries against a worsening exchange rate for the Straits dollar.

He served on the Sarawak State Advisory Council at Westminster, helped prepare the Sarawak pavilion for the 1924 British Empire Exhibition at Wembley, made several return visits to Sarawak, and through collections and publishing managed to convert his jungle experience into deserved prestige and some income. Perhaps the most important instance in which this paid dividends was when he deftly helped the Anglo-Saxon Petroleum Company to develop the oilfield near the coast at Miri. As if to compensate for the loss of income occasioned by the delay of his last promotion, the deal benefited not only the Rajah but also

Hose himself. In part, it repaid his diligence in recording evidence of oil while in government service, but more especially (since Hose's predecessor, C. C. de Crespigny, had noted it first) his consistent faith that oil production was economically viable despite an unenthusiastic earlier survey by a consultant geologist. In biding his time, pressing his argument only after he had retired from the Sarawak service, Hose may well have had his own financial interest in mind, and in eventually negotiating a commercial contract he used managerial skills probably learnt as much in the Residency or Fort at Marudi as in Kuching. If this was the intelligently executed strategy of a man out for compensation for under-rewarded service, the Rajah could hardly complain. Appropriately enough, production at Miri declined after a maximum of five and a half million barrels in 1929, the year Hose died.

In this as in other activities connected with Borneo that occupied his later years, Hose was perhaps justified in trading on the past. When this book first appeared, the experiences it recorded were already twenty-two years old; but far from reducing their interest, this enhances their status as episodes and reflections the mature author thought most worth recording from a life spent observing and trying to understand indigenous Sarawak. His past was so full of interest and adventure, and the bankable benefit he derived from it so meagre by contrast, that we can be thankful that the author, who was no sluggard even near the end of his days, chose to share it at all. If little or no evidence survives of his talks, lectures and fireside anecdotes, we at least have his books, published papers, photographs and artefact collections—the latter scattered among several museums—to give a flavour of Borneo as Hose knew it.

* * *

Natural Man was rightly acclaimed as a useful précis of *The Pagan Tribes of Borneo* (1912), the standard two-volume treatise Hose wrote with the assistance of Professor William McDougall, then of Oxford. In his review in the anthropological journal *Man*, Professor A. C. Haddon of Cambridge calls it a 'skilful abridgement', but complains that while it includes many photographs not previously published in the larger work, some descriptions are harder to understand in their revised form, and that Hose fails to present much new information about the natives themselves.

Haddon was perhaps the most eminent anthropologist to review the book, and was certainly highly respected by Hose himself, but his criticisms now seem narrow-minded. Others made similar comments but it must be remembered that these were all specialists judging the book according to specialist standards and addressing a select audience that was almost certainly not the one for whom the book was primarily written. If he was unfair to criticize the shorter book for omitting new details, Haddon at least perceived that *Natural Man* 'will be useful to those who cannot afford the larger book'. With hindsight, we can recognize Hose's book as much more than a 'skilful abridgement'. *Natural Man* remains in its own right a valuable introduction to some of the inland peoples of Borneo, vividly written and testifying to the author's deep involvement with his subject. However, the book is also historically informative precisely because, as a popularization of the larger work, it presents, like *Pagan Tribes* and the great anthropological classics of the day, the kind of ethnology that aroused the interest of the more general public Hose was addressing, but in a more accessible package. *Pagan Tribes* sold at forty-two shillings in 1912; in 1926, *Natural Man* could be bought for thirty. Adjusted for changes in the value of money and cost of living over the fourteen years in between, this made *Natural Man* about 40 per cent more affordable in real terms.

Who were the intended readers of the original edition of *Natural Man?* They were not restricted to those subscribing to specialist journals, but neither was Hose writing for the masses. They were probably like himself, from a similar social and cultural background. He would in any case have found it natural to address an audience of this kind, perhaps because one of his main objectives was to set out evidence in such a way as to convince his readers that the interpretations he put forward were relevant to the way they would encounter their own society, in the same terms—deference and authority, compassion and discipline—that structured his own upbringing and outlook.

In this respect, it is interesting to note that only a few months after *Pagan Tribes* was published, Hose wrote to his publisher, Daniel Macmillan, saying he had declined an offer from another publisher, Hutchinson, to follow this up with a popular book on the peoples of Borneo. Almost certainly, Hutchinson's had in mind a book similar in scope and style to what eventually appeared as *Natural Man*. In the same letter, Hose tried to persuade Macmillan to publish a sequel to *Pagan Tribes* which would also be written with William McDougall, with the aim of answering all the important questions raised in reviews of the two-volume work, and claimed that Sir James George Frazer and other leading anthropologists backed this idea. There were certainly strong academic grounds for writing at greater length on aspects of traditional Sarawak inadequately covered in the earlier work. But perhaps because of Hose's preoccupation with the war effort, the book was never commissioned and it was not until April 1925, by which time the author may have realized he might not have another chance to write it at all, that Macmillan's undertook instead to publish the present book.

Although aimed at a wider market than the earlier work, *Natural Man* is no simplified version; its content is not rendered-down so much as selectively extracted and revised from the earlier two volumes. We get a distinct impression that its intended readership was just as interested in tribal cultures and their implications for interpreting the human condition as were the specialists for whom the original work was written. The two audiences differed not only in income and motivation but also in the uses to which they might conceivably put Hose's arguments and insights.

Besides presenting copies of *Pagan Tribes* to all the prominent anthropologists of his day, Hose was especially pleased to learn that by 1924 his book was recommended reading for cadets in the Sarawak administration. He was not only out to impress experts—something he achieved, with reservations—but it is important to realize he also wanted to influence the lay reader. A less expensive précis of the larger book might reasonably be expected to appeal to a wider public as the work of an already established authority, and justifiably so. At one point, the publisher suggested the book should be called 'Borneo and its

Jungle-Folk', but Hose dissuaded him. The title eventually chosen implies that Hose wanted his book to contribute to the contemporary debate about the plasticity of 'human nature' and social institutions. However patronizing it may seem to us, the term 'jungle-folk' was retained by Hose in the text itself to attack the predominant idea that these people were contemptible savages. This is a point that now seems worth considering, as it did to the diffusionist Professor Elliot Smith in his thoughtful introduction to the book; but this argument, with its reference to the popular ideology of the time, was ignored by most specialist reviewers who were therefore unable to set the book in its proper context.

In his sympathetic descriptions of their cultures, Hose champions the right of at least some colonial subjects to be assessed on their own terms, and even suggests that the Edwardian English might learn lessons in living from the native peoples of Sarawak. This makes him sound remarkably modern. At the same time, he had fairly predictable prejudices of his own. He particularly respected the Kenyah and Kayan peoples, with whom he had close connections. As a middle-class late Victorian, he found much to admire in their hierarchical societies and their readiness to follow their leaders. Administering such people was a relatively straightforward matter of winning over a few chiefs, even if some of them might later change their minds. He also liked the nomadic Punan, who lived in small, unstratified groups and threatened nobody, least of all Europeans. But the Iban, although 'agreeable companions', had 'too little respect for their chiefs' and were 'truculent'. It seems no coincidence that they were historically the main resistance to Brooke rule. As a major force, the Iban had been subjugated with real British savagery under James Brooke and even if they still caused the government problems in the first few years of the twentieth century, their use by the regime as punishment squads against other peoples is a measure of how thoroughly their resistance was broken. To Hose, an aggressive mien like that of the Kayan, or an egalitarian one like that of the Punan, was acceptable as long as it did not threaten British power. While this view of Hose's seems to have been deep-seated and accords with a wider prejudice among Sarawak's Europeans at the time, in his case it is also a function of the area in which he spent most of his time. On the Baram, he would in any case have had much more to do with Kenyah–Kayan groups than with the Iban.

* * *

It would be easy to criticize the style and content of the book with the hindsight of sixty years. We now know a great deal more about the cultures of Borneo than Charles Hose did. Haddon's review noted the misleading title, among other defects. Few would now agree with Haddon that even the Punan can be regarded as near to a state of nature, but he was certainly right to argue that other Bornean peoples, with complex social systems and long histories of interacting with others, are very far from 'natural'. While several of Hose's speculative ideas about the origins and culture histories of Bornean peoples have been justifiably criticized, specialists have failed to grasp the popular, imaginative appeal that such speculations had and were doubtless meant to have, and to assess Hose's work in its true context. Within dominant anthropological circles, culture-historical speculation was only partly discredited on its own terms; more important in its eventual demise was the tendency of many of the background assumptions to quietly slip out of anthropological currency. If in this book Hose argued simplistically from inadequate data, at least his speculations have some imaginative interest. Even now, the archaeology of South-East Asia is insufficiently clear to properly test hypotheses like that of cultural connections between the upland peoples of the peninsula and archipelago, which Hose repeats in this book from the earlier *Pagan Tribes*; but the issues, if more complex than Hose believed them to be, still retain some interest and cannot be written off just yet.

The value of *Natural Man*, as of Hose's other books, lies not only in what it got right but also in provoking us to think about the circumstances of its author, including his intellectual universe. It helps us understand at least part of Borneo, and, by extension, part of the larger linkage of colonial domination and social science, by drawing attention not just to an 'object' of knowledge (in this case, some Bornean cultures) but especially to how that knowledge is constructed. Certain themes recur in Hose's writing—for example, the question-begging but, for its time, progressive idea that subject peoples cannot be considered savages since their mental processes are like those of Europeans; or that the best way to rule is through example and under-standing, although still relying on the far-sighted leadership supposedly innate to the British middle and upper classes. But he hardly invented such views; they were part of the common currency of late Victorian imperialism.

If there was a strong and pre-existing demand for Hose's brand of scientific exoticism, his response was revealingly individual—rather than some anonymous ideology, we get the considered and therefore plausible voice of experience. This is hardly surprising, since Hose had already absorbed this style of thinking and made it his own before contributing to it himself. A further reminder of the man behind the prose is his habit of peppering his books with personal views and selective accounts of his background. It seems obvious that this was never meant to enhance his scholarly reputation, but it certainly made the author much more accessible than most academics ever are to a lay reader. Getting an honorary D.Sc. out of Cambridge may have had more to do with his ethnographic collection in the University Museum than with publicizing himself as a 'jungle-wallah', but it also acknowledged genuine contributions to ethnography. His style of writing made him accessible not only to the wider public of his own time, but also to us. For the writer himself alerts us not simply to the landscape but to the figure: Borneo with Hose looking on, or Hose against a Bornean backdrop. In either case, the picture is fascinating, and, like all good pictures, invites us to ask how it came to be.

London
November 1987

BRIAN DURRANS

References

Balfour, Henry, 'Hose, Charles (1863–1929)', *Dictionary of National Biography*, 1922–30, pp. 431–3.

Crisswell, Colin N., *Rajah Charles Brooke: Monarch of All He Surveyed*, Kuala Lumpur, Oxford University Press, 1978.

Doering, Otto C., III, 'Government in Sarawak under Charles Brooke', *Journal of the Malay Branch of the Royal Asiatic Society*, Vol. 39, Part 2, December 1966.

Haddon, A. C., Review of 'Hose, *Natural Man. A Record from Borneo*', *Man*, March 1927, No. 34, pp. 55–6.

Harper, G. C., 'The Miri Field 1910–1972', *Sarawak Museum Journal*, Vol. XX, Nos. 40–1 (New Series), 1972, pp. 21–30.

Harrisson, Tom and Brunig, B., 'Hose's Irrawaddy Pioneers', *Sarawak Museum Journal*, Vol. VI, No. 6 (New Series), 1955, pp. 518–21.

Hose, Charles, *Natural Man. A Record from Borneo*, London, Macmillan, 1926.

———, *Fifty Years of Romance and Research or A Jungle-Wallah At Large*, London, Hutchinson, 1927.

Hose, Charles and McDougall, William, *The Pagan Tribes of Borneo*, London, Macmillan, 1912.

Rutter, Owen, Review of 'Hose, *Natural Man. A Record from Borneo*', *Geographical Journal*, Vol. LXIX, 1927, pp. 272–3.

Charles Hose to Daniel Macmillan, 14 July 1913; unpublished correspondence with Charles Hose, 1911–29, Macmillan archive, British Library, Add MS 55157.

PREFACE

IT is surely unnecessary to introduce Dr. Charles Hose either to men of science or the general public. His services to biology are well known throughout the world. Mainly as the result of his investigations the fauna of Sarawak is perhaps better known than that of any territory of equal extent elsewhere. Moreover, Dr. Hose has generously supplied museums and comparative anatomists in various countries of the Old World and the New with material for some of the most significant researches that have been made in vertebrate morphology during the last thirty years, in particular those relating to the study of the problems of man's ancestry. But Dr. Hose's contribution to our knowledge of cultural anthropology is even more widely known than his services to zoology. The general results of this work were made known in 1912 by the publication of the important volumes on *The Pagan Tribes of Borneo*, written in collaboration with Dr. William McDougall, which are now generally admitted to be the classical treatise on the ethnology of Borneo.

But if Dr. Hose's achievements are so well known as to make this Preface unnecessary, nevertheless I welcome the opportunity that his generous insistence offers of adding a brief reference to the wider significance of the problems he discusses in this volume.

The customs and beliefs of the various peoples at present living under Rajah Brooke's beneficent rule in Sarawak present an epitome of the early history of civilisation, representing as they do a series of primitive phases of culture that in most other parts of the world have been profoundly modified or even completely suppressed by

the disturbing influences of higher types of civilisation.
In Borneo some of the most interesting and significant
of the earlier phases have been crystallised and fixed for
us to study at the present day.

From its far-reaching significance and bearing upon
anthropological doctrine the survival among the Punans
of an almost complete lack of culture is a fact of cardinal
importance. In Chapter V, Dr. Hose has rendered an
important service in once more emphasising the fact that
a competent, intelligent and good-natured population
should remain simple nomad hunters after being in contact
with more cultured people for many centuries. They
build no houses, cultivate no crops, have no property,
except what can be carried about with them, and have
no dogs. They are good-natured and peaceful people.
Although they are almost wholly devoid of culture they
are the very antithesis of what is usually understood by
the term " savage." The instinctive kindliness and morality of people who are exempt from the exasperations
and the greed that civilisation creates are clearly set forth
by Dr. Hose. If his book achieves no other purpose
than to establish the fact of fundamental importance that
man is by nature peaceful and good-natured he will
have achieved a revolution in anthropological doctrine.

Borneo, however, affords many other clear-cut facts
that have an intimate bearing upon the solution of the
problems that divide ethnologists into two conflicting
camps.

Centuries ago Mohammedanism was introduced into
Borneo and certain of its people are still devoted to Islam.
Not even the most obstinate opponent of the idea of cultural diffusion can deny that the influence of a particular
type of Arabic or Arabo-African beliefs and customs still
persists in Borneo. But several centuries before the teaching
of Mohammed reached as far as the Malay Archipelago,
Buddhism and Brahmanism had already spread from India
and left their indelible impress upon the customs and beliefs.

It is a problem of special interest to determine why such influence was more potent and enduring in Java than in Borneo. Nor is one justified in assuming that Hinduism was the earliest alien influence to intrude into this area. The survival of the Babylonian methods of hepatoscopy and procedures for reading omens and auspices such as the Romans and Etruscans used to practise is so complete, as Dr. Hose and Professor McDougall have been at pains to emphasise, that no one can question the influence in Sarawak of a Western culture much more ancient than Brahmanism. The interest of these similarities does not necessarily depend upon the acceptance of the idea that they are the result of a spread of culture from Babylonia and the Mediterranean area. For if the reading of omens and all the peculiar formalities incidental to the interpretation of auspices were devised quite independently in Borneo and in Italy, the study of these practices by a living people does not lose any of its interest. To many scholars, however, the identities seem to be too exact to be explained by the chance of independent origin.[1] Hence Dr. Hose's study of the practical details of the auspices in Sarawak become a matter of particular interest to the interpreter of Latin literature and to all students of early civilisation.

But there are indications in Sarawak of the survival of yet more ancient practices, the fuller understanding of which will eventually illuminate the earliest of all beliefs. Dr. Hose has set forth in this book all that he could discover of the ideas involved in the Ngarong, which the Ibans regard as the Unknown Helper. It probably represents what the Karens of Burma call the *Kelah*, the *Fravashi* of the Persian Avesta, the Babylonian " God who walks by my side," the Roman *Genius* and the Egyptian *Ka*.

[1] The late Dr. Warde Fowler, who disclaims to pass judgment on this issue, has provided the most decisive evidence in demonstration of diffusion ("Ancient Italy and Modern Borneo" in *Roman Essays and Interpretations*, Oxford, 1920).

From the discussion of this belief will, I am convinced, eventually emerge the true explanation of totemism, how there developed the idea of the soul, the meaning of animal standards, heraldic crests and the sanctity of the flag. In 1924 I put forward a tentative interpretation [1] of the important evidence Dr. Hose has been able to collect. Since then further scraps of information, and especially the new facts recorded in this volume, have convinced me that in the interpretation of the Iban Ngarong lies the germ of the true understanding of the origin of the most fundamental belief of all mankind.

G. ELLIOT SMITH.

[1] "Animal Standards in Indonesia," *The Year Book of Oriental Art and Culture*, 1924–1925, edited by Arthur Waley (London, 1925), p. 70.

CONTENTS

CONTENTS

PART V

CREEDS AND SUPERSTITIONS

PART VI

LIST OF ILLUSTRATIONS

xiii

LIST OF ILLUSTRATIONS XV

PART I

ANTHROPOLOGICAL

CHAPTER I

INTRODUCTORY

An isle of Romance—Nature and Man

The fascination which the " East Indies," to use a good old term, and especially the Islands, have always exercised over Western minds is due to a combination of Natural Beauty and Natural Resources. From the days when the first Greek navigators, fired with the Romance of an adventurous trade, sailed down the Red Sea, the call of the East has been insistent; and it is hardly too much to say that the call of Borneo has been imperative. It is not enough that it is a land of far distances; the island is about four times the size of England and Wales combined, a land of rivers and forest, of torrential rains and golden sunsets : it is, above all, a land of the Unexpected and of the Unknown. Its setting, if that were all, is, in the highest sense, romantic : to the North lies China, with its quaint and formal beauty ; to the West, the desolate solitude of the Indian Ocean ; to the East, the spaces of the Pacific.

But it is not merely to its setting that Borneo owes its charm. It possesses the double advantage that what is known is fascinating, but what might be known, and is not yet known, appeals to all that is best in man ; giving him thus a scope for his artistic or scientific designs, and a satisfaction in work done, perhaps with inconvenience and discomfort, but at least with thoroughness. For the labours of the pioneer have been concerned with a strange breed of men, savages perhaps they may be called, pirates,

B

organised murderers; and yet, at bottom, very little different from those who are to be found, any day of the week, in St. John's Wood or the Boulevard Vaugirard.

In the preparation of this book I have not had the benefit of the co-operation and advice of Dr. W. McDougall, with whom I collaborated in *The Pagan Tribes of Borneo*. But this new book derives some measure of advantage from the invaluable chapters in the first, for which Dr. McDougall was chiefly responsible, and I know and appreciate the fact that I have his cordial good wishes in my latest effort to trace the problem of Natural Man in Borneo.

I am indebted to Ranee Margaret of Sarawak, who first stimulated my interest in the people of the country, and to many kind friends for helpful advice, especially to Mr. T. O. Hodges for assistance in the revision of the proofs, as well as for some valuable suggestions. To my friend Dr. Elliot Smith I am indebted for kindly writing a Preface which in my grateful judgment adds distinction to my own humble efforts.

I must also cordially acknowledge the personal interest which the Publishers have taken in the work, and the uniform courtesy which they have shown in their dealings with me.

The illustrations are from photographs taken by myself, with the exception of the painting of the burial jar, which was drawn by my daughter Violet, and there are also a few photographs for which I tender my thanks to Professor Harrison Smith of Boston, U.S.A., Professor Le Gros Clark, late Principal Medical Officer, Sarawak, and the Rajah for his photograph of a large fish speared by himself, and permission to include his portrait in the book.

Captain Bertram Brooke, Tuan Muda of Sarawak, very kindly permitted me, with the sanction of the Rajah, to reproduce, for the first time, a photograph of the original document which was granted to Sir James Brooke by the Sultan of Brunei whereby the country of Sarawak was ceded to Sir James Brooke and his heirs for ever.

CHAPTER II

THE FIRST PEOPLE OF THE ISLAND

Indonesians—Caucasic and Mongoloid—Kayans, Muruts and Ibans—
Kayans and Burmese—A thousand-years-old culture—Muruts and
Philippines—" Sea-Dayaks "—" We of this country."

WHILE it is impossible to make any confident assertion
as to the origin of the aboriginal tribes from which the
present inhabitants of Borneo are descended, this much
may be said, that the island, together with the other
great islands of Java and Sumatra, at one time formed part
of the mainland of South-east Asia. To the peoples
who inhabited this " dead " region, the term " Indonesian "
is most properly applicable. They would appear to be a
blend of Caucasic and Mongoloid elements; and their
survivals are to be found in the Punans, Kenyahs, and
Klemantans of to-day. The fairness of the skin, the wavy,
and even, in some individuals, the curly character of the
hair; the regular and comparatively refined features
of many individuals; the frequent occurrence of straight
and aquiline noses; the comparatively large, horizontal,
or only slightly oblique, eyelid-aperture; the not infrequent absence of all trace of the Mongolian fold of the
eyelid and its slightness when present—all these characters
point to the predominance of the Caucasic element.

On the other hand, among many members of these
tribes we find smooth yellowish skin, long dark thick hair,
and a scantiness of hair on the cheeks, chin, and lips;
rather broad cheek-bones, a prevailing slight obliquity
of the eyes, a rather narrow eyelid-aperture, and the
presence of a slight Mongolian fold—these characters
(all of which are found in a considerable proportion

3

of these peoples) are features that point to Mongol ancestry.

After the separation of Borneo from the mainland, there came a long period throughout which it remained an isolated area, the population of which received no important accessions from other areas. It is probable that during this period the Indonesian population of the mainland continued to receive further infusions of Mongol blood, for there is abundant evidence that for a long time past there had been a drifting of Mongol peoples southward from China into the Indo-Chinese area.

During this period the knowledge and practice of working iron, of building Long Houses and boats, and of cultivating rice became diffused through the greater part of the population of this corner of the Asiatic continent; and this advance of culture encouraged the migration of Northern peoples to the islands.

These civilised or semi-civilised visitors and settlers from China, Java and elsewhere were separated from the indigenous Borneans by a great culture gap, and they probably had but little friendly intercourse with them and affected their culture but little, if at all ; and though it is possible that they bartered salt, metal, tools, and weapons for camphor and other jungle produce, their influence, in most parts of the island, probably extended but a little way from the coast. The higher culture of the indigenous tribes of the interior was introduced by invasions of peoples less widely separated from them in cultural level, who penetrated far into the interior and mingled intimately with them.

Three such invasions may be distinguished as of principal importance : that of the Kayans in the South and the South-east, of the Muruts in the North, and of the Ibans in the South-west. Each of these three invading populations followed the course of the rivers to the interior and established its communities over large areas. Of the three principal invasions that of the Kayans seems to have been of most effect in spreading a higher culture among the aboriginal population.

There can be little doubt that the Kayans of to-day are the descendants of emigrants from the mainland, and that they brought with them thence all or most of their characteristic culture.

The Kayans migrated to Borneo from the basin of the Irrawaddy by way of Tenasserim, the Malay Peninsula, and Sumatra. They represent a part of the Indonesian stock which had remained in the basin of the Irrawaddy and adjacent rivers from the time of the separation of Borneo. The highland tribes of those districts have still a striking resemblance to the lank-haired inland Bornean jungle people, and even in the most minute details of legend, superstition, customs, habits, arts and even language, amazing analogies can be found between Borneo, Burma, and Assam.

Among the Kayans themselves there is a tradition of having crossed the sea; and they seem to have entered Borneo by way of the rivers opening on the South coast. Gradually they penetrated to the central highlands by following up these rivers, pushing out communities every few years to build new villages higher up the river in the course of their unceasing search for new areas adapted to their farming operations. But, what is most important, from the time of their arrival in Borneo, the Kayans played the part of a dominating and conquering people among tribes of lower culture, and imposed their customs upon those tribes, without blending with them or accepting from them any important cultural elements; and the presumption is that the Kayans have to this day preserved the culture which they had a thousand years ago.

Further, the view that the Kayans have played this large civilising rôle is supported by the fact that Kayan is the language most widely understood in the interior and that it is largely used for inter-communication between tribes neither of whose vernacular it is.

A second invasion would appear to be that of the Muruts, who probably immigrated from the Philippines, or directly from Annam.

The Muruts have coarser but less Mongolian features than the Kayans, and are lankier in build. Their culture is so distinct that it must have had a completely different origin from that of the Kayans. They build Long Houses; but these are flimsy structures compared to those of the Kayans, and they are often situated at a distance from any navigable stream. The Muruts are not sea or river folk : they have little or no skill in boat-building, and they prefer to make their journeys by land, being great walkers, rather than by water. Their most distinctive peculiarity is their system of agriculture, in terraces very like that of the Angami Naga tribes of Assam, which involves irrigation with the use of the buffalo, in the raising of two crops a year from the same land. Other distinctive features are their peculiar long sword and short spear ; the absence of any axe and blow-pipe, and the custom according to which the women propose marriage to the men.

Distinct from their predecessors are the third group, the Ibans, both by reason of their physical and mental peculiarities, and of the many differences of their culture.

The Ibans have for many years been known to Europeans as *Sea Dayaks*, a name utterly incorrect ; in the first place, the term is self-contradictory, for, if it meant anything at all, it could only mean "The Sea-farers who live up-country"; and, secondly, it is not a name by which they have ever called themselves, or which they would ever recognise if called by it. It is, in fact, a Malay term, alien and inaccurate.

These are the latest of the immigrants, and their arrival is comparatively recent. But, although they are new-comers, so to speak, they brought with them something which is older than themselves, namely, their language. Iban would seem to be a tongue out of which Malay, as

Landing-place at a farm.

Mountain range in Upper Sarawak.

Mount Mulu from the Tuto river.

Santubong mountain from the sea.

spoken to-day, has been evolved under Arab influence; [1] for the Iban employs many words which are no longer current in Malay, but which, in the eighteenth century, were in use in Sumatra.

Another interesting fact about the Iban is that although, both by his language and by his physical characteristics, he can be easily distinguished from the other peoples, and although all Ibans recognise themselves as one race, they have no common word for the whole group. They normally speak of themselves as *Kami Menoa* (" We of this country "), a term which hardly disarms suspicion; but the name by which they are generally known is that given them by the Kayans, namely, *Ivan* (wanderer), which is commonly modified into *Iban*, so that the expression *Kami Iban* (" We wanderers ") is frequently used by them.

The Iban probably turned up in Borneo less than three hundred years ago: his place of origin was possibly Sumatra. At a date, which, in the absence of credible evidence, no one can discover, a number of Malay nobles were authorised by the Sultan of Brunei to govern the five rivers of Sarawak proper, namely, the Samarahan, the Sadong, the Batang Lupar, the Saribas, and the Klaka rivers. These Malays were leaders of pirate gangs, and were glad to enrol large numbers of pagan fighting men among their followers; for the professional fighter was glad to do most of the hard work, claiming the heads of the pirates' victims as his principal remuneration, while the Malays retained that part of the booty which had a marketable value. These Malay leaders found, no doubt, that their pagan relatives of Sumatra lent themselves more readily to this service than the less warlike Klemantans of Borneo, and brought over considerable numbers of them and settled them about the mouths of these rivers.

Such was the entrance of the Iban.   But there is reason

---

[1] Malay is written in Arabic characters, and contains a large number of Arabian words, grafted upon the original language.

to think that some of them had settled at an earlier date in this part of Borneo and rather farther southward. In most respects these earlier settlers closely resemble the other Iban tribes, but they are distinguished by some peculiarities of language and accent : their manners are gentler, their bearing is less boastful and they are less given to wandering. They are recognised by themselves and by other Ibans as belonging to the same people ; but they are slightly looked down upon by Ibans of the other tribes as any home-staying rural population is looked down upon by travelled cosmopolitans.

NOTE.—Reference has already been made to the characteristics of the tribes, but one is constantly asked the question, Who are the people of Borneo, and whence do they come ? This ethnological problem has for many years been prominently before my mind, and even now I can claim only an approximate exactitude for the classification finally adopted. The so-called Malays of the coast regions, who are, by the way, Mohammedans without tribal organisation, are ethnically a " mixed lot." The rest of the islanders are usually lumped together as Dayaks, but physically no less than culturally they show considerable diversities amongst themselves. Six principal groups, already referred to, can be distinguished. Intermarriage, however, takes place continually in some degree between these groups, so that besides typical communities, which, however, constitute the main bulk of the population, there are others that present decidedly intermediate characteristics. So far as I know there are no Negritoes, or, in other words, Pygmies, in Borneo, though these are found in the Malay Peninsula, the Philippines, and elsewhere in this region. The most backward amongst the existing inhabitants of Borneo are the Punans, forest-dwellers without fixed abode, who live by what their blow-pipe brings them. The Kenyahs and Klemantans are in my opinion akin physically to the Punans, there being visible in each case a certain blending of Caucasoid and Mongoloid elements, of which the former predominates. Dr. Haddon, however, in an interesting appendix on the physical characters of the races of Borneo published in my former work in collaboration with Dr. McDougall, and entitled *The Pagan Tribes of Borneo*, which embodies somatological measurements made by himself in company with Dr. McDougall and myself, would seem to regard the Punans and Klemantan-Kenyahs as, on the contrary, pre-eminently Mongoloid or " Proto-Malayan " in type. Though he does not definitely express such a conviction, his admirable statistical tables are everywhere eloquently suggestive of the anomalies attendant on race-mixture. Be these things as they may, I still have reason to think that these three people together constitute the true aboriginals, the blend which they represent going back possibly to the time when Borneo was still continental. The Muruts, Ibans and Kayans, on the other hand, I hold to be later immigrants.

These groups differ considerably from one another in respect of material and moral culture as well as of mental and physical character. To the reader it may appear that the names have been used as though the groups denoted by them were well defined and easily to be distinguished from one another. But this is by no means the case. These descriptions are intended to depict the typical communities of each group, those which present the largest number of group-marks. Besides these more typical communities, which constitute the main bulk of the population, there are many communities or sub-tribes which combine in some measure the characteristics of two or more of the principal groups. It is this fact that renders so extremely difficult the attempt to classify the tribes and sub-tribes in any consistent fashion, and to which is largely due the confusion that reigns in most of the accounts hitherto given of the inhabitants of Borneo.

The wide distribution of remnants of the Negrito race in

the islands round about Borneo and in the adjacent parts
of the mainland of Asia renders it highly probable that at a
remote period Negritoes lived in Borneo ; but at the present
time there exists no Negrito community and no distinct
traces of the race, whether in the form of fossil remains or
of physical characteristics in the present population, unless
the curly hair and coarse features of a few individuals to be
met with in almost all the tribes may be regarded as such
traces.   It is best to leave open the question of an ancient
Negrito population, and go on to the statement that the
present population is derived from four principal sources.

It seems not improbable that at an early period, perhaps
one preceding the separation of Borneo, Sumatra, and
Java from the mainland, bands of nomads closely
resembling the Punans and Klemantans of Borneo were
scattered over a large part of this area.   For in several
of the wilder parts, where the great forest areas remain
untouched, bands of nomads closely resembling the Punans
of Borneo are still to be found, notably the Orang Kubu of
Sumatra.   The principal characteristics of this primitive
culture are the absence of houses or any fixed abode ; the
ignorance of agriculture, of metal working, and of boat-
making ;   and the nomadic hunting life, in which the
blow-pipe is the principal instrument.   The chief and only
important improvement effected in the condition of the
Punans since that early period would seem to be the introduction of the superior form of blow-pipe made of hardwood in the place of the more primitive instrument
fashioned from a bamboo or some soft wood stem from
which the pith had been extracted.   This cannot be made
without the use of a metal rod for boring, and since none
of the Bornean tribes which still lead a nomad life know
how to work metals, it may be inferred that they learnt
the craft of boring this hardwood blow-pipe from more
cultured neighbours, procuring from them by barter the
iron tools required.

Keane describes the Indonesians as a Proto-Caucasic

race which must have occupied Malaysia and the Philippines in the New Stone Age.

If these oldest inhabitants of Borneo may be regarded as typical Indonesians, the most plausible view seems to be that they are the product of an ancient blood of Southern Mongols with a Caucasic stock. It seems probable that the blending was effected by the infusion of successive doses of Mongol blood from the North into a Caucasic population that had previously diffused itself over this corner of Asia from the West. After the separation of Borneo from the mainland there came a long period throughout which it remained an isolated area, the population of which received no important accessions from other sources. It is probable that during this period the Indonesian population of the mainland continued to receive further infusions of Mongol blood ; for there is abundant evidence that for a long time past there has been a drifting of Mongol peoples, such as the Shans, Nagas, Karens, and other tribes of Assam and Burma southwards.

The Kayans seem to have entered Borneo by way of the rivers opening on the southern coast and gradually to have followed them up to the central highlands, and there can be little doubt that they are the descendants of emigrants from the mainland and that they brought with them thence all or most of their characteristic culture. But what part exactly of the mainland, and by what route they came, and how long a time was occupied in the migration, are questions in answer to which one cannot do more than throw out some vague suggestions.

I believe that the Kayans migrated to Borneo from the basin of the Irrawaddy by way of Tenasserim, the Malay Peninsula, and Sumatra ; and that they represent a part of the Indonesian stock which had remained in the basin of the Irrawaddy and adjacent rivers from the time of the separation of Borneo, and through contact with the southward drift of peoples from the north had received fresh infusions of Mongol blood ; in that case they would be a part of the Indonesians which is more Mongoloid in character than that part which at a remote period was shut up in Borneo by the separation from the mainland. During this long period the Kayans acquired or developed a type of culture characterised by the cultivation of rice on land newly cleared of forest by burning, the building of Long Houses on the banks of rivers, the use of boats, and the working of iron.

The way in which the Kayans hang together and keep in touch with one another, even though scattered through districts in which numerous communities of other tribes are settled, preserving their characteristic culture with extreme faithfulness, lends colour to the supposition that the whole tribe may thus have been displaced step by step, passing on from one region and from one island to another without leaving behind any part of their tribe. The parts of this tribal migration that are the most difficult to imagine are the passage of the straits between the peninsula and Sumatra, and between Sumatra and Borneo. But we know that Kayans do not fear to put to sea in their long war boats, and follow the coast round the island for considerable distances.

As long ago as the year 1850, J. R. Logan, writing of the highland tribes of the basins of the Kolodan and Irrawaddy, and the south-eastern part of the Brahmaputra, asserted that " the habits of these tribes have a wonderful resemblance to those of the inland lank-haired races of Indonesia." Dr. Hutton, Colonel L. W. Shakespear, Mr. T. P. Mills, and others have written very valuable and interesting books on the Naga tribes, and more particularly those tribes which have come under the administration of the Government of Assam, and there seems to me to be a very close similarity in the legends, superstitions, customs, habits and arts of these tribes and the adjacent highlands of the remainder of the Brahmaputra basin, which is characteristic of one or other of the ruder lank-haired tribes of Borneo, Sumatra, the Philippines, and the other islands of the Malay Archipelago. It is not possible as yet, however, to find any one tribe of this part of the mainland which agrees really closely with the Kayans or any other single tribe in respect of physical characteristics and essential cultural features. But people generally recognised as closely akin are the Karens, the Chins (known as Khyens of the basin of the Chindwina tributary of the Irrawaddy), the Kakkhyens (also called Kachins), who occupy the hills east of Bhamo and the basin of the river Tapang in the border-lands of Burma and Yunnan, and the Nagas of Manipur and the hills of Assam.

It seems highly probable that all these, together with the Kayans of Borneo, are the surviving branches of a people which occupied a large area of south-eastern Asia, more especially the basin of the Irrawaddy, for a considerable period before the first of the successful invasions which have given rise to the existing Burmese and Shan nations, and represent the original Indonesian population, of which the Klemantans of Borneo are the purest type modified by later infusions of Mongol blood.

This is, however, a branch of ethnological study which, despite its interest, space will not permit me to pursue further in this volume. Its relation to the people of the other Pacific islands and their origins from Samoa to New Zealand are parts of the same problem, a field to which much attention has been devoted. Borneo is a link in the great chain connecting the various primitive peoples and is a stepping-stone in the migrations of peoples from the earliest times, when doubtless the geographical conditions of land and water on that part of the earth's surface were vastly different from the present.

CHAPTER III

EARLY DAYS IN BORNEO

Early Chinese visitors—*Poli*—Cotton and the Mynah—Brunei a Buddhist kingdom—King Hianzta sends tribute to China—Majapahit and Malacca—*Puni*—Again tributary to China—Early Chinese influence in Borneo—" Moorish " kings in Bruni—Sultan Mohammed—Nakoda Ragam : his distant expeditions : his lasting work—The new city of Brunei (Bornei)—Pigafetta's account—Decadence followed by European intervention—The Dutch at Banjermasin—English attempts—James Brooke—A Romance of Empire—Brooke becomes Rajah—The agreement with Muda Hasim—Permanence of Brooke's work.

WHEN Europeans first visited the island, the Arab-Malay population, dwelling for the most part, as it still does, in villages and small towns upon the coast and in or near the mouths of the rivers, owed allegiance to several Malay sultans and a number of subordinate rulers, the local rajahs and pangerans. The principal sultans had as their capitals, from which they took their titles, Brunei on the North-west, Sambas in the West, Pontianak at the mouth of the Kapuas river, Banjermasin in the South at the mouth of the river of the same name, Pasir at the South-east corner, Koti and Balungan on the East at the mouths of the rivers of those names ; while the Sultan of Jolo, the capital of the Sulu islands, which lie off the North coast, claimed sovereignty over the northern end of Borneo. But these Malay sultans were not the first representatives in the island of culture and of civilised or semi-civilised rule ; for History preserves some faint records of still earlier times, of which some slight confirmation is afforded by surviving traces of the culture then introduced.

14

In the beautiful Hindu temple of Boro-Budur in Java commenced about A.D 850—its construction must have lasted over many years—are long terraces the walls of which are adorned with a series of superb reliefs. These have been hewn out of lava-blocks and are crowded with an amazing wealth of sculptures.

It is probable that the Hindu architects must have employed a large number of local native artists, and to some extent left them a free hand, as there are non-Indian elements in this decoration. This beautiful work shows in many cases people with ear-lobes drawn down by heavy weights much in the same manner as that practised by the people of Borneo at the present time. This peculiar method of adornment also occurs in many of the sculptures in the famous temple of Angkor hidden away in the jungles of Northern Cambodia in the Mekong basin. The Khmer people who no doubt helped largely in the construction of this temple probably show close affinity both with the peoples of Borneo and Java.

The Klings,[1] still the principal Indian traders in the Far East, visited the Malay Archipelago in the first or at any rate the second century after Christ, and introduced their writing and chronology. But their early histories are meagre and unsatisfactory in the extreme. The Arab culture of the Malays, which took root in Sumatra in the twelfth century, is of course of no assistance in regard to events of earlier date, and does not give trustworthy and detailed accounts until the fifteenth century; and the aboriginal Pagan tribes have no written records, and only faint traditions as to their past. The Chinese, on the other hand, always a literary people, carefully preserved in their archives all that could be gathered with regard to the " Southern Seas."

The first account from such a source is a description in a sixth-century Chinese manuscript, referring to a place named Poli. This place is said to have been on an island in the sea south-east of Camboja or Cambodia, and two months' journey south-east of Canton. (The voyage was, of course, a coastal one, by way of the Gulf of Siam and the Malay Peninsula—a route still followed by Chinese junks.) Envoys were sent to the Imperial court in A.D. 518, 523, and 616. "The people of this country," one authority says, " are skilled in throwing a circular knife the edge of which is like a saw; when they throw it at a man, they never fail to hit him. Their other arms are much the same as in China. Their customs resemble those of Camboja, and the products of the country are the same as of Siam. If a man commits a murder or theft his hands are cut off, and in cases of adultery the culprit has his legs chained for the period of a year. For their sacrifices they choose a time when there is no moon; they then fill a bowl with wine and eatables and let it float down on the surface of the water. The Great Sacrifice

---

[1] The word Kling is applied by speakers of Malay to natives of India, and in particular to the Hindus of the South, of whom the merchant classes of Tamils are the most numerous.

is in the eleventh month. They get corals from the sea, and they have a bird called *s'ari*, which can talk. . . . They carry the teeth of wild beasts in their ears, and wrap a sheet of cotton round their loins; from the cotton plant they collect the seed-pods to make cloth : the coarser kind is called *kupa*, and the finer cloth *t'ieh*. They hold their markets at night, and cover their faces. . . . At the East of this country is situated the land of the Rakshas, which has the same customs as Poli."

How, one asks, do known facts corroborate this account ?

In this way. Sacrifices made at a time when there is no moon are found to-day among the more primitive of the Kadayans, who are forbidden certain kinds of food until they have performed this duty. Small rafts laden with food are sent down the rivers by the Melano and other tribes, to propitiate the spirits of the sea. The very names of the two kinds of cotton, which, at the time of the record, was a novelty to the Chinese, are preserved to-day. Kupa, which is Kapok, is the well-known Malay word for the vegetable down of the silk-cotton *tree* (*Bombax malabaricum*). T'ieh, or Taya, is the name commonly applied by the Ibans to the cotton-*plant*. The use of teeth as an ornament is found among the Kenyahs and Kayans. These instances should be sufficient to prove the correctness of the Chinese records, and to identify Poli with Brunei. The " bird called s'ari " is a mynah, which is most common in Borneo, but unknown in China.

Brunei, it is almost certain, before it became Mohammedan, was a Bisaya kingdom under Buddhist sovereigns; and nearly all the particulars given with regard to the people of Borneo are true of one or other of the tribes allied to Bisayas and living near Brunei to-day. The discus-knife, a wooden weapon, is not now in use, but is known to have been used formerly.

In any case it would seem that the kingdom, though not a great one, had attained a certain civilisation and even

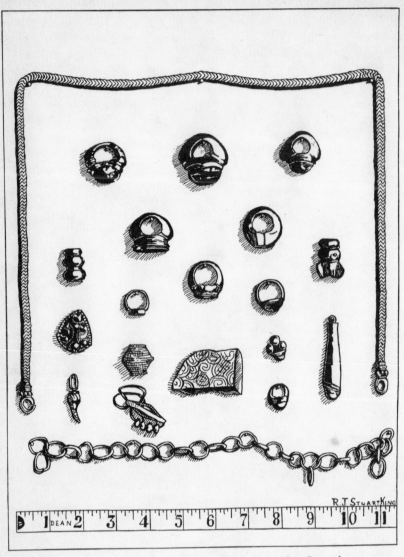

Gold and Ornaments found in the Limbang District, Sarawak

luxury. A Buddhist monarch was on the throne, and was served with much ceremony. He was clad, according to records, in flowered silk or cotton, adorned with pearls, and sat on a golden throne attended by servants with white dusters and fans of peacock feathers. When he went out of his palace, his chariot, canopied with feathers and embroidered curtains, was drawn by elephants, whilst gongs, drums, and conches made appropriate music. Now, Hindu ornaments have been found in the Limbang district near Brunei, and the names of many offices of state are Sanskritic; while until a few years ago the people of Sarawak used to speak of " the days of the Hindus." On the other hand, Chinese ornaments and coins of great antiquity have been found in the same localities. When these facts are put together, it seems reasonable to believe that a Chinese account describing part of Borneo as ruled by Buddhists is substantially correct.

Whether it is correct or not to identify Poli with Brunei, there is another city mentioned by Chinese travellers, as being distant, with a fair wind, forty-five days from Java, forty from Palembang, and thirty from Champa. The name given by the Chinese to the State and City was Puni, which is the way the Chinese to-day, having neither the letters " b " and " r " nor double consonants in their language, pronounce the word Brunei. This State is said to have been forty-five days' journey from Java, forty from Palembang, and thirty from Champa (the exact locality of which is doubtful).

In the annals of the Sung dynasty, which, though only ruling over Southern China, had a complete monopoly of the ocean trade for three centuries (A.D. 960 to 1279), this State is mentioned frequently, Puni being apparently a town of some 10,000 inhabitants, protected by a stockade of timber. The king's palace, like the houses of modern Brunei, was thatched with palm leaves, the cottages of the people with grass. Warriors carried spears and protected themselves with copper armour. When any native died,

c

his corpse was exposed in the jungle, and once a year for seven years sacrifices were made to the departed spirit. Bamboos and large green leaves, thrown away after every meal, sufficed for crockery. The products of the country, or at least such as were sent as tribute, were camphor, tortoiseshell, ivory, and areca nuts.

The year 977 opens a new era, for then Hianzta, king of Puni, sent envoys to China, who presented tribute, together with a letter from the king, to this effect : " May the Emperor live thousands and tens of thousands of years, and may he not despise the humble offerings of my little country." The letter was written on what looked like the very thin bark or the leaf of a palm ; it was glossy, slightly green, several feet long, and somewhat broader than one inch ; the characters in which it was written were small, and had to be read horizontally. In all these particulars the letter resembled the books of magic which are still written by the Battas of inland Sumatra.

The message ran : " I, Hianzta, King of Puni, offer my submission to the Great Emperor, praying for him ten thousand years of life. I send envoys with tribute ; for, although I knew before that there was an Emperor, I could not send ships. But recently a merchant called Pu-lu arrived with his ship at the mouth of my river ; him I invited to my palace, and he told me that he came from China. The people of my country were much delighted at this, and, preparing a ship, asked this stranger to guide them to the Court. The envoys I have sent wish no more than to see Your Majesty in peace ; but every year I will send tribute. But when I do so I fear that my ships may perhaps be blown to Champa, and I therefore hope that Your Majesty will send orders to that country that, if a ship belonging to Hianzta arrives there, it be not detained. My country has no other produce than this, and I pray Your Majesty not to be angry with me." The envoys were entertained and sent home with presents. A hundred years later (in A.D. 1082), Sri Maja, king of Puni, sent tribute again, but the promise of yearly homage was not kept. When, gradually, the Sung dynasty declined in power, the East Indian potentates became less humble.

In the thirteenth and the early part of the fourteenth centuries Brunei owed allegiance alternately to two powers much younger than herself (being founded in the thirteenth century) namely, Majapahit in Java, and Malacca on the west coast of the Malay Peninsula. Majapahit, originally only one of several Javan kingdoms, rapidly acquired strength and subjugated her neighbours and the nearest portions of the islands around. Malacca, formed when the Malay colony of Singapore was overwhelmed by Javanese, became the great commercial depot of the Straits and the chief centre of Mohammedanism in the Archipelago. The two powers therefore stood for two faiths and two cultures : Majapahit for Brahminism and Hindu influence, Malacca for Islam and the more practical civilisation of Arabia.

In the early years of the fourteenth century Brunei was a dependency of Majapahit, but, taking advantage of a rather weak ruler, who was a minor, recovered its independence. It is to this time that the tradition of the Kapuas Malays ascribes the arrival of the Kayans in Borneo. Somewhat later Angka Wijaya extended the power of Majapahit over Palembang in Sumatra, Timor, Ternate, Luzon, and the coasts of Borneo; and in 1368 Javanese soldiers drove from Brunei certain local marauders who had sacked the town. Yet a few years later the ungrateful king transferred his allegiance to China, and not long afterwards, with calculating humility, paid tribute to Mansur Shah, who in 1374 had succeeded to the throne of Malacca. However, the influence of Majapahit and of the Buddhistic culture of Java must have been much more powerful and enduring than the paying of tribute and the maintenance of relations would suggest ; and Javanese influence is not merely confined to Brunei, but evidence of it is found in the southern half of the island, where among some Klemantans is practised the cremation of the dead, in the

Koti district the carving in low relief of bulls in stone, and in various other districts the manufacture of gold ornaments of a distinctly Buddhist or Hindu character, survive until to-day.

At the beginning of the fifteenth century an extraordinary incident occurred which again—and for the last time—draws our attention to the Chinese Court. The Ming emperors, who were of Chinese rather than Mongol blood, and came to power in 1368, soon developed the maritime influence of the empire. Their predecessors, the great Mongol conquerors, Genghis and Kublai Khan, had had little to do with the Malay Archipelago, though the latter sent an unsuccessful expedition against Java in 1292. But for a few years after the Ming accession there was a continual stream of East Indian embassies. During the last twenty years of the century these became more rare, and in 1405 the Chinese Emperor found it necessary to send a trusted minister, by name Cheng-Ho, to visit the vassal States in the South. Cheng-Ho made several journeys, travelling as far as the shores of Africa, in most cases with immediate and profitable results. Among other rulers, Maraja Kali, king of Puni, although Cheng-Ho does not appear to have called on him in person, sent tribute in 1405; and so impressed was he with the embroidered silk presented in return that, three years later, he visited the Son of Heaven. Landing in Fuk-kien, he was conducted, among scenes of riotous enthusiasm, to the capital. Here he was received by the Emperor, who at once made him a mandarin of the first rank, and loaded him with gifts. The effort appears to have been rather too much for our friend, for, having accomplished his one great ambition of " seeing the face of the Son of Heaven," the obsequious monarch died in the Imperial City, leaving his son Hia-wang to succeed to the throne of Puni. His unfilial offspring, preferring his own country to China, put off the Imperial Power with a promise of tribute in place of actual payment, and returned to his own country, in hopes of independence. His plans seem to have worked out well, for between 1410 and 1425 he paid tribute six times, but afterwards entirely ignored his suzerain.

Apart from this, there appears to have been a permanent Chinese colony, or colonies, in the neighbourhood of the great mountain of Borneo, Kina Balu, and of the river Kina Batangan which flows from it. It is reasonable to think that these settlers came during the Ming dynasty, as several old writers refer to the founding of colonies, and local traditions to the same effect survive. Further, among several tribes are to be found legends (differing in detail, and therefore more likely to be essentially correct) to the effect that the Chinese came to seize the great jewel of the Kina Balu dragon (which has always existed in tradition, but never been encountered in fact), but quarrelled about the spoil and separated, some (apparently optimists) remaining behind. One tribe in North Borneo go so far as to claim descent from these settlers, a claim which can only be true in a limited sense.

Since the breaking-off of relations with China, following the fall and decay of the Ming Empire, the predominating influences on the manners and politics of the East Indies have been those of Europe and Islam. The Mohammedan influence was the earliest to make itself felt, and for some years it shared a precarious supremacy with Java; but Java was not destined to last long. In 1478, Majapahit was utterly destroyed, and thirty years later Malacca was captured by the Portuguese. In 1521, within a hundred years of King Hia-wang's last visit to China to pay homage, Pigafetta, the chronicler of Magellan's great voyage round the world, was calling on a " Moorish " king in Brunei. The change had come.

At exactly what point, or what date, this all-important transformation occurred it is impossible to say. Tradition in Brunei ascribes the introduction of Islamic influences to a potentate locally famous as Sultan Mohammed, but whose original name was *Al Akbar Tata*. This hardy

warrior is the earliest monarch of whom the present
inhabitants of Brunei have any knowledge—a fact to be
accounted for by the brilliance of his alleged exploits
and to the introduction—undoubtedly about this period—
of Arabic writing. Like most of his subjects in Brunei he
was, probably, a Bisaya; and in early life was neither a
Mohammedan nor any other kind of civilised ruler, if conventional standards are to be a criterion, for the chief mark
of his royal dignity was an immense loin-cloth, carried, as he
walked in procession, by eighty men, forty in front and forty
behind. The account sounds less like history than Hans
Christian Andersen's story about another Eastern monarch.

Sultan Mohammed, after much fighting, subdued the
river-peoples of Northern Borneo, and compelled them to
pay him tribute. On the other hand, he definitely refused
to pay an annual tribute to Majapahit. During his reign
the Muruts were brought under Brunei rule by peaceful
measures, while the Chinese colony were propitiated by a
convenient marriage. His actual conversion to Islam is
said to have taken place at Johore, where another marriage
helped him to make good his claims over Sarawak and the
North coast generally. Sultan Mohammed was succeeded
by his brother Akhmad, son-in-law of the Chinese chief,
and he was in turn succeeded by an Arab from Taif who
had married his daughter. Thus the present royal house
of Brunei is derived from three sources—Arab, Klemantan,
and Chinese.

The coronation ceremony as still maintained affords an
interesting confirmation of this account. On that occasion
the principal minister wears a turban and Haji outfit, the
two next in rank are dressed in Chinese and Hindu fashion,
while the fourth wears a waist-cloth over his trousers to
represent the Bisayas; and each of these ministers declares
the Sultan to be divinely appointed. Then after the
demonstration of loyalty the two gongs—one from Menang-
kabau in Sumatra, the other from Johore—are beaten, and
the Moslem high priest proclaims the Sultan and preaches

a sermon, declaring him to be a descendant of Sri Turi Buana, the Palambang chief who founded the early king- dom of Singapore in A.D. 1160, who reigned in that island for forty-eight years, and whose descendants became the royal family of Malacca.

The sultans who followed Sultan Mohammed did very little of note except to build up Islam as a Power and make Brunei a practically Mohammedan city. But, about the year 1500 we come to an heroic figure, Sultan Bulkiah, better known by his earlier name, Nakoda Ragam. Under this prince, whose exploits have been celebrated in prose and verse, Brunei attained an eminence that she had never possessed before, and never recovered after. She was no longer a vassal State, paying tribute to an overlord, but was a sovereign Power, dictating her terms to those whom she conquered. Nakoda Ragam himself journeyed to distant lands, and conquered the Sulu islands and Eastern Borneo. Over the throne of Sambas he set a weak- minded brother of his own. He even sent an expedition to Manila, and on the second attempt seized that place. Tribute poured into his coffers from all sides. His wife was a Javanese princess, who brought many people to Brunei. These intermarried with the Bisayas, and from them it is said are sprung the Kadayans, a quiet agricultural folk, skilled in various arts, but rendered timid by continual oppression.

Nakoda Ragam's reign ended prematurely and tragically, for he was accidentally given his quietus with a bare bodkin—his wife's. His work, however, was destined to last for another generation ; and, strangely enough, the best evidence which we have for his constructive powers comes from one who visited the country after his death. This is Pigafetta, who in 1521, with the surviving com- panions of Magellan, visited the capital and Court at the city of Brunei, the new pile-built water-city which took the place of Nakoda Ragam's own capital, Buang Tawa.

Pigafetta's is the first good account, from a European

source, of the town, which he calls Bornei, and whose latitude he estimated with an error of less than ten miles. From it it is clear that at his visit the splendour of Nakoda Ragam's exploits had not evaporated. The magnificence of the Court and the large population the city is said to have contained were presumably the result of the conquests he had made in neighbouring islands. The king, like the princes of Malacca before the conquest, had his elephants, and he and his courtiers were clothed in Chinese satins and Indian brocades. He was in possession of artillery, and the appearance and ceremonial of his Court were imposing.

From this time, however, the power of Brunei continuously declined. Recurrent civil wars invited the occasional interventions of the Portuguese and of the Spanish governors of the Philippines, which, although they did not result in the subjugation of the Malay power, nevertheless sapped its strength.

The interest of the later history of Borneo lies in the successive attempts, many of them fruitless, made by Dutch and English to gain a footing on the island. The Dutch arrived off Brunei in the year 1600, but, after a ten days' stay, were glad to leave with a certain amount of pepper, being convinced that the place was nothing better than a den of thieves. This short acquaintance was not pressed, although factories were shortly after started at Sambas, with considerable success. In 1685 an English captain named Cowley arrived in Brunei ; but his experience concurred with that of the Dutch in declining to take up the commerce which the Portuguese had abandoned.

At Banjermasin, on the southern coast, more progress was made, where the Dutch arrived before their English rivals, but were soon compelled by intrigues to withdraw. On the other hand, in 1704 the English factors on the Chinese island of Chu-san, expelled by the Imperial authorities and subsequently driven from Pulo-Condar off the Cochin-China coast by a mutiny, arrived here. They had every reason to be gratified with the prospects which the port offered ; for they could sell the local pepper to the Chinese at three times the cost price. But their bitter experiences in the China seas had not taught them wisdom : they soon fell out with the Javanese Sultan, whose hospitality they were enjoying, and after some bloody struggles were obliged to withdraw from this part of the island.

In 1747 the Dutch East India Company, which had recently established its authority over all the north-eastern coast of Java, obtained, by forcible methods, a monopoly of trade at Banjermasin and set up a factory. Nearly forty years later, the reigning prince having rendered himself odious to his subjects, the country was invaded by 3000 natives of Celebes. These were expelled by the Dutch, who dethroned the Sultan, placing his younger brother on the throne ; and he, in reward for their services, ceded to them his entire dominions, con-senting to hold them as a vassal. This is the treaty under which the Dutch claim the sovereignty of Banjermasin and whatever was once dependent on it. In this way the Dutch obtained a hold on the country which they have never relaxed ; but gradually, year by year, they strength-ened that hold, until now two-thirds or more of the island is under their flag and feels the benefits of their rule. If, indeed, there still remain any districts of this large area where Dutch influence has not made itself felt, they will not long remain in their isolation ; for the *Contrôleurs* are extending their influence even into the most remote corners of the territory.

English attempts to found settlements were less intensive and systematic than those of the Dutch : in the eighteenth century some minor concessions were given to trading companies, but none of them lasted. The chief reason for this was that in the last quarter of the century the Malays of Brunei, Sulu, and Mindanao, inspired possibly by the example of their European visitors, resumed, with increased vigour, an old profession—that of piracy. English traders, indeed, tried to pay occasional visits to the North coast, but after the loss of the *May* in 1788, the *Susanna* in 1803, and the *Commerce* in 1806, with the murder of their crews, the Admiralty warned merchants that to venture up the river to Brunei was " certain destruction." For forty years this instruction was left on British charts, and British seamen followed the humiliating counsel. Not until the early 'forties was peace restored, and then only after an event of the most romantic and improbable kind, the accession to the throne of Sarawak of an English gentleman, James Brooke.

Brooke was a young Englishman, who, having resigned his commission in the army of the British East India Company, invested his fortune in a yacht of 140 tons, with which he set sail in 1838 for the Eastern Archipelago. At Singapore he heard that the Malays of Sarawak, a district forming the south-western extremity of the Sultanate of Brunei, had rebelled against the Brunei nobles, and had in vain appealed to the Dutch Governor-General at Batavia for deliverance from their oppressors. Under the nominal authority of the Sultan, these Brunei nobles, many of whom were of Arab descent, had brought all the north-western part of Borneo to a state of chronic rebellion. They had taught the Ibans of the Batang Lupar and the neighbouring rivers to join them in their piratical excursions, and, being to some extent dependent upon their aid, were compelled to treat them with a certain consideration ; but all other communities were treated by them with a rapacity and cruelty which was causing a rapid depopulation and the return to jungle of much cultivated land.

Brooke sailed for Sarawak in August 1839, and found a country torn by internal conflicts. The Sultan had recently sent Muda Hasim, his uncle and heir-presumptive to the throne of Brunei, to restore order ; but this weak though amiable noble had found himself quite incapable of coping with the situation. Brooke spent some time surveying the coast and studying the people and country, and gained the confidence of Muda Hasim. After an

Sir James Brooke, K.C.B., 1st Rajah of Sarawak, who reigned from 1841–1868.

excursion to Celebes, Brooke sailed for a second visit to Sarawak just a year after the first, and found the country going from bad to worse. Muda Hasim besought him to take command of his forces and to suppress the rebellion. Brooke consented, and soon offered to secure the submission of the rebel leaders on the condition that he himself, and not any Brunei noble, should be the Governor and Rajah of Sarawak. When, however, the rebellion was quelled, Muda Hasim having saved his own face, showed himself disinclined to carry out this arrangement. Brooke, feeling himself bound by his agreement with the rebel leaders, whose lives he had with difficulty preserved from the vengeance of the Brunei nobles, insisted upon it with some show of force ; and on September 24, 1841, he was pro-claimed Rajah and Governor of Sarawak amid the rejoicings of the populace. Muda Hasim, as representative of the Sultan, signed the document which conferred this title and authority ; but since he was not in any proper sense Rajah of Sarawak (which, in fact, was not a raj, but a district hitherto ruled or misruled by Brunei governors not bearing the title of Rajah), this transaction cannot properly be described as an abdication by Muda Hasim in favour of Brooke. Brooke accordingly felt that it was desirable to secure from the Sultan himself a formal recognition of his authority and title. To this end he visited the Sultan in the year 1842, and obtained from him the desired confirmation of the action of his agent, Muda Hasim, of which the following is a translation.

SARAWAK TREATIES
SARAWAK, 1841.

TRANSFER by Pangeran Muda Hasim of the Govern-ment of Sarawak.

(*Translation.*)

This Agreement made in the year of the Prophet one thousand two hundred and fifty-seven at twelve o'clock on

Wednesday the thirtieth day of the month of Rejab showeth that with a pure heart and high integrity PANGERAN MUDA HASIM son of the late Sultan Muhammad hereby transfers to JAMES BROOKE Esquire the Government of Sarawak together with the dependencies thereof its revenues and all its future responsibilities. Moreover he James Brooke Esquire shall be the sole owner of its revenues and will be alone responsible for the public expenditure necessary for the good of Sarawak.

Moreover James Brooke Esquire acting with the same integrity and pureness of heart accepts this Agreement as set forth and further undertakes from the date hereof to pay to the Sultan of Brunei one thousand dollars to Pangeran Muda one thousand dollars to the Pettinggi three hundred dollars to the Bandar one hundred and fifty dollars and to the Temenggong one hundred dollars.

Moreover James Brooke Esquire undertakes that the laws and customs of the Malays of Sarawak shall for ever be respected since the country of Sarawak has hitherto been subject to the government of the Sultan of Brunei the Pangeran Muda and Malayan rajas.

Moreover should intrigues arise either within or without the State of Sarawak detrimental to its interests whether caused by peoples or princes or rulers who may be inimical to Sarawak the Sultan and his brother the Pangeran Muda shall uphold James Brooke Esquire as the lawfully appointed Ruler of Sarawak subject to no interference by any other person.

Moreover the Pangeran Muda and James Brooke Esquire do themselves make this Contract and the Pangeran agrees to relinquish all further activities in the Government of Sarawak except such as may be carried out by the consent of James Brooke Esquire and anything which they may severally or individually do in regard to the Government of Sarawak must be in accordance with the terms of this Agreement.

Document granted to Sir James Brooke by H.H. the Sultan of Brunei in 1841, whereby the country of Sarawak was made over to him and his successors for ever.

Written in Sarawak on the night of Friday the second day of Shaaban 1257 at ten o'clock.

James Brooke was a man of instinctive and resourceful courage : a man of keen intellect, a born fighter, an organiser and an administrator.   His mental powers were reflected in his physical qualities of alertness and precision of movement.   He was quite without fear, and in the presence of danger alone was he quite normal.   A characteristic story tells how, when he was sitting at dinner with some friends, the room was suddenly filled with a body of armed pirates under Lingire, the Dayak pirate chief, hoping to add to their grisly collection the head of their chief enemy.   Brooke, who was weaponless, professed to treat the visit as one of courtesy, and proceeded to fetch for the delectation of his guests a bottle of old brown sherry.   The discussion of the wine was followed by an interchange of narratives of a humorous nature ; and the entertainment was only interrupted by the entry of a large body of Brooke's Malay friends, to whom he had sent a message during the decanting of the wine, and who now rounded up the pirates, and proceeded to treat them as they had intended to treat the Rajah.

The British Government of the day treated Brooke with the ingratitude and neglect which are commonly the lot of European pioneers in the East.   However, the work endures.   Brooke gave to the Empire a new country of almost inexhaustible wealth, which he ruled with moderation and justice ; and his own tradition has been worthily carried on by his successors.

The other important British settlement is in the Northern end of Borneo.   This territory had long been a hunting-ground for slaves for the nobles of Brunei and Sulu, whose sultans claimed, but did not exercise, the right to rule over it.   In 1877 Mr. (later Sir) Alfred Dent, a Shanghai merchant, induced the two sultans to resign to him their sovereign rights over this territory in return for a money payment.   The British North Borneo Company, which was formed for the commercial development of it, undertook the necessary tasks of pacification and administration.   In 1881 the Company was granted a royal charter by the British Government.   In 1888 Sarawak and British North Borneo were formally brought under the protection of the British Government; but the territories remained under the rule of the Rajah and officials of the Chartered Company respectively, except in regard to their foreign relations.   In the year 1906 the Sultan of Brunei placed himself and his capital, together with the small territory over which he still retained undivided authority, under the protection of the British Government; and thus was completed the passing of the great island of Borneo under European control.

Note.—The author is indebted to Sir Percy Cunyng-hame for information regarding the old ornaments (see plate facing p. 17) which were discovered in 1899 in a landslip on the hill behind the Resident's bungalow at Limbang, Sarawak.   They are all of solid gold, and consist of rings, chains, part of the top of a gold box, and other ornaments, including two which seem to be associated with Phallic worship.   They are certainly very old, and appear to be of Hindu origin, and were probably brought from Java when Brunei was a dependency of Majapahit.

The drawing kindly made by Mr. R. T. Stuart King of these gold ornaments is from a photograph taken by Mr. J. A. Smith at the Sarawak Government Offices, Westminster.

Gathering of native chiefs after the Rajah's coronation ceremony.

CHAPTER IV

JUNGLE-FOLK TO-DAY

The chief tribal groups—Ibans: agreeable companions but quarrel-some—Kayans: warlike but industrious and retiring—Kenyahs: handsome, courageous and reliable—Klemantans (the term a con-ventional one): a careful and artistic people—Muruts: agriculturists —Punans: houseless hunters—Types and characteristics of the various tribes—The village community—Diversity of language.

THE present-day population of Borneo may be described as falling naturally into two great classes; on the one hand those who have accepted, nominally at least, the Moham-medan religion and civilisation, and on the other hand the Pagan peoples. In Brunei and in all the coast regions the majority of the people are Mohammedan, have no tribal organisation, and call themselves Malays (*Orang Malayu*). All other natives of Borneo, with the exception of these partially civilised " Malays " of the coast regions and such imported elements as Europeans, Chinese, and Klings, live under tribal organisation, their cultures ranging from the extreme simplicity of the nomadic Punans to a moder-ately developed barbarism. All these Pagan tribes have often been classed together indiscriminately under the name Dyaks or Dayaks, though many groups may be clearly distinguished from one another by differences of culture, belief, and custom, and peculiarities of their physical and mental constitutions.

Of these there are six principal groups: (1) Ibans, (2) Kayans, (3) Kenyahs, (4) Klemantans, (5) Muruts, (6) Punans. It will be recalled that the Kenyahs, Klemantans, and Punans are more or less aboriginal tribes; while the Ibans, Kayans, and Muruts are results of various invasions. Any estimate of the numbers of the

31

people of each of these six divisions is necessarily a very rough one, but it is about as follows : Klemantans, rather more than 1,500,000; Kenyahs, about 300,000; Muruts, 250,000; Ibans, 500,000; Kayans, 250,000; Punans and other peoples of similar nomadic habits, 150,000—*i.e.* a total of about 3,000,000.

Of all these six peoples the Ibans have become best known to Europeans, largely on account of their restless disposition, and to the fact that they are more numerous in Sarawak than any of the others. They have spread northwards over Sarawak during the latter half of the last century, chiefly from the region of the Batang Lupar and Saribas rivers, where they are still numerous. They are still spreading northward, encroaching upon the more peaceful Klemantan tribes. They are most densely distributed in the lower reaches of the main rivers of Sarawak, especially the Batang Lupar, Rejang, and Saribas rivers, which are now almost exclusively occupied by them ; but they are found also in scattered communities throughout almost all parts of Sarawak, and even in British North Borneo, and they extend from their centre in Sarawak into the adjacent regions of Dutch Borneo, which are drained by the northern tributaries of the Great Kapuas River.

The Iban is of a well-marked and fairly uniform physical type. His skin is distinctly darker than that of the other peoples of the interior, though not quite so dark as that of most of the true Malays. The hair of his head is more abundant, and longer than that of other peoples. His figure is well-proportioned, neat, and generally somewhat boyish. His expression is bright and mobile, his lips are generally distorted, and his teeth discoloured by the constant chewing of betel-nut. They are a vain, dressy, boastful, excitable, not to say frivolous people : cheerful, talkative, sociable, fond of fun and jokes and lively stories ; and, though prone to exaggeration, their statements can generally be accepted as founded on fact; they are industrious and energetic, and are great wanderers; to

His Highness Charles Vyner Brooke, 3rd Rajah of Sarawak.

the last peculiarity they owe the name of Iban, which has been given them by the Kayans, and which has now been generally adopted even by the Sea Dayaks themselves.

The good qualities enumerated above render the Iban an agreeable companion and a useful citizen. But there is another side to the picture : they have too little respect for their chiefs, a peculiarity which renders their social organisation somewhat defective and chaotic; they are quarrelsome and litigious, and were formerly the most inveterate head-hunters of the country ; unlike most of the other peoples, they followed the principle " Art for Art's sake," and took heads for the mere glory which the act brought them.

The Kayans are widely distributed throughout Central Borneo, and are to be found in large villages situated on the middle reaches of all the principal rivers with the exception of those that run to the north coast. They occupy in the main a zone dividing the districts of the lower reaches of the rivers from the central highlands, from which all the principal rivers flow.

The Kayans are a warlike people, but less truculent than the Ibans, more staid and conservative and religious, and less sociable. They do not wantonly enter into quarrels, and they respect and obey their chiefs. They are equally industrious with the Ibans, and though somewhat slow and heavy in both mind and body, they are more skilled in the handicrafts than any of the other peoples.

The Kenyahs predominate in the highlands a little to the north of the centre of Borneo where all the large rivers have their sources; but they are found also in widely scattered villages throughout the Kayan areas. In all respects they show much closer affinities with the Kayans than with the other peoples : as regards custom and mode of life they closely resemble the Kayans, with whom they are generally on friendly terms ; but they are easily distinguished from the Kayans by well-marked differences of bodily and mental characters, as well as by language.

D

Physically they are without question the finest people of the country, and are perhaps the most courageous and intelligent of the peoples. Pugnacious, but less quarrelsome than the Ibans : more energetic and excitable than the Kayan : hospitable and somewhat improvident, sociable and of pleasant manners : less reserved and of more buoyant temperament than the Kayan : very loyal and obedient to their chiefs ; more to be depended upon under all circumstances than any of the other peoples, except possibly the Kayans.

The term Klemantan is one recently devised to cover a number of peoples, who although widely-scattered throughout Borneo, and differing largely in language and customs, yet present to the experienced observer certain peculiar characteristics. The name Pulo Klemantan (the Mango Country) is that given by Malays to the whole island. It follows that there is no one tribe, or set of tribes, calling themselves by the title. In physical and mental characters they show affinities to the Kenyahs of the interior on the one hand and to the Muruts on the other. They are less bellicose than the peoples mentioned above, and have suffered much at their hands. They are a careful, intelligent, and sociable, though somewhat timid, people ; skilful in handicrafts, but less energetic than the Kayans and Kenyahs, and inferior to them in metal-work and the making of swords, spears, and boats. Amongst many of the Klemantan tribes the blow-pipe is the characteristic weapon, and they are more devoted to hunting than any others, except perhaps the Punans. They are to be found in every part of the island, but most of their villages are situated on the lower reaches of the rivers. They are most abundant in the south, constituting the greater part of the population of Dutch Borneo.

The Muruts constitute a very large part of the population of the North of the island. In British North Borneo they predominate over all the other peoples combined : in Sarawak and in Dutch Borneo they are found in small

Iban woman.

Kayan woman.

Punan woman carrying baby in a
basket.

scattered communities. To a certain degree they resemble the Klemantans, but their features are less regular and pleasing, and their skin is of a more ruddy colour. The Murut tribes living in the highlands are a fine, muscular, and comparatively tall people : their agriculture is superior to that of the majority of the other Bornean peoples, but they are addicted to the drinking of rice-spirit. Their social organisation is less stable than that of either the Kayans or the Kenyahs, and the authority of their chiefs finds no great respect.

Of the Punans, a nomadic people, and possibly the oldest of all the tribes inhabiting the island, more will be said hereafter. They live in small groups, and are so primitive that they are not even agricultural. They are found throughout the interior of Borneo, but are difficult to meet with, as they remain hidden in the depths of the forests. They support themselves by hunting with the blow-pipe, by gathering wild jungle fruits, and by collecting jungle products and bartering them with the more settled peoples. They are shy people, timid, reserved and inoffensive ; and they never engage in open warfare, although they will avenge injuries by stealthy attacks on individuals with the blow-pipe and poisoned darts. Their only handicrafts are the making of baskets, mats, blow-pipes, and the implements used for working the wild sago ; but in these and in the use of the blow-pipe they are very expert. All other manufactured articles used by them— cloths, swords, and spears—are obtained by barter from the other tribes.

All these six tribes bear the superficial physical character-istics which might be expected from them. They are all of medium height, while the colour of their skin varies from a rich medium brown to a very light *café-au-lait*. The nose varies largely, being normally rather wide at the nostrils, while in many cases the plane of the nostrils is tilted a little upwards and forwards. Of the whole the pure-bred Kenyah presents, perhaps, the most distinctive and the noblest physical type. He has a light yellow skin and wavy hair. The Kayan has a rather darker skin and of a redder tone. His legs are not so disproportionately short to his body, but his features are less regular, and are coarser and heavier. The chief characteristic of the Murut is his length of leg : his intonation is melodious and pleasant, when contrasted with the staccato of the Kenyah.

The Klemantans, who, naturally, are less of a homogeneous group, are generally less muscular and active than the Kenyahs. They are, however, a handsome race.

A common feature of all these peoples, with the exception of certain nomad tribes, is that they live in village communities, situated on the banks of rivers. These villages vary in size most curiously, the smallest comprising twenty or thirty inhabitants only, while the larger may hold as many as 1500. There seems to be no local distribution of peoples—villages of various tribes are found everywhere closely adjacent. The Ibans alone seemed to be afforded isolation—the result, probably, of their truculent disposition. These village communities have little or no political organisation, beyond the fact that each has a " head-man," and occasionally unites with a neighbouring village for defensive purposes. Except for these informal alliances obtaining between neighbouring villages of the people of any one stock, each village forms an independent community, making alliances and selecting patches of land for cultivation much at its own pleasure. No village community remains on the same spot for any long period ; but after fifteen, ten, or even fewer years a new site is sought, often at a considerable distance, and a new village is built. The principal reasons for this habit of frequent migration, which has produced the intimate mingling throughout large areas of the peoples of different stocks, are two : first, the necessity of finding virgin soil for cultivation ; and secondly the occurrence of epidemics or other calamities which lead them to believe that the place of their abode is unpropitious.

One of the most peculiar features of the people of Borneo is the great diversity of language obtaining among them. The migratory habits of the people and the consequent mingling of communities of different stocks within the same areas, far from having resulted in the genesis by fusion of a common language, have resulted in the formation of a great number of dialects; so that in following the course of a river one may sometimes find in a day's journey of a score of miles villages, the people of which speak a dialect almost unintelligible to their neighbours. The natural result is that, with the exception of the Ibans, almost all adults speak or at least understand two or more dialects of the same language, while most of the chiefs and leading men speak several dialects fluently, and partially understand a larger number. The language most widely understood by those to whom it is not native is the Kayan; but since the recent spread of trade through large areas protected by European Governments, a simplified form of the Malay language has been rapidly establishing itself as a *lingua franca* for the whole country.

CHAPTER V

THE PUNANS : NOMAD HUNTERS

"Living in their boxes"—People without houses, crops, or dogs—Common commodities—Punans attached to villages of other tribes—Their shyness—Tribal and social habits—Marriage—Bali Penyalong—The crocodile—Magic and sorcery—Hunting and singing.

In practically every part of Borneo there may be found, if one can penetrate to the remotest jungle, certain nomad hunting tribes. Such are the Ukits, the Sians, the Bukitans, the Lugats, the Lisums, and the Punans. All these tribes present certain physical similarities, although as regards language they differ widely; and of them the most typical, as well as the most interesting, are the Punans.

These people enjoy certain amazing habits. They possess no houses; they own no more property than they can carry on their backs (and so may be said perpetually to "live in their boxes"); they cultivate no crops, relying for all their food on what the jungle can provide; and—most amazing of all—although they are a hunting people, they possess no dogs, and do not even manufacture their arms of precision.

When to these curious facts it is added that they in every way come up to the ideal of the "gentle" or "noble" savage, and that, although nomads and hunters, they show no signs of exposure to the elements, surprise increases.

For physical development the Punan stands very high among the Bornean peoples. Of the important tribes mentioned above, he bears the greatest resemblance to the Kenyah, for he is short of stature with a comparatively long body, and is very sturdily built. His head is comparatively

The toothless scaly ant-eater and its young.

Tarsius spectrum.
From a photograph by
Dr. Le Gros Clark.

A baby orang-utan.

short (sub-brachycephalic) and is inclined to squareness : the features are regular, and the most distinctive characteristics are a relatively well-developed nasal bridge, the nostrils being shot so far forward and upward that one seems almost to be able to look through them into their heads.   The skin of a Punan is of a fine silky texture, and is either of a pale yellow or even of a greenish shade ; for the Punan rarely exposes himself to even indirect sunlight, preferring always the deep twilight of the jungle.

Having no crops and no domestic animals, the Punans live exclusively on jungle produce, animal and vegetable. Animals of all kinds are eaten, being obtained chiefly by means of the blow-pipe, in the use of which they are surprisingly expert.   The vegetable food consists of wild sago and a form of vegetable tallow contained in the seed of a large forest tree, Shorea.   What food is obtained is shared by all the members of the group.   A hunter, on returning to camp with a piece of game, throws it down before his fellows and invites them to treat it as common property.   If his " bag " is too big to be brought in without aid (as with a large pig or a deer), he returns to camp, but modestly keeps silence as to his achievement, until he is questioned as to his luck : he then remarks, casually, that he has left a small piece of game—something quite inconsiderable—in the jungle.   At once some three or four men start out to find the quarry, being guided by the bent twigs of trees and bushes which the hunter has used to mark his trail.

Commodities gained by other means (as by gift, or barter) are similarly shared in common : if a present of tobacco (a most welcome gift to a Punan) is made to one member of a group, the whole mass is divided up into as many little heaps as there are members present : each of whom, men and women alike, takes one.

The weapons and other implements usually carried by a Punan are naturally few and light.   He carries a sword, a small knife, a blow-pipe with a spear-head attached, and a small narrow-bladed axe with which to extract camphor from the heart of the tree in which it is found. For domestic purposes the family possesses mallets and sieves for the preparation of sago, dishes and spoons of hard wood, tongs of bamboo for the eating of the sago, a few iron pots (obtained by barter), large baskets carried on the back, a few mats of plaited rattan, and small bamboo boxes for miscellaneous purposes. Perhaps the most important of these impedimenta is a double-ended spatula, with which the head of the family first stirs the boiled sago, and then, with one end, conveys it to his own mouth, and, with the other, to his wife's.

A company of Punans, although perpetually wandering in their exploitation of the forest, will yet commonly attach itself to an undefined general area. For this they have two excellent reasons : the first, that they are thus able to familiarise themselves with the local resources of Nature; and the second, because they can establish friendly relations with the settled inhabitants of the region, and can barter jungle produce with them for their mutual advantage. The local community looks on such a proposition with the highest approval : it learns the language of the new-comers, and definitely (and often practically) resents any attempt made to disparage the established relations. Any village, of whatsoever tribe, welcomes the Punan, and at the same time regards him with a friendly sense of proprietorship, and is jealous of interference by other tribes. It has found the Goose, and methodically collects the Golden Eggs; but the Goose loses very little, having found a gold mine, which it knows perfectly well how to exploit.

Punans are incredibly shy, and even among friends they rarely appear to be at their ease. When gathered in friendly talk with strangers, even such as they have every reason to trust (for years they knew of the European, but were shy of him), they prefer to remain squatting on their heels, instead of sitting down on a mat like other tribes.

They seem always to be prepared for an unpleasant emergency; and the tension of their muscles, combined with the unrelenting watchfulness of their faces, gives the impression of some sort of wild animal, shy but friendly, and ready at any moment to fight for its life.

A Punan will never wantonly slay or attack a man of another tribe, and he never goes on the war-path except when he is accidentally roped in with some other tribe. Head-hunting is not practised, for tribal tradition does not require it. If, however, he is attacked, he will not merely defend himself adequately, but he will call to his assistance other Punans in the same area (which often is a big one). It should be said that, in many cases, vengeance is delayed for a long period—a fact which, being known to the other peoples, procures him a certain immunity from wanton attacks.

A Punan community usually has, as titular chief, one of its older members, whose authority is not formally defined, but depends on his reputation and age. There is very little of the Dictator about this functionary, for, in important matters, he generally finds a strong body of public opinion, of which he is the mouthpiece. He is, further, responsible for the reading of omens, and has charge of such household gods and altars as his group carries with it, such as the wooden image of a crocodile, which is always prominent in a Punan camp.

Monogamy is the rule among these people, but occasionally polyandry occurs, particularly when a woman has lived with a man for a long time without giving him a child. Marriage is for life, although the chief can order a separation; and chastity, as with other tribes, is more common after than before marriage. Endogamy within the group is not countenanced.

The actual ceremony consists in a joint feast of the two communities, at which the chiefs " say a few words," exhorting the husband to be zealous in hunting and in the collecting of camphor, and the wife to the claims of

her children, and the virtue of cooking.   After this simple
ceremony, the husband joins the wife's community, and
usually remains a member of it : no definite payment is
made to the bride's parents, although a small gift, such as
a pound or so of tobacco, or a skein of beads, is considered
" good form."

Adverse omens, such as the call of the barking deer,
may cause a marriage to be postponed ; but, beyond this,
there is practically no appeal for divine or supernatural
sanction, except that an appeal is made for protection
to Bali Penyalong (their god), to whom an offering of
food is made, placed on a stake beneath the image of a
crocodile.

This creature is, as with other tribes in Borneo, treated
with respectful fear ; although, since the Punans have no
boats (among other things in which they are lacking), he
is hardly so immanent and formidable as he is to others.
His image is, however, treated as a sort of altar, and the
title given to him, Bali Penyalong, is that which other
Bornean tribes confine exclusively to the Supreme Being.
The wooden image of the crocodile is carried round by a
Punan group wherever it goes ; and to it appeals are made
in the case of sickness, by the medicine-man.   Other
religious beliefs that they possess are similar to those of the
Kayans, but simpler.   Omens are obtained from civet-cats,
grasshoppers, lizards, and the barking deer.   Their rites,
however, involve no taking of life, and they do not look
for guidance from the entrails of animals.   This may,
possibly, be evidence that they are of later origin than
other tribes.

Burial and funeral rites are unknown, and the Punan
view of life after death seems to contain no doctrine of
Retribution   or   Sin,   and   practically   has   no   moral
significance.

Punans are great believers in charms and sorcery : their
medicine-men are famed for their knowledge and skill,
and are in much request among other tribes for the

Punans.

Kayan youths wrestling.

" catching of souls," and for the extraction of pain and
disease. They have great faith in charms, especially for
the bringing of good luck in hunting. The selection
of the talismans is arbitrary, and commonly confined to
the grotesque.

It has been said above that the Punan cannot make his
own tools. This is only partially true. He can make no
metal tools, all of which he obtains from the tribes that
patronise him, especially the Kayans. The iron rod which
he, like other peoples, uses to bore out his blow-pipe is not
of his manufacture. This fact would seem to prove that
the blow-pipe, at least as it is to-day, cannot have been of
his invention, although he is the most skilful of all Borneans in its use. Apart from metal implements he shows
remarkable skill in the plaiting of rattan-strips to make
baskets, mats, and sieves. Besides this a certain amount
of wood and bone-carving is done, mostly knife-handles
and decorative pieces for the sword-sheaths.

It will be understood that the chief art of the Punan
is that of the Hunter ; tracking and trapping come
naturally to him, and in these pursuits he displays an
incredible skill in the interpretation of forest signs. He can
infer, from tracks, the number of a preceding party : he
can cover his own tracks by leaving the firm earth and
making his way by the boughs of trees : he can follow
a hostile tribe for days without a chance of discovery.

The only other art that this interesting creature seems
to possess is that of Song. His principal instrument may
be described, for want of a better term, as a stringed
cylinder : it consists, in its body, of a length of thick
bamboo, about twenty-four inches by four. This is
hollowed out, and on the outer surface six little narrow
strips are cut to a length of about twenty inches. These
strips are not detached from the main body, but the ends
are kept unsevered : the strip between each end is raised
by means of little " bridges " of wood. Thus there are
six strips, or strings, on which, by a variation of the

bridges, different notes can be produced.   Another instrument is a sort of dulcimer, laid across the shins of the performer, and beaten with little sticks.

Curiously, however, the best songs of the Punan are those sung without accompaniment. To hear, in the dense blackness of the jungle, when a few torches alone light up the solemn circle, a Punan recite with dramatic gestures the story of a departing soul, gives an impression which is not without its solemnity or beauty.

The Punan pretends that he can dance ; but his efforts in this line are confined to imitations of animals, and to posturing—which may be seen in London.

Such are these strange people—isolated, not even self-supporting ; unresourceful, yet able to make a livelihood at others' expense ; simple, yet wise ; untrained, and with a fear of the unfamiliar, yet knowing instinctively what is right ; a type of civilisation, and a civilisation of no mean kind.

PART II

TRIBAL AND VILLAGE LIFE

CHAPTER I

TRIBAL LIFE (KAYANS AND KENYAHS)

Homogeneity of the Kayans—Long Houses—House chiefs and the village chief—The chief's powers—Succession and election—Kenyah chiefs paternal rulers : their special training—Social classes among Kayans and Kenyahs—The lowest class : war-captives and servants—Marriages out of class—Forbidden degrees—Divorce—Adoption—Kith and kin—Inheritance of property.

WHEN one comes to examine the social habits of the Bornean, one finds the Kayan and Kenyah most typical, because they are most homogeneous.

Although a similar tribal and village system is found in all parts of the island, it is among the Kayans—and to a certain extent the Kenyahs—that it finds its highest and most characteristic development. Among the Muruts, Ibans, Dusuns, and Klemantans the headman is little more than an arbitrator in household disputes. Among the Kayans he is an essential part of their polity.

Although their villages are scattered over a wide area, yet the Kayan people everywhere speak the same language and follow the same customs, have the same traditions, beliefs, and ceremonies. Such small local differences as they present are hardly greater than those obtaining between the villagers of adjoining English counties. Although communication between the widely separated branches of the people is very slight and infrequent, yet all are bound together by a common sentiment for the tribal name. The chiefs keep in mind and hand down from generation to generation the history of the migrations of the principal branches of the tribe, the names and genealogies of the principal chiefs, and important incidents affecting any one branch. At least fifteen sub-tribes of Kayans, each bearing a distinctive name, are recognised. The word *Uma*, which appears in the names of each group, means village-house or settlement, and it seems probable that these sub-tribes represent so many original Kayan villages which at some remote period, before the tribe became so wholly scattered, may have contained the whole Kayan population in Borneo.

There exist, however, no formal bonds between the various sub-tribes and villages. Each village is absolutely independent of all others, save in so far as custom and caution prescribe that, before undertaking any important affair (such as a removal of the village or a warlike expedition), the chief will seek the advice and, if necessary, the co-operation of the chiefs of neighbouring Kayan villages. The people of neighbouring villages, especially the families of the chiefs, are also bound together by many ties of kinship ; for intermarriage is frequent.

As was said above, a Kayan village almost invariably consists of several Long Houses. Each house is ruled by a chief; but one such chief is recognised as the head chief of the village. The purely domestic affairs of each house are settled by the house chief, but all important matters of general interest are brought before the village chief. In the former category fall disputes as to ownership of domestic property, questions of compensation for personal injury or loss, marriage and divorce. The matters to be settled by the head chief sitting in council with the subordinate chiefs are those affecting the whole village, questions of war and peace and of removal of the village to a new site, disputes between houses, and trials for serious personal injuries.

The degree of authority of the chiefs and the nature and degree of the penalties imposed by them are pre-

Outside verandah of an Iban house.

Kayans making fire by friction.

scribed in a general way by custom, though as regards the former much depends upon the personal qualities of each chief, and as regards the latter much is left to his discretion. The punishment which these chiefs are allowed to impose are generally fines of so many gongs, swords, or spears. On the whole the chief plays the part of a referee or mediator, awarding compensation to the injured party, rather than that of a judge. In the case of offences against the whole house, a fine may also be imposed; and the articles of the required value are placed under the charge of the chief, who holds them on behalf of the community, and uses them in the making of payments or presents in return for services rendered to the whole community.

The chief also is responsible for the proper observation of omens and for the regulation of *malan* (restrictions) affecting the whole house; and he takes the leading part in social ceremonies and in most of the religious rites collectively performed by the village. He is regarded by other chiefs as responsible for the behaviour of his people, and above all, in war he is responsible for both strategy and tactics.

For the maintenance of his authority and the enforcement of his commands the chief relies upon the force of public opinion, which, so long as he is capable and just, will always support him, and will bring severe moral pressure to bear upon any member of the household who hesitates to submit.

In return for his labours on behalf of the household or village the Kayan chief gains little or nothing in the shape of material reward. He may receive a little voluntary assistance in the cultivation of his field; in travelling by river he is accorded the place of honour amidships; but his principal rewards are the social precedence and deference accorded him and the satisfaction found in the exercise of authority.

The office of chief is elective rather than hereditary, but the electors' choice is strongly biassed in favour of the

most capable son of the late chief; and in practice a chief
is usually followed by one of his sons. Indeed, in the
case of a chief dying with only young sons, these boys
would feel that they held the reversion of the headship
when they grew up. If the *interim* chief, however, left
capable descendants, there would be at least two claimants :
in which case the village would, probably, literally split
up into two new villages. A similar break-up is found
in the rare cases when a chief fails to give satisfaction.

The Kenyahs form a less homogeneous and clearly
defined tribe than the Kayans; yet in the main their
social organisation is very similar to that of the Kayans,
although, as regards physical characters and language, they
present closer affinities with other peoples.

Among the Kenyahs the position of the chief is one of
greater authority and consideration than even among the
Kayans. The people voluntarily work for their chief
both in his private and public capacities, obeying his
commands cheerfully, and accepting his decisions with
more deference than is accorded by the Kayans. The
chief in return shows himself more generous and paternal
towards his people, interesting himself more intimately
in their individual affairs. Hence the Kenyah chief stands
out more prominently as leader and representative of his
people, and the cohesion of the whole community is
stronger. The chief owes this great influence over his
people, in large measure, to his training, for, while still a
youth, the son or the nephew of a chief is accustomed to
responsibility by being sent in charge of small bodies of
followers upon missions to distant villages, to gather or
convey information, or to investigate disturbing rumours.
He is also frequently called upon to speak on public
occasions, and thus early becomes a practised orator.

Among both Kayans and Kenyahs in every village three
social strata are clearly distinguishable and are recognised
by the people themselves. The upper class consists of the
family of the chief and his near relatives, his aunts and

uncles, brothers, sisters, and cousins. These upper-class families are generally in easier circumstances than the others, thanks to the possession of property such as brass ware, valuable heads, caves containing edible birds' nests, and a supply of various other material possessions in a larger quantity and a superior quality to those of the middle- and lower-class families.

The man of the upper class can generally be distinguished at a glance by the regularity of his features, his superior bearing, the neatness and cleanliness of his person, and his more valuable weapons and personal ornaments. The woman of the upper class also exhibits to the eye similar marks of her superior birth and breeding. The tattooing of her skin is more finely executed, greater care is taken with the elongation of the lobe of the ear, so that the status of the woman is often indicated by the length of the lobe. Her dress and person are cleaner, and generally better cared for, and her skin is fairer than that of other women, owing, no doubt, to her having been less exposed to the sun in her duties.

Both men and women of the upper class work in the rice-fields and bear their share of all the labours of the village; but they are able to cultivate larger areas than others, and the labours of the field and the house are rendered less severe by the assistance of servants.

The chief's room, which is usually about twice as long as that of any other room, is usually in the middle of the house; and those of the other upper-class families, which also are commonly larger than the other rooms, adjoin it on either side.

In all social gatherings, and in the performance of public rites and ceremonies, the men of the upper class are accorded leading parts, and they usually group themselves about the chief. Social intercourse is freer and more intimate among the people of the upper class than between them and the rest of the household.

The middle class in most cases comprises the majority

E

of the people of a house. They may enjoy all the forms of property, though generally their possessions are of smaller extent and value, and they seldom possess dependents. Their voices carry less weight in public affairs; but among this class are generally a few men of exceptional capacity or experience whose advice and co-operation are specially valued by the chief. Among this class, too, are usually a few men in each house on whom devolve, often hereditarily, special duties demanding peculiar skill or knowledge, e.g. the working of iron at the forge, the making of boats, and the finding of camphor.

The lowest class is made up of people captured in war and of their descendants, and for this reason its members are of a very varied physical type. An unmarried captive of either sex lives with the family, and is treated almost as a member of it, eating and in some cases sleeping in the family room. If they acquire families, they are allowed to acquire a room in the house, and they then begin to acquire a less dependent position and though they still retain the status of dependents, are spoken of as " servants outside-the-room," the room-holder generally finds it impossible to command their labour beyond a very limited extent, and in some cases will voluntarily resign his rights over the whole family. But in such a case the family still continues to belong to the lowest class.

On the whole the dependents are treated with so much consideration that they have little to complain of, and most of them seem to have little desire to return to their own people. A capable man may become the confidant and companion of the chief, and may attain a position of considerable influence in the village. A young boy or girl is commonly addressed by the chief as " My child." The most severe punishment is, usually, scolding, and the children bear their part in the life of the family, sharing in its labours and its recreations. Nothing in the dress or appearance of this class distinguishes them from the other members of the village.

In each of these three classes marriage is confined to within that class, although not always to the village. In the upper class unions are largely a matter of personal choice, subject to the approval of the relatives and the chief.

As regards marriages out of the class, a youth of the upper class, becoming fond of some girl of the middle class, and not being allowed to marry her (although this is occasionally permitted), will live with her for a year or two. Then, when the time for his marriage arrives (it may perhaps have been postponed for some years after being arranged, owing to evil omens, or to lack of means or of house accommodation), he may separate from his mistress, leaving in her care any children born of their union, and make over to her such property as public opinion demands. She may, and usually will, subsequently marry a man of her own class, but the children born of her irregular union may claim and may be accorded some of the privileges of their father's class. In this way there is formed in most villages a class of persons of ambiguous status, debarred from full membership in the upper class by the bar-sinister. Such persons tend to become wholly identified with the upper or middle class according to the degrees of their personal merits.

Marriages are sometimes contracted between persons of the middle and lower classes. In the case of a young man marrying a lower-class woman, the owner of the room in which the woman lives will endeavour to persuade him to live with her in their room, when he becomes a subordinate member of their household. If they succeed in this, the room-holder will claim as their property half the children born to the couple. On the other hand, if the man insists on establishing himself in possession of a room, he may succeed in practically emancipating his wife, by making some compensation to her room-holder in the shape of personal service, brass ware or jungle products. In this case the children of the couple would be regarded

as freeborn.   It is possible for an energetic member of the
lower class to buy his or her freedom should they desire
to do so.

Less frequent is the marriage of a man of the lower class
with a woman of the middle class.   In this case the man
will generally manage to secure his emancipation and to
establish himself as master of a room, and to merge himself
in the middle class.   In the case of marriage between two
lower-class people, they continue to live in the rooms of
their owners, spending by arrangement periods of two or
three years alternately as members of the two households.
The children born of such a couple are more or less
divided as they grow up between the room-holders of their
parents.

Very few men have more than one wife.   Occasionally a chief, whose wife has borne him no children, will
with her consent, or even at her request, take a second
younger wife.   In such a case each wife has her own
sleeping apartment within the chief's large chamber, and
the younger wife is expected to defer to the older, and to
help her in the work of the house and of the field.   The
second wife would be chosen of rather lower social standing
than the first wife, who in virtue of this fact maintains her
ascendancy more easily.   A third wife is probably unknown : public opinion does not easily condone a second
wife, and would hardly tolerate a third.   In spite of the
presence of women descendants of captives in the houses,
concubinage is not recognised or tolerated.

Incest is regarded very seriously, and the forbidden
degrees of kinship are clearly defined.   They are very
similar to those recognised among ourselves.   First cousins
may marry, but such marriages are not regarded with
favour, and certain special ceremonies are necessitated ;
and it seems to be the general opinion that such marriages
are not likely to prove happy.

Divorce is rare but not unknown.   The principal grounds
of divorce are misconduct, desertion, incompatibility of

temper, and family quarrels; or a couple may terminate their state of wedlock by mutual consent on payment of a moderate fine to the chief. Such separation by mutual consent is occasioned not infrequently by the sterility of the marriage, especially if the couple fails to obtain a child for adoption : the parties hope to procure offspring by taking new partners; for the desire for children and pride and joy in the possession of them are strongly felt by all. The husband of a sterile wife may leave the house for a long period, living in the forest and visiting other houses, in the hope that his wife may divorce him on the ground of desertion, or give him grounds for divorcing her. On discovery of misconduct on the woman's part the husband will usually divorce her; the man then retains all property accumulated since the marriage, and the children are divided between the parents. Misconduct on the part of the man must be flagrant before it constitutes a sufficient ground for divorce by the wife.

Adoption is by no means uncommon. When a woman has remained barren for some years after her marriage, the couple usually seek to adopt one or more children. They generally prefer the child of a relative, but may take any child, even a captive or a slave-born child, whose parents are willing to resign all rights in it. A child is often taken over from poor parents, some article of value or a supply of rice being given in exchange. Not infrequently the parents wish to have the child returned to them when their affairs, owing to a good harvest or some stroke of luck, take a turn for the better, and this is a frequent cause of dissensions. Usually the adopted child takes in every way the position of a child born to the parents.

During its first few years the child remains nameless, and is spoken of as *Ukat* if a boy, *Owing* if a girl, both of which seem to be best translated as Thingumybob; among the Ibans *Ulat* (grub) is the name commonly used. It is felt that to give the child a name whilst its hold of life is still feeble is undesirable, because the name would tend to draw the attention of evil spirits to it. During its third or fourth year it is given a name at the same time as a number of other children of the same house. The name is chosen with much deliberation, the eldest son and daughter usually receiving the names of a grandfather and grand-mother respectively.

The name first given to any person is rarely carried through life : it is usually changed after any severe illness or serious accident, in order that the evil influences that have pursued him may fail to recognise him under the new name. Among the Klemantans it is usual under these circumstances to name the child after some offensive object, e.g. *Tai* (dung), in order to render it inconspicuous, and thus withdraw it from the attention of malign powers.

The terms used to denote degrees of kinship are few, and are used in a very elastic manner. The word of widest connotation is *Parin Igat*, which is equivalent to our cousin or the Scottish " sib " : it is applied to all blood relatives of the same generation, and is some-times used in a metaphorical sense like the Romany " pal." There are no words corresponding to our words son and daughter, *Anak* meaning merely child of either sex. There are no words corresponding to brother and sister ; both are spoken of as *Parin*, but this word is often used as a title of endearment in addressing or speaking of a friend of either sex of the same social standing and age as the speaker. The children of the same parents speak of them-selves as *Panak* ; this term also is sometimes used loosely and metaphorically. The terms applied to other relatives are merely descriptive, and are not terms of address.

At a man's death his property is divided between his widow and children. But in order to prevent disputes, an old man may divide his property before his death. The widow becomes the head of the room, though a married son or daughter or several unmarried children may share it with her. She inherits all or most of the household

utensils.   Such things as gongs and other brass ware,
weapons, war-coats, and boats are divided equally among
the sons, the eldest perhaps getting a little more than the
others.   The girls divide the old beads, cloth, bead-boxes,
and various trifles.   The male dependents go to the sons,
the females to the daughters.   Such property as birds'-
nest caves and honey-trees may be divided among all the
children.

CHAPTER II

CHILDHOOD AND YOUTH OF A KAYAN

Birth : ceremonies and superstitions—Restrictions on parents during
infancy—Giving of names—Laki Pesong—A naming ceremony on
the Upper Rejang—The *Dayong*—Boys' games—The first garment—
A Spencerian training—Music and dancing—The *Keluri*—The war-
dance—Manhood : head-striking—" Seeking tobacco "—Betrothal
—Pre-wedding presents—" Fixing the day "—The bridal beads—
The wedding—Taking the omens—The honeymoon.

AMONG the firmest superstitions among the Kayans
is the belief that a child, from the moment of its existence until its actual birth, is subject to religious restrictions, or taboos. (In their own language they are *malan*,
and certain objects and acts are *lali* to them.) The belief
that an expectant mother is influenced by what she
happens to see is universal : she must avoid the sight
of the long-nosed monkey (*Nasalis larvatus*) and the
Maias, the great Anthropoid Ape of Borneo, and must
refrain from sundry kinds of flesh and fish. There are
certain other matters which are forbidden both to her and
to her husband.

To ensure a successful delivery certain definite measures
are taken. A young pig is sacrificed, his mission being
to propitiate Doh Tenangan, the wife of the Supreme
Being, Laki Tenangan ; and in case of any untoward
incident the sacrifice is repeated.

In every Kayan house are certain elderly women who
have a reputation for special knowledge and skill in all
matters connected with pregnancy and childbirth. One
of these is called in at an early stage, and she makes from
time to time a careful examination. She has also a number
of charms, which she hangs in the woman's room, and
various unguents, which she applies externally.

56

In all other respects the pregnant woman follows her ordinary mode of life until the pains of labour begin. Then she is attended by the wise woman and several elderly relatives or friends. She sits in her room, which is *lali* to all but her attendants and her husband; and she is hidden from the latter by a screen of mats.

If labour is unusually difficult or prolonged, the whole household is thrown into consternation, for death in childbirth is regarded with peculiar horror. All the men of the house, including the chief and boys, fly from the house, or, if it is night, clamber up among the beams of the roof and there hide in abject fear; and, if the worst happens, they remain there until the woman's corpse has been taken out of the house for burial. In such a case the burial is effected with the utmost despatch. Old men and women, who are indifferent to death, undertake the work; but they expect a large fee, for the soul of the woman who dies in childbirth goes, with the souls of those who fall in battle, or die by violence of any kind, to Bawang Daha (the Lake of Blood).

If twins are born of different sexes, the girl is commonly sacrificed [1] by exposure in the jungle. It is held that twins necessarily must incur double sorrows; while the practical difficulty of nursing two children at one time is held to be prejudicial to both. Moreover, the Kayan is so fond of slightly older children that he is less sensitive to the claims of an infant.

At the moment the child is completely born, a gong or a drum (according as it is male or female) is beaten in the gallery with a peculiar rhythm. All the inhabitants of the Long House who are within at the moment have the right to a handful of salt from the parents of the child; and all members who are not under the roof are expected to make a present of some piece of iron to the child. This is an ancient custom, which is no longer

[1] Needless to say, this custom is passing away with the increased influence of European Governments.

strictly observed, and which seems to be undergoing a natural decay.

During the confinement of a woman, Kayans (more especially those of the Upper Rejang) sometimes perform a dance which is supposed to facilitate delivery. It is commonly performed by a woman (a friend or relative of the mother), who takes in her arms a bundle of cloth, which she handles like a baby while she dances, afterwards putting it into the cradle, in which a child is carried on the back. It is related that this custom dates back to a woman who, receiving a child from a dying mother, afterwards acquired great prosperity. After the actual birth the mother for seventeen days wears threads tied round the thumbs and big toes, and she is expected to avoid heavy labour, such as farm-work and the pounding of rice.

Both the father and the mother observe certain restrictions during the early months and years of the child's life, with diminishing strictness as the child grows older. The general aim of all these restrictions seems to be to establish and maintain about the child a certain atmosphere, or, as they say, a certain odour, in which alone it can thrive. This notion of an atmosphere attaching to material objects pervades the thought and practice of Kayans. Analogous to it is the fact that a Kayan will wear for a long time, and will often refuse to wash, a garment which has been worn and afterwards given to him by a European whom he respects.

During the child's infancy neither father nor mother will eat or touch anything the properties of which are thought to be harmful or undesirable for the child, such as the skin of the deer or of the tiger-cat; and the child himself is still more strictly preserved from such contact. Further, nothing used by or about the child—toys, garments, cradle or beads—must be allowed to pass out of the possession of the parents. No stranger may handle or gaze too closely upon the child; and when it is put down to sleep in the parents' room, the mat or cradle on which it lies is generally surrounded by a rough screen. The more influential the stranger, the more is his contact to be feared; for any such contact or notice may attract to the infant the unwelcome and probably injurious attentions of the Spirits. For the same reason it is forbidden, or *parit*, to a child to lie down on the spot where a chief has been sitting or where he usually reposes. It is a grave offence for a child to jump over the legs of a reclining chief; although in this case the disrespect shown is probably the more important ground of the disapprobation incurred.

In its first year of life the infant is carried by the mother almost continuously during its waking hours : it is generally suspended by a sling made of wood or of basket-work, resembling in shape the swing familiar to our nurseries : the child sits on a semicircular piece of board, its legs dependent, its knees and belly against the mother's back, and its own back supported by the two vertical pieces of the cradle. The father hardly handles it during its first year, but older children are dandled for hours together in the most affectionate manner; and, if the child's grandfather is living, he generally becomes its devoted slave.

Until the boy is five or six years of age he remains under the care of his mother. He spends the day running about the house and among the boats at the landing-place, playing with his fellows, chasing the pigs and fowls, and bathing in the river. The children are in the main what is commonly called good, they cry but little, and quarrels and outbreaks of temper are few. During the boy's third year a hole is punched in the shell of each ear. A single blow with a sharp bamboo punch takes out a round piece; into this a plug of wax or wood is inserted. The girl, on the other hand, has more rings added to the lobes of her ears, which gradually yield to the weight, and begin to assume the desired character of slender loops. During these years the boy normally takes the first step of his initiation as a warrior by striking a blow at a freshly-taken head, or, if need be, at an old one.

It is at some time in the course of these years, usually not earlier than the beginning of the child's third year, that he first receives a name. Normally all the children in one Long House are given names at the same time, usually the conclusion of a successful harvest; for a general feast is made for which much rice and rice-spirit are required, and these cannot be spared in a year of poor harvest. For each child who is to be named a small human image in soft wood is prepared. This is an effigy of Laki Pesong, the god whose special function it is to care for the welfare of children. A small mat is woven and a few strips of rattan are provided for each child. The child sits with a near relative in the gallery beside the door of their room, and the parents announce the name they propose for the child. Then the father, or some other man, after killing a chick or a young pig, lays the image on a small mat before the child, passes one of the rattan strips beneath it, and, holding the image firmly with a big toe on each end of it, pulls the strip rapidly to and fro, until it is made hot by its friction against the image and smoke begins to rise. While this goes on, the same man, or another, pours out a string of words addressed to Laki Pesong, asking whether the proposed name will be suitable and auspicious. He continues the sawing movement until a spark is produced and the strip breaks in two. The two pieces are then compared: if they are of unequal length, this result is regarded as expressing the approval of the proposed name by Laki Pesong; if they are of approximately equal length, the god is held to have expressed his disapproval, and another name is proposed and submitted to the same test. Should disapproval be thus expressed more than once, the naming is postponed to another occasion.

If a name has been approved, the little image and

Small children out for a ride.

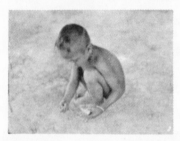

Child playing with pebbles on the road.

Happy Iban children.

strip of rattan, together with the knife used in killing the pig or chicken, are wrapped up in the small mat ; and the bundle is thrust behind the rafters of the gallery opposite the door of the child's room as a permanent record.

When this ceremony is over, a general feast begins, the parents of the newly-named children contributing the chief part of the good things ; and a number of specially invited guests participate.

The name so given is usually borne until the child becomes a parent, when he or she resigns it in favour of the name given to his child with the title *Taman* (father) prefixed, or *Tinan* (mother) in the case of a woman.

Among the Kayans of the Upper Rejang the naming ceremonies differ widely from those described above, and are even more elaborate. The following description was given to the writer by Laki Bo, a Kayan *Penghulu* (the leading chief of a district). A child is named some time between its third month and the end of its second year, the date depending partly on the family's capacity to afford the expenses of the ceremony. The father and his friends obtain specimens of various edible animals and fish, and after drying them over the fire, set them up in his room in attitudes as lifelike as possible. He procures also the leaves of a certain species of plantain ; and having procured the services of a female *dayong*, who has a reputation for skill in naming, he calls all the friends and relatives of the family to the feast. The *dayong* enters the room where the child is, bearing a fowl's egg, while gongs and drums are beaten and guns discharged. She strokes the child from forehead to navel with the egg, calling out some name at each stroke, until she feels that she has found a suitable name. The whole company then pretends to fall asleep ; and, to complete the illusion, some go out into the gallery. The *dayong* then calls upon sixteen of the women to enter the room ; they enter led by a woman who, pretending to be a fowl, clucks and crows, and says : " Why are you all

asleep here ? It has been daylight for a long time. Do
you not hear me crowing ? Wake up ! " The child,
which has been kept in its parents' cubicle during this
first part of the ceremony, is then brought into the large
room, and a fowl and small pig are slaughtered, and
their entrails examined. If these yield favourable omens,
the *dayong* in a chant invokes the protection of good
spirits for the child. The actual feast then begins, some
person eating on behalf of the child, if it is too young
to partake of the feast. Eight days later the *dayong*
again invokes the protection of the kindly spirits, and
the child is taken out into the gallery and shown to all
the household. Some near relative makes a cross upon
its right foot with a piece of charcoal, and the child is
taken to the door of each room to receive some small
present from each room-hold. The child must then
return to its parents' room and remain there eight days.
After the next harvest a similar feast of pigs' flesh and
dried meat of other animals is made, and the name is
confirmed. But if in the meantime the child has been
ill, or any other untoward event has happened, a new
name is given to it. In this case it would be usual to
choose the well-tried name of some prosperous uncle or
aunt. Again the child must be confined to its parents'
room for eight days following the feast : after that time
it is free to go where it will, or, rather, wherever children
are allowed to go.

For five or six years onwards the boy more and more
accompanies the men in their excursions on the river
and in the jungle, and is taught to make himself generally
useful, and also in the rice-fields, where he helps in scaring pests and in other odd jobs. But he still has much
leisure, which is chiefly devoted to playing with his
fellows.

The most popular boys' games are kite-flying and
top-spinning. The last operation is conducted on principles like our own, the aim being the knocking-out of

the opponent's " wood." Other sports are the throwing of mock-spears at the domestic animals, tilting at the ring (*i.e.* throwing a spear through a bounding hoop), and running games, like " Prisoner's Base." The games are but little organised, and the rules are arbitrary ; but their aim is to train the players to be hunters and warriors.

Indoors, there is a form of Cat's-cradle, and a game, less fatal than might appear, in which a glowing ember is quickly passed from hand to hand, and which is a mixture of " Catch " and " Old Maid," the loser being the player who holds it when the last spark goes out.

Domestic pets are kept in the gallery, especially horn-bills, parrakeets, squirrels, porcupines, and small birds.

About the age of ten the Kayan boy begins to wear a waist-cloth—his first garment—his sister having assumed the apron some two or three years earlier. From this time onward he begins to accompany his father on the longer excursions of the men, especially on expeditions in search of jungle produce, and is expected to take an active part in the labours of the party. Participation in such expeditions affords, perhaps, the most important part of his education. Another important part of the training of older boys, and perhaps the most popular sport, is wrestling. In this each grips his antagonist by the back of the waist-cloth, and endeavours to throw him.

There is little or no attempt made to impart instruction to the children, whether moral or other, but they fall naturally under the spell of custom and public opinion ; and they absorb the lore and traditions of their tribe while listening to their elders. They learn also the prohibitions and taboo by being constantly checked ; a sharp word generally suffices to secure obedience. Punishments are almost unknown, especially physical punishments ; though in extreme cases of disobedience a child's ear may be tweaked, while it is asked if it is deaf. A sound scolding also is not infrequent, and an incorrigible offender, especially if his conduct has been offensive to persons outside his family, may be haled before the chief, who rates him soundly, and who may, in a more serious case, award compensation to be paid by the delinquent's father. But in the main a Spencerian method of training is followed. A parent warns his child of the ill effects that may be expected from the line of behaviour he is taking, and when those effects are realised, he says, " Well, what did I tell you ? "

At about fifteen years, or rather earlier, the boys begin to assert their independence by clubbing together with those of their own age, and taking up their sleeping quarters with the bachelors in the gallery. At an earlier age the children have picked up a number of songs and spontaneously sing them in groups, but now they begin to develop their powers of musical expression by practising with the *keluri*, mouth-harp, drum, and gong.

Of these instruments the first is the most used, especially by the youths. It is a rude form of bagpipes, and consists of a dried gourd shaped like an oval flask with a long neck. The closed ends of a bundle of six narrow bamboo pipes are inserted in the body of the gourd through a hole cut in its wall, and are fixed hermetically with wax. Their free ends are open, and each pipe has a small stop cut at a carefully determined distance from the open end. The artist blows through the neck of the gourd, and the air enters the base of each pipe by an oblong aperture, which is filled by a vibrating tongue or reed weighted with wax.

As regards dancing, both girls and boys learn early to execute a solo dance, largely consisting in a rhythmical movement of the hands and feet. But, besides this, the boys are taught a war-dance, or rather a musical march, representing the return of warriors from the war-path. A party of young men in full war-dress form up in single line ; the leader, and perhaps two or three others, play a battle-march on the *keluri*. The line advances slowly up the gallery, each performer turning half about at every third step, the even numbers turning to the one hand, the odd to the other hand, alternately, and all stamping together as they complete the turn at each third step. The turning to right and left symbolises the alert guarding of the heads which are supposed to be carried by the victorious warriors.

A more violent display of warlike feeling is given in the war-dance which is executed by one or two warriors only. The boy, in full panoply of war, and brandishing a sword and shield, goes through the movements of a single combat. He crouches beneath his shield, and springs violently hither and thither, emitting piercing yells of defiance and rage, cutting and striking at his imaginary foe or his partner in the dance. It is characteristic, however, that neither in this dance nor in the actual practice of fencing do the opponents attempt to strike one another. The Kayan has a strong feeling that the symbolical art brings about that which it symbolises; and, apart from this, to draw the blood of a house-mate would be *lali*, and would incur a fine.

Manhood is reached without any elaborate ceremony. All that is required of a boy to qualify him for taking his place as a full-fledged member of the community is the second occasion on which he strikes at the heads which have been taken in battle. We have seen that he performs this ceremonial act for the first time when still of tender age. The age at which he repeats it depends in part upon the occurrence of an opportunity; but, since no boy is allowed to go out to war until he has passed this test, there is a general desire to get it through as soon as possible : it commonly falls between his eighth and fifteenth year. If in the house there are a number of big lads who have not performed this rite, owing to no heads having been taken for some years, a head may be borrowed for the purpose from a friendly household; and in this case the borrowed head is brought into the

F

house with all the pomp and circumstance of successful war.

As the *soi-disant* war-party approaches the village, the boys who are to take part in the rite are marshalled before the house by a master of the ceremonies. He kills a fowl and thrusts a sharpened stake right through it, so that the point projects from its beak, and slashes the carcase into three pieces, one for the adults of the house, one for the boys, and one for the infants. He then takes a small bamboo knife and a bunch of palm leaves, and, after making a short address to the boys, ties a band of palm leaf round the wrist of each of them, and, diluting the blood of the fowl with water, smears some of the mixture on each boy's wrist-band. He puts a handful of rice on a burning log and gives a grain of it to each of the boys to eat.

The war-party is met by one of the elders of the house, who brings up the head and holds it out, while the master of ceremonies, holding the portion of the fowl's carcase assigned to the boys, leads up each boy in turn to strike at the head with a sword. Having done this, the boys go down to the river; and, while they bathe, a bunch of palm leaves with which the head has been decorated is waved over them.

Courting is sensible and easy. When the youth begins to feel strongly the attraction of the other sex, he finds opportunities of paying visits, with a few companions, in friendly houses. It is then said in his own house that he has gone "to seek tobacco," a phrase which is well understood to mean that he has gone to seek female companionship. A youth of average presentability will usually succeed, if not in "walking out" with a girl, at least in "sitting in" with her; and he is usually not much over twenty years of age when he becomes accepted as the future husband of a girl some years his junior.

The initiative is taken in nearly all cases by the young

man. He begins by paying attentions somewhat furtively to a " fancy-girl." He will often be found passing the evening in her company in her parents' room. There he displays his skill on the *keluri*, or sings the favourite love-song of his people. If the girl looks with favour on his advances and wishes him to stay, she gives him a cigarette tied in a peculiar manner, winding the strip which ties its sheath of dried banana leaf close to the narrow mouth-piece. On all other occasions this strip is wound about the middle of the cigarette.

Thus encouraged, the young man repeats his visits. If his suit makes progress he may hope that the fair one will draw out the hairs of his eyebrows and lashes with a pair of brass tweezers while he reclines on his back with his head in her lap.

When the courtship has advanced to this stage, the girl may attract her suitor to the room by playing on the mouth-harp : on this she speaks to him what is presumably the language of the heart. The youth thus encouraged may presume to remain beside his sweetheart till early morning, or when the rest of the house have retired, to return to her side.

At this stage it becomes necessary to secure that public recognition which constitutes a formal betrothal. The prospective husband charges some elderly friend of either sex, in many cases his father or mother, to inform the chief of his desire.

If the chief and parents favour the match, the young man presents a brass gong or a valuable bead to the girl's family as pledge of his sincerity. If for any reason beyond his control the match is broken off, this is returned to him.

The actual wedding usually takes place after the harvest. If, however, the omens are regarded as evil, the wedding is postponed for a year. Such omens are hardly ever disregarded, even if the girl is far advanced in pregnancy. The wife incurs no odium, but is treated as if she were a married woman, and her child is regarded as legitimate.

When the appointed time draws near, the " best man " is sent to open negotiations with the bride's family. He carries with him a number of presents, varying according to the position of the bridegroom's parents. For some time each side fences about, neither pretending to know the reason for the visit, until finally the legate comes to the point and asks on behalf of his friend a definite date at which he may marry the daughter.

If the parents accept the proposal (which is not always the case), the best man hands to them five sets each of sixteen beads, the beads of each set being of uniform shape and colour, namely, (1) small yellow beads; (2) black beads; (3) a set known as *habarani*, which may not be worn by the bride before the naming of her first child; (4) light blue beads; (5) dark blue beads. Each of these sets of beads is held to ensure to the bride some moral benefit. The date of the marriage is fixed with regard to the phases of the moon, the time of the new moon being considered the most favourable. Tally is kept by both parties of the date agreed upon. On two long strips of rattan an equal number of knots is tied. Each party keeps one of these tallies (often it is carried tied below the knee) and cuts off one knot each morning, until none are left.

On the actual day the parties on both sides invite their friends and relatives, who crowd the gallery of the bride's house. Early in the morning the bridegroom arrives with his best man and a party of young friends in full war-dress; they land from a boat even though they have come but a few yards by water. They march up to the house, some of them carrying large brass gongs; ascending the ladder, they lay the gongs along the gallery from the head of the ladder towards the door of the bride's room at intervals of about eighteen inches. It is understood that these gongs become the property of the bride and her parents. Others of the bridegroom's band bring other articles of value, which they offer to the family, under the fiction that the bridegroom, being a sort of invader, must pay for admission. A mock conference between the two parties now takes place; which having failed, a sham fight takes place : the men of the defending party make a sortie from the room fully armed, and repel the attackers with every show of violence.

At last the bridegroom and his supporters are admitted to the room, and they rush in, only to find, perhaps, that the bride has slipped away through the small door which generally gives access to a neighbouring room. The impatient suitor cannot discover where she is, and so he and his men resignedly sit down in the room and accept cigarettes. Presently the bride relents and returns to her parents' room accompanied by a number of her girl friends. The bridegroom has now changed his tactics, and affects to take no notice of her entry. Meanwhile the inevitable pig decked in skeins of beads has been laid in the gallery, together with a few gifts for the *dayong* who is to " read " its liver. Here the final steps of the bargaining are conducted by the friends of the bridegroom. (It is impossible to say in each case how far this bargaining is genuine and how far pre-arranged.) More gongs are added to the row upon the floor, until the row extends to the door of the bride's room. The pig is then slaughtered and its liver examined; if it proves unpropitious, other pigs are killed, until one whose liver permits of favourable interpretation is found. A series of unsatisfactory livers would lead to the postponement of the marriage.

The *dayong* now sprinkles pig's blood and water from a gong upon all the assembly, invoking the blessing of the gods upon the young couple, asking for them long life and many children. Then the bride and bridegroom walk up and down the row of gongs eight times, stepping only upon the metal. In some cases the bridegroom descends to his boat at the landing-stage during these processions, as if to prove that he is free to come and go as he pleases, and that he is under no obligation. In this degenerate age this act terminates the ceremony, except for feasting and speech-making. But in the old days the bride descended with the groom and his party to his boat, and was then carried off at full speed, pursued by several boat-loads of her family. The fleeing party would then check the pursuit by throwing out on to the bank every article of value still remaining among them; each article in turn would be snapped up by the pursuers, who then, having thus extorted the highest possible price from the bridegroom, would make a truce, and welcome back the Prodigal Children.

After the marriage the bridegroom usually becomes a member of the room of his father-in-law and remains there for some years before carrying off his wife once more to his own house. During this time he works in the fields of his father-in-law, and generally helps in the support of the household, showing due deference towards his wife's parents. If the bride is the only child of a chief her husband may remain permanently in her home and succeed her father as chief. But in most cases the young couple, before the end of the third year of marriage, migrate to the husband's house. This move takes place generally on the occasion of the building of a new Long House, or on the death of the husband's father, either of which events affords him the opportunity of becoming the head of a room and of a family.

CHAPTER III

THE LONG HOUSE

Many families in one house—General plan and dimensions—The interior
—Private chambers—Window and chimney in one—The " village
street "—The outside : barns and store-houses—Kenyah villages
smaller than Kayan—Iban houses—Daily life in a Kayan house—
Women before pigs, pigs before men—Work-time—Woman's work—
The evening bath.

THE most typical, and perhaps the most striking
phenomenon in the whole of Borneo is the communal
Long House. It is interesting, for it is found amongst
most of the hill tribes of Burma and Assam and in the
South Sea Islands of the Pacific, a fact which raises
questions as to its origin. But whatever doubts may
exist, one thing is certain, that it exists all over Borneo.
All the tribes build these houses; and all except, of
course, the Punans, build them of one type; but the
size and proportions, the strength of the materials used,
and the skill and care displayed in the work of construction show wide differences. The houses of the Kayans
are perhaps better and more solidly built than any others
and may be taken as the type. Each house is built to
accommodate many families; an average house may
contain some forty to fifty, making up with children
some two or three hundred persons; while some of the
larger houses are built for as many as a hundred and
twenty families, or some five to six hundred persons.
The house is always close to a river, and it usually lies
along the bank at a distance of from twenty to fifty yards
from the water, parallel to the course of the river.

Its roof is always a simple ridge extending the whole
length of the building and is made of shingles of iron-

wood or some other durable kind. The framework of the roof is supported at a height of some twenty to thirty feet from the ground on massive piles of ironwood, and the floor is supported by the same piles at a level some seven or eight feet below the cross-beams of the roof. The floor consists of cross-beams mortised through the piles, and of very large planks of hard wood laid upon them parallel to the length of the house. The projecting eaves of the roof come down to a level midway between that of the roof-beams and that of the floor, and the interval of some four to five feet between the eaves and the floor remains open along the whole length of the front of the house, save for a low parapet which bounds the floor along its outer edge. This space serves to admit both light and air, and affords an easy view over the river to those sitting in the gallery.

The length of the house is in some cases as much as 400 yards, but the average length is probably about 200 yards. The width of the floor varies from about thirty to sixty feet; the whole space between roof and floor is divided into two parts by a longitudinal wall of vertical planks, which runs the whole length of the building. This wall lies not quite in the middle line, but a little to the river side of it. Of the two lengthwise divisions of the house, that which adjoins the river is thus somewhat narrower than the other in its whole length; it remains undivided. The other and wider part is divided by transverse walls at intervals of some twenty or thirty feet, so as to form a single row of spacious chambers of approximately equal size.

Each such chamber is the private apartment of one family; in it father, mother, daughters, and the younger sons sleep and eat. Within each chamber are usually several sleeping-places or alcoves more or less completely screened or walled off from the central space. The chamber contains a fire-place, generally merely a slab of clay in a wooden framework placed near the centre.

The outside wall on this side of the house is carried up to meet the roof, except for a square section which works on a hinge and with a strut, something like a sun-blind. This serves as both window, ventilator, and chimney. This aperture can be easily closed, during heavy rain, by removing the prop and allowing the flap to fall into its original position.

The front part of the house is undivided, and forms a single long gallery serving as a common antechamber to all the private rooms. It is in a sense, though roofed and raised some twenty feet above the ground, the village street as well as a common living and reception hall. Along the outer border of the floor runs a low platform on which the inmates sit on mats. One part of this, usually that opposite the chief's apartment in the middle of the house, is formed of several large slabs of hardwood, sometimes raised above the floor on crudely carved wooden figures. These platforms are specially reserved for the reception of guests and for formal meetings. Between them there are smaller platforms, which are the sleeping quarters assigned to the bachelors and male visitors. At intervals of some thirty or forty feet throughout the gallery are fire-places similar to those in the private chambers; on some of these fire constantly smoulders. Over them and generally near the middle of the great gallery is hung a row of trophies obtained in war, together with a number of charms and objects used in various rites.

Alongside the inner wall of the gallery stand the large wooden mortars used by the women in husking the rice. Above these hang the winnowing trays and mats, and along this wall are various implements of common use—hats, paddles, fish-traps, and so forth.

The gallery is reached from the ground by several ladders, each of which consists of a notched beam sloping at an angle of about 75°, and furnished with a slender handrail. The more carefully made ladder is fashioned

from a single log, but the wood is so cut as to leave a
handrail projecting forwards a few inches on either side
of the notched gully or trough in which the feet are
placed. From the foot of each ladder a row of logs,
laid end to end, forms a footway to the water's edge. In
wet weather such a footway is a necessity, because pigs,
fowls, and dogs, and in some cases goats, run freely
beneath and around the house, and churn the surface of
the ground into a thick layer of slippery mire. Here
and there along the front of the house are open platforms
raised to the level of the floor, on which the rice-grain is
exposed to the sun to be dried before being husked.

Under the house, among the piles on which it is raised,
such boats as are not in daily use are stored. Round
about the house, and especially on the space between it
and the brink of the river, are numerous rice-barns.
Each of these, the storehouse of the grain harvested by
one family, is a large wooden bin about ten feet square,
raised on piles some seven feet from the ground. Just
below the floor-level each pile passes through a large
circular disc, which serves to keep out rats. In the clear
space round the house there are generally a few fruit
trees and tobacco plants, and between it and the river
are usually some rudely carved wooden figures, around
which rites and ceremonies are performed from time to
time.

Kayan villages generally consist of several, in some
cases as many as seven or eight, such houses of various
lengths, grouped closely together. The favourite situation for such a village is a peninsula formed by a sharp
bend of the river.

Of the houses built by the other peoples, those of the
Kenyahs very closely resemble those of the Kayans.
The Kenyah village frequently consists of a single Long
House (and with the Ibans this is invariably the case),
and it is in many cases perched on a high steep bank
immediately above the river. Some of the Klemantans

Early morning bathe.

Klemantan rice barn.

also build houses little if at all inferior to those of the Kayans, and very similar to them in general plan. But in this as in all other respects the Klemantans exhibit great diversities, some of their houses being built in a comparatively flimsy manner, light timber and even bamboos being used, and the roof being made of leaves. The houses of the Muruts are usually small and low, and of poorer construction.

The Iban house differs from that of the Kayan more than any of the others. The general plan is the same; but the place of the few massive piles is taken by a much larger number of slender piles which pass up to the roof through the gallery and chambers. Of the gallery only a narrow passage-way alongside the main partition-wall is kept clear of piles and other obstructions. The floor is of split bamboo covered with coarse mats. An open platform at the level of the floor runs along the whole length of the open side of the house. There are no rice-barns about the house, the rice being kept in bins in the roofs. The roof itself is low, giving little head space. The gallery of the house makes an impression of lack of space, very different from that made by the long, wide gallery of a Kayan or Kenyah house.

Although the more solidly built houses, such as those of the Kayans, would be habitable for many generations, few of them are inhabited for more than fifteen or twenty years, and some are used for much shorter periods only. Villages are constantly being broken up or removed, either because of accidents, such as fires or epidemics, or for superstitious reasons, but most commonly because the soil of the neighbourhood has been worked out.

Daily life in a Kayan Long House is methodical and almost unvarying. A little before dawn the first actors, or, perhaps one should say, the Overture begins : cocks crow, pigs grunt and squeal, and dogs trot noisily along the gallery. Before the first streaks of daylight comes the next Turn : the women light the fires in the private rooms or blow up the smouldering embers; then most of them descend from the house, each carrying in a basket slung on her back several bamboo water-vessels to be filled from the river. Many of them bathe at this time in the shallow water beside the bank : the toilet of others consists in dashing water over their faces, washing their mouths, and rubbing their teeth with the forefinger. Returning to the house with their loads of water, they boil rice for the household breakfasts and for the dinner of those who are to spend the day in the rice-field or jungle. The boiled rice intended for the latter use is made up in packets wrapped in tough green leaves, each containing sufficient for a meal for one person.

About half-past six, when the daylight is fully come, the Third Act is provided by the pigs, who, expectant of their meal, are clamouring loudly for it. The women descend to them, and each gives to the pigs of her household some mash consisting of rice dust and the leavings of the meals of the previous day. Last of all, the men begin to bestir themselves sluggishly. Some descend to bathe, while others smoke the fag-ends of the cigarettes that were unfinished when they fell asleep. Then the men breakfast in their rooms, for not until they are satisfied do the women and children sit down to their meal. During all this time the chronically hungry dogs, attracted by the odours of food, make persistent efforts to get into their owners' rooms. Success in this manœuvre is immediately followed by their sudden and noisy reappearance in the gallery, caused by a kick or smart blow with a piece of firewood. In the busy seasons the workers often take their breakfast with them.

After breakfast the men disperse to their various tasks. The old women and invalids remain all day long in the rooms : the old men lounge in the gallery, smoking many home-made cigarettes, and perhaps doing a bit of carving or other light work and keeping an eye on the children. The young children play in and about the house, chasing

Durian fruit.

Mangosteen.

Ibans with boatloads of Durian fruit.

the animals, and dabbling among the boats moored at the bank.

A few of the able-bodied men employ themselves about the house, making boats, forging swords, spear-heads, iron hoes, and axes, repairing weapons or imple-ments. Others go in small parties to the forest to hunt deer and pig, or to gather jungle produce—fruit, rubber, rattans, or bamboos—or spend the day hunting or fishing. During the months of December and January the jungle fruits—the durian, rambutan, mangosteen, lansat, mango, and numerous small sour fruits—are much more abundant than at other times ; whilst this fruit season lasts most of their other work is neglected, while the people devote themselves to gathering the fruit which forms for a time almost their only food.

When work has to be done in the rice-fields, everyone turns out to take his part ; but at other times the women's work lies wholly within the house. The heaviest part of their household labour is the preparation of the rice. After breakfast they proceed to spread out rice on mats on the open platforms adjoining the gallery. While the rice is being dried by the exposure to sun and wind on these platforms, it must be protected from the domestic fowls by a guardian, who, sitting comfortably in the gallery, drives them away by means of a long bamboo slung by a cord above the platform. Others fill in the time between breakfast and the noonday dinner by making and repairing clothing, hats, mats, and baskets, fetching water, cleaning the rooms, and preparing dinner. This meal consists of boiled rice with perhaps a piece of fish, pork, fowl, or vegetable, and, like breakfast and supper, is eaten in the private rooms.

As soon as dinner is over the pounding of the rice begins. Each mortar usually consists of a massive log of timber roughly shaped, and having sunk in its upper surface, which is a little hollowed, a pit about five inches in diameter and nine inches in depth. Into this pit about a quarter of a bushel of rice is put. Two women stand on the mortar facing one another on either side of the pit, each holding by the middle a large wooden pestle. This is a solid bar of hardwood about seven feet long, its ends rounded and polished by use. Each woman raises her pestle to the full height of her reach, and brings it smartly down upon the grain in the pit, the two women striking alternately with a regular rhythm. As each one lifts her pestle, she deftly sweeps back into the pit with her foot the grain scattered by her stroke.

After pounding the grain for some minutes without interruption, one woman takes a winnowing pan, a mat-basket made in the shape of an English housemaid's dustpan, but rather larger than this article, and receives in it the pounded grain which the other scoops out of the pit with her foot.

Both women then kneel upon a large mat laid beside the mortar; the one holding the winnowing pan keeps throwing the grain into the air with a movement which causes the heavier grain to fall to the back of the pan, while the chaff, bran, and dust are thrown forward on to the mat. Her companion separates the broken grain and rice dust from the chaff by sifting it through a sieve. A considerable quantity of the dust or finely broken rice is formed by the pounding in the mortar, and is the principal food given to the pigs. The winnowed grain is then usually returned to the mortar to be put through the whole process a second time. The husked rice thus prepared is ready for the cooking-pot.

When this task is completed, the women, covered with dust, descend again to the river, and bathe themselves and the children once more. They may gather some vegetables and then proceed to prepare supper with their rice and whatever food the men may have brought home from the forest or the river. For now, about an hour before sundown, the men return from hunting expeditions, often bringing a wild pig, a monkey, a porcupine,

Kenyah women husking rice with pestle and mortar.

Iban woman at work at her rice mill.

jungle fruit, or the young shoots of bamboo, as their contribution to the supper-table; others return from fishing or from the rice-fields, and during the sunset hour at a large village a constant stream of boats arrives at the landing-place before the house.

Most of the home-comers bathe in the river before ascending to the house. This evening bath is taken in more leisurely fashion than the morning dip. A man will strip off his waist-cloth and rush into the water, falling flat on his chest with a great splash. Then standing with the water up to his waist he will souse his head and face, then perhaps swim a few double overhand strokes, his head going under at each stroke. After rubbing himself down with a smooth pebble, he returns to the bank and, having resumed his waist-cloth, squeezes the water from his hair, picks up his paddle, spear, hat, and other belongings, and ascends to the gallery. There he hangs up his spear by jabbing its point into a roof-beam beside the door of his chamber, and sits down on a large floor-mat to smoke a cigarette and to relate the events of his day while the meal is preparing. As darkness falls, he goes to his room to sup. By the time the women also have supped, the tropical night has fallen, and the house is lit by the fires and resin torches, and nowadays by a few kerosene oil lamps. The men gather round the fire-places in the gallery and discuss politics, the events of the day, the state of the crops and weather, the news obtained by meetings with the people of neighbouring houses, hunting experiences, and relate myths and legends, folk-tales and animal stories. The women, having put the children to bed, visit one another's rooms for friendly gossip; and young men drop in to join their parties, smoke cigarettes, and play the *keluri*, the nose-flute, and the mouth-harp. About nine o'clock all retire to bed, save a few old men who sit smoking and talking round the fires far into the night. The dogs, after some final skirmishes, subside among the warm ashes of the fire-places; the pigs emit a final squeal, and within the house quietness reigns. The villagers sleep soundly till cock-crow; but the European guest, lying in the place of honour almost beneath the row of human heads which adorns the gallery, is, if unused to sleeping in a Bornean Long House, apt to be wakened from time to time throughout the night by an outburst of dreadful yelpings from dogs squabbling for the best places among the ashes, by the prolonged fit of coughing of an old man, by an old crone making up the fire, by goats squealing and scampering over the boats beneath the house, or by some weird cry from the depths of the forest.

In olden days the peace of the night was occasionally broken an hour before the dawn by the yells of an attacking force, and by the flames roaring up from bundles of lighted shavings thrown beneath the house. But happily attacks of this kind are no longer made, save perhaps occasionally in some few remoter parts of the far interior where the European Governments have not yet quite fully established their authority.

CHAPTER IV

PERSONAL POSSESSIONS

Male dress—Ear-rings—Iban dandies—Weapons—Women's dress—A practical apron-skirt—Necklaces, ear-rings, and bracelets—Enlarged ear-lobes—Beads : valuable collections—Head-broadening (Melanos) —Boats—Paddling and poling—Basket-work—Baskets and mats— Gongs and drums—China jars.

WITH few exceptions, the main features of the dress, adornment, and weapons of all the peoples of Borneo are similar, showing only minor local differences. The universal article of male attire is the waist-cloth, a strip of cloth about one yard wide and four to eight yards in length. Formerly most of these garments were made of bark-cloth, but now cotton obtained from the Chinese and Malay traders has largely superseded the local fabric, except in the remoter regions : here and there a well-to-do man may be seen wearing a cloth of more expensive stuff, sometimes even of silk. One end of such a cloth is passed between the legs from behind forwards, about eighteen inches being left dependent : the rest of it is then passed several times round the waist and tucked in at the back. The man wears in addition when out of doors a coat of bark-cloth or white cotton stuff, and a wide sun-hat of palm leaves, in shape like an inverted and very shallow basin, which shelters him from both sun and rain ; many wear also a small seat-mat of plaited rattan strips hanging behind from a cord passed round the waist and serving as a seat when the wearer sits down. At home he wears nothing more than the waist-cloth, save some narrow plaited bands of palm fibre below the knee, and, in most cases, some adornment in the ears or about the neck and on the arms. The hair is allowed to grow long on the crown of the scalp, and to hang freely over the back of the neck, in some cases reaching as far as the middle of the back. This long hair is never plaited, but is sometimes screwed up in a knot on the top of the head and fastened with a skewer. The latter mode of wearing the hair is the rule among the Muruts, who use elaborately carved hair-pins made from the shin-bone of the deer. The front hair is cut to form a straight fringe across the forehead. All the rest of the head is kept shaven, except at times of mourning for the death of relatives.

When in the house the man commonly wears on his head a band of plaited rattan, which varies from a mere band around the brows to a complete skull-cap. The free ends of the rattan strips are generally allowed to project, forming a dependent tassel or fringe. A well-to-do Kayan man usually wears a necklace consisting of a single string of beads, which in many cases are old and of considerable value. Every Kayan and Kenyah has the shell of the ear perforated, and when fully dressed wears, thrust forward through the hole in each shell, the big upper canine tooth of the tiger-cat; but he is not entitled to wear this until he has been on the war-path. Those who have taken a head or otherwise distinguished themselves in war may wear, instead of the teeth, pieces of similar shape carved from the solid beak of the helmeted hornbill. Youths who have not qualified themselves for these adornments, and warriors during mourning, usually wear a small disc of wood or wax in their places.

The lobe of the ear is perforated and distended to a loop some two inches in length, in which a brass ring is worn. Just above this loop a small hole through the shell is usually made, and from this a little skein of small beads depends. Similar ear ornaments are worn by Kenyahs and some of the Klemantans, but not by Muruts, and by few individuals only among Punans and Ibans. Many of the latter wear rows of small brass rings inserted through

Youthful Ibans in Gala Dress

From a photograph by the Author, by permission of "Peoples of All Nations"

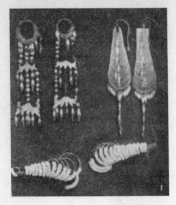

Iban ear-rings.

Murut hairpins.

Klemantan necklaces.

Iban corsets.

the margin of the shell of each ear. Many wear above the elbow bracelets of shell or hard wood.

Although the dress of the men is so uniform in essentials throughout the country, it gives considerable opportunity for the display of personal tastes, and the Iban especially delights in winding many yards of brilliantly coloured cloth about his waist, in brilliant coats, gorgeous turbans, feathers, and other ornaments. By means of these he manages to make himself appear as a very dressy person in comparison with the sober Kayan and with most of the people of the remoter inland regions, who often have little but scanty strips of bark- or cotton-cloth about the loins.

The universal weapons of the country are sword and spear, and no man travels far from home without these and his oblong wooden shield. Many of the peoples are expert in the use of the blow-pipe and poisoned dart. The blow-pipe and the recently introduced fire-arms are the only missile weapons; the bow is practically unknown save as a plaything for children.

Women's dress in Borneo is less uniform than that of the men. The Iban woman wears a short skirt of cotton thread woven in various patterns of several colours, reaching from the waist almost to the knee; a long-sleeved jacket of the same material, and a sort of corset consisting of many rings of rattan built up one above another so as to enclose the body from breast to thigh. Each rattan ring is sheathed in small rings of beaten brass. The corset is made to open partially or completely down the front, but is often worn continuously for long periods. The hair is tied in a knot at the back of the head.

The principal garment of the women of all the other peoples is a skirt of bark or cotton cloth, which is tied by a string a little below the level of the crest of the hip-bone. It reaches almost to the ankle, but is open at the left side along its whole depth. It is thus a large apron rather than a skirt. When the woman is at work in the house or elsewhere, she tucks up the apron by drawing the front flap backwards between her legs, and tucking it tightly into the band behind, thus reducing it to the proportions and appearance of a small pair of bathing-drawers. Each woman possesses also a long-sleeved, long-bodied jacket of white cotton similar to that worn by the men; this coat is generally worn by both sexes when working in the fields or travelling in boats, chiefly as a protection against the rays of the sun. The women wear also a large mushroom-shaped hat similar to that worn by the men. With few exceptions all the women allow the hair to grow uncut and to fall naturally from the ridge of the cranium, confined only by a circular band of rattan or beadwork passing over the back of the skull and above the eyebrows.

Their principal ornaments are necklaces and girdles of beads, ear-rings, and bracelets. The bracelets are of ivory, and both forearms are sometimes completely sheathed in a series of such bracelets. The ear-rings are the most distinctive feature of the Kayan woman's adornment. The perforated lobes of the ears are gradually drawn down during childhood and youth, until each lobe forms a slender loop which reaches to the collar-bone, or lower. Each loop bears several massive rings of copper whose combined weight is in some cases as much as two pounds. Accidental tearing of the lobe inevitably occurs occasionally; and if this is attributed to the carelessness of any other person a brass *tawak* or gong must be paid in compensation. Repair of a torn lobe is sometimes effected by overlapping the raw ends and keeping them tied in this position for some weeks. Most of the Kenyah women also wear similar ear-rings, but these are usually lighter and more numerous and the lobe is not so much distended. The women of many of the Klemantan tribes wear a large wooden disc in the distended lobe of each ear, and those of other Klemantan tribes wear a smaller wooden plug with a boss.

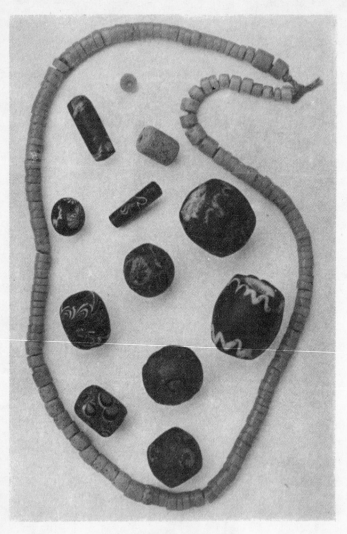

Old Beads worn by Kayan Women

The most treasured ornaments, however, especially
among the Kayans, are various kinds of beads. Few
families of the upper class do not possess a certain number
of them, while the richer women often have what must
be quite valuable collections. At one time, indeed, they
seem to have been used as currency. Most of them are
of foreign manufacture, although a few made of shell
or agate may perhaps be indigenous. The foreign-
made beads were probably imported by Arab, Malay,
and Chinese traders at various dates. Some of them are
probably of Chinese manufacture, others perhaps came
from the Near East and even from Venice. Some are of
glass curiously marked and coloured, others of stone
inlaid with different colours, others of some hard substance whose composition defies description. Certain
rare kinds are especially valued and can hardly be bought
at any price; they are reckoned to be worth at least
100 dollars apiece. The most valuable of all is known as
the *lukut sekala* ; the ownership of each such bead is as
accurately known throughout a large district as the
ownership of a masterpiece of ancient art in our own
country. The wife of a rich chief may possess old beads
to the value of thousands of pounds, and will wear a large
part of them on any occasion of display. They are worn
threaded together to form necklaces and girdles, being
arranged with some reference to harmony of size and
colour and to value, the most valuable being placed in
the middle, where they can be shown to best advantage.
A single costly bead is sometimes worn on the wrist.

A woman who possesses a good stock of such beads
will seldom be seen without some of them on her person.
She will occasionally exchange a few for other varieties,
and is generally eager to add to her collection ; she may
occasionally make a present of one or two to some highly
esteemed friend or relative, and will generally assign
them, but without handing them over, to various female
relatives before her death.

Besides these valuable old beads there are in use among all the tribes many small glass beads of modern European manufacture. These are threaded to form a variety of designs, generally in two colours, the combination of black and yellow being the most commonly preferred. These strips of bead-work are put to many decorative uses : they are applied to the women's head-bands, to the centre of the sun-hat, to sword sheaths, to cigarette boxes, to the war-coat at the nape of the neck, and, by some Klemantans, to the jackets of the women.

Among the Melano of Sarawak (a branch of the Klemantans) there exists the curious habit of broadening the heads of children, especially girls. The apparatus used consists of a flat bar of wood about seven inches long, and three inches broad at its widest point. On the inside it has a soft pad ; while on the outside it has strings which are brought round to the front of the bar, where they are tied together through a copper coin perforated in the centre, extra pressure being applied by the twisting of the coin. The Melano are a handsome people, with a typical roundness of head and breadth of brow ; and, by this artificial process, they would seem to have tried to perpetuate a racial peculiarity. The process starts, usually, within the first month after birth ; and it would seem that the operation carried on for about fifteen minutes on from ten to twenty successive days is enough to bring about the desired result. The pressure is applied while the child sleeps and is at once relaxed if it appears to be oppressive.

The most important possession of a Bornean family after the house is the boats. Each family possesses at least one small boat capable of carrying seven or eight persons, and used chiefly for going to and from the rice-fields, but also for fishing and short journeys of all kinds. In addition to these the community possesses several larger boats used for longer journeys, and, formerly at least, one long war-boat, capable of carrying fifty to one hundred men.

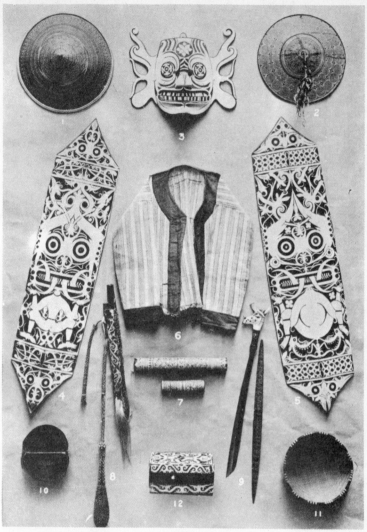

(1) An Iban woman's sun-hat. (2) A Land Dayak woman's sun-hat. (3) A Klemantan medicine-man's mask. (4) A Kenyah shield. (5) A Kenyah shield. (6) A Klemantan man's coat made from cloth and woven by one of their women. (7) Bamboo carved vessels. (8) Sheath of Kenyah sword. (9) Iban woman's shuttle and Kenyah sword. (10) Klemantan water bucket made from the sheath of a palm leaf. (11) A Klemantan shallow basket used as a strainer. (12) Klemantan cigarette box with beadwork pattern in yellow and black.

Each boat, even one of the largest size, is hollowed from a single log, the freeboard being raised by narrow planks lashed to the edge of the log. Amidships on a large boat is a section, the freeboard of which is raised still higher, and is covered by an arched roof of palm leaves. The boat is crossed at intervals of some three feet by seats formed of short planks. In travelling on the lower reaches of the rivers, the paddlers sit two on each bench, side by side. On the upper reaches, where rapids abound, a sort of deck is made by laying split bamboos along the length of the boat upon the benches, on which the crew sit when paddling, or stand when poling the boat over rapids.

Other important possessions are baskets and mats. The baskets are of various shapes and sizes, adapted to a variety of uses. The largest hold about two bushels of rice, and are chiefly used for transporting grain from the fields to the house. They are almost cylindrical in shape, but rather wider at the upper end. Four strips of wood running down from near the upper edge project slightly below, forming short legs on which the basket stands. The upper end is closed by a detachable cap, which fits inside the upper lip of the basket. The whole is provided with a pair of shoulder-straps, and a strap which is passed over the crown of the head. These straps are made of a single strip of tough beaten bark. One end of it is attached to the foot of the basket; a second attachment is made half-way up, forming a loop for the one shoulder; the strip is then looped over to the corresponding point on the other side, forming the loop for the head, and then carried down to the foot of the basket on that side to form the loop for the other shoulder.

A smaller cylindrical basket, very neatly plaited of thin and very pliable strips of rattan, is used for carrying the few articles which a man takes with him in travelling— rice and tobacco, a spare waist-cloth, a sleeping-mat, perhaps a second mat of palm leaves used as a protection against rain, a roll of dried banana leaves for making cigarettes, perhaps a cap for wear in the house, and, not infrequently nowadays, a bright coloured handkerchief of Chinese silk. The lip of the basket is surrounded by a close set row of loops through which a cord is passed. To this cord a net is attached, and is drawn together in the centre of the opening of the basket by a second cord, in order to confine its contents. This basket is provided with shoulder-straps only. In addition to these two principal baskets, each family has a number of smaller baskets of various shapes for storing their personal belongings, and for containing food in course of preparation.

The mats are of many shapes and sizes. The largest are spread on the raised part of the floor, both of the gallery and of the private chambers, when a party sits down to eat or converse. Each individual has his own sleeping-mat, and each family has a number of mats used for drying, husking, winnowing, and sieving rice.

For the carrying of water the Bornean uses a vessel made of a section of the stem of the bamboo, having a spout at the top of the section for drinking purposes; while a short length of branch is kept uncut, to form a sort of handle. These vessels are used also for carrying rice-spirit.

In every house is a number of large brass gongs (*tawak*), which are used in various ceremonies, for dancing and for signalling, and constitute also one of the best recognised standards of value and the most important form of currency. Besides these largest gongs, smaller ones of various shapes and sizes are kept and used on festive occasions.

Beside the gongs a Kayan house generally contains, as the common property of the whole household, several long, narrow drums. Each is a hollow cylinder of wood, tapering at its middle, open at one end, and closed at the other with a sheet of deer-skin. This is stretched by means of slips of rattan attached to its edges, and carried

Valuable old Chinese Jar, as used for the burial of a Klemantan Chief

Presented to Rajah Sir Charles Brooke, 1887—now in the possession of the Author

back to a stout rattan ring woven about the middle of the drum : the skin is tightened by inserting wedges under this ring.

In most houses two or three small brass swivel guns may be seen in the gallery, and a small stock of powder for their service is usually kept by the chief. They are sometimes discharged to salute a distinguished visitor, and formerly played some small part in repelling attacks.

The personal possessions of the various peoples are, generally, much the same as those of the Kayans. The Ibans, however, have a habit of collecting large vases of china-ware, which they prize highly. The ordinary jar stands about three feet high and is made of plain brown earthenware ornamented with mythological creatures moulded in relief. Still more prized is an older type of jar with perforated " ears " projecting beyond the rim, commonly of a dark green hue. These jars should be of old Chinese manufacture; but, although the Iban is by way of being a connoisseur in such matters, he is quite often put off with modern Chinese counterfeits. However, in many houses valuable vases, from Siam or China, are still to be found.

CHAPTER V

FESTIVALS AND VISITS OF CEREMONY

Reception formalities—The social cigarette—The dinner-party—A jovial
evening—The libation—The loving-cup—The chiefs' speeches—
" I am drunk."

THE even tenor of village life is interrupted from time
to time by certain festivals or other incidents : the harvest
festival; the marriage or the naming of a chief's son or
daughter; the arrival of important guests—one or more
chiefs with bands of followers coming to make peace or
renew their acquaintance, or nowadays the visit of the
District Officer or the Resident of the Division; the
funeral of an important chief; the preparations for an
expedition or for a long journey in search of trade; the
necessity of removing to a new site ; an epidemic of disease ;
and various acts of religion or superstition.

When a chief visits a neighbouring village he remains
seated in his boat until one of his followers has announced
his arrival and ascertained that there is no *malan* (restriction) upon the house which would make the presence of
visitors unwelcome. If a favourable answer is returned,
the visitor will probably remain seated in his boat some
few minutes longer, and then make his way into the
gallery, followed by most of his men, who leave their
spears and shields behind in the boats. If the visitor is
an intimate friend, the chief of the house will usually send
a son or brother to welcome him, or will even go himself.

Arrived in the gallery, the visitor advances to the central
platform where the chief of the house awaits him, unbuckles
his sword and hangs it upon any convenient hook, and
then sits down beside his host ; while his men, following

Peace-making ceremony.

Interior of a Kenyah Long House.

his example, seat themselves with the men of the house in a semicircle facing the two chiefs. The followers may greet, and even embrace, or grasp by the forearm, their personal friends; but the demeanour of the chiefs if they are less intimate is more formal. Neither one utters a word, or even glances at the other for some few moments; the host remains seated, fidgeting with a cigarette; the visitor looks stolidly over the heads of his followers, and perhaps clears his throat or coughs. Presently a woman thrusts into the semicircle a tray of freshly made cigarettes. One of the men of the house pushes it forward towards the principal visitor, who makes a sign of acceptance by lightly touching the tray; the other, crouching on his heels, lights a cigarette with an ember from the fire, blowing it into a glow as he waddles up to present it to the visiting chief. The latter takes it, but usually allows it to go out. By this time the chief of the house is ready to open the conversation, and, after clearing his throat, suddenly throws out a question, usually, "Where did you start from to-day?" The embarrassing silence thus broken, question and answer are freely exchanged, the cigarette of the visitor is again lighted at the fire by a member of the household, and conversation becomes general.

In the meantime the women are busy preparing a meal, a pig having been killed and hastily cut up. When it is ready, the visitors, if old friends, are invited to partake of it in the chief's room. Otherwise the meal is spread for them in the gallery on platters placed in a long row, one for each guest; each platter containing cubes of boiled pork, and boiled rice wrapped in leaves. The space is surrounded with a slight bamboo fence to keep away the dogs. In either case the visitors eat alone, their hosts retiring until the meal is finished. As the chief's wife retires, she sometimes says, "Eat slowly, my children, our food is but poor stuff. There is no pork, no fish, nothing that is good to eat." Before withdrawing, one of the people of the house pours a little water from a bamboo vessel on the right hand of the visiting chief, who then passes on the vessel to his followers. With the hand thus cleansed each guest conveys the food to his mouth, dipping his pieces of pork in coarse salt placed in a leaf beside his platter; and when he has finished eating, he drinks water from a bamboo vessel. The chief, and perhaps one or more also of his upper-class companions, leaves a little of the pork and perhaps a few grains of rice on the platter " for manners "; and good taste demands that he should prove his satisfaction with the meal by a loud and prolonged belching which is echoed by his followers to the best of their ability. After thus publicly expressing his appreciation of his host's hospitality, he rinses out his mouth, squirting out the water towards the nearest gap between the floor-boards, rubs his teeth with his forefinger, again rinses his mouth, and washes his hand. Then re-lighting his cigarette, which he has kept behind his ear or thrust through the hole in its shell, he rejoins his host, who awaits him on the daïs.

On such an occasion, and in fact on any other occasion of festivity, the evening is enlivened with oratory, song, and drink. After supper the men gather together about the chiefs, sitting in close-set ranks on and before the daïs. At a sign from the chief a jar of *burak* (rice-spirit) is brought into the circle. A little is poured into a vessel and handed to the house chief, who first makes a libation to the omen-birds and to other friendly spirits, by pouring a little on to the ground through a crevice of the floor, or by throwing a few drops out under the eaves, saying, as he does so, " To all the friendly powers ! " He then drinks a little and hands back the cup to the young man who is in charge of the jar. The latter, remaining crouched upon his heels, ladles out another cupful of spirit and offers it in both hands to the principal guest, who drinks it off, and expresses by a grunt, a smack of the lips, and even perhaps a shiver, his appreciation of its quality. The cup is then handed in similar formal

Offerings made to the omen-birds on the return of a
victorious war-party.

Altars for sacrificial purposes to the gods.

fashion to each of the principal guests in turn; after which more cups are brought into use, and the circulation of the drink becomes more rapid and informal.

When all have drunk, the house chief stands up, and, addressing his guest, expresses the pleasure his people feel at this visit; then, in a deprecating manner, and suggesting that perhaps he is talking in his sleep, he delicately introduces the subject of local politics. As he goes on, he warms to his theme, speaking more plainly and excitedly, at times leaping into the air or comprising his audience with a sweep of the arm; but, whether he warns, reproaches, or threatens, he never exceeds the strictest bounds of courtesy. He then takes from the attendant a bowl of spirit and breaks into song, reminding his guests of the long-standing union between the villages, of the antiquity and glories of their common race. The song is in rhythm and rhymed; and, at the end of each sentence, all the men of both parties repeat, in long-drawn-out cadence, the refrain. At the conclusion he hands the bowl to his guest, who takes it in one long draught, while the chorus swells to a deep musical roar. At this moment the circle of auditors, if much excited, will spring to their feet and swell the noise by stamping vigorously and jumping heavily on the resounding planks, while the house chief smilingly strokes his guest from the shoulder downwards and resumes his seat.

Gradually the commotion dies away, and there follow some minutes of silence. Then the guest begins his reply; and the manner of it is as antistrophic as a Greek chorus. He thanks his hosts for their kindness; and then, gradually and humbly, puts forward his own views, which he represents as being those of a third party. Still, he exhorts both parties to agreement, using similar gesticulations to those of the house chief; and then, with similar deprecation, sits down beside his host, saying, " Make allowance for my words : I am drunk." The cup-bearer approaches with the bowl; and the guest, rising again, addresses the

company with song, the refrain being again taken up by
the public. The bowl is presented to the house chief,
who, in his turn, drains it, with no heel-taps.

The cup, hereafter, circulates freely, and cigarettes are
smoked; a few shorter speeches may follow, but the
formality is over, and affection and joviality take its place.
Intoxication, however, and quarrelsomeness are practically
unknown : if a man becomes too boisterous he is quite
simply led away and put to bed. Indeed among the
Kayans, Kenyahs, and most of the Klemantans, intoxication is most uncommon, except at the big Harvest Festival,
or after the return of a successful expedition. Noise and
bonhomie there may be, but little more; and drunkenness is unknown, because the rice-spirit is never drunk in
private, but only on festive occasions.

The flow of speech and song goes on bravely (apart
from interruptions by dogs) until midnight, the women
meanwhile congregating in the neighbouring rooms, or
even about the doors opening on to the gallery. At last
the circle breaks up, by twos and threes, the curtain being
rung down when the visiting chief expresses a desire for
sleep. The guests spread their mats on the platform
assigned to them, while the men of the house retire to
their own rooms.

In an Iban house the reception and entertainment of
guests are less ceremonious but none the less hospitable,
and are carried out largely by the unorganised efforts of
individuals, rather than by the household as a whole with
the chief at its head. On the arrival of a party of visitors,
the people of each room clamorously invite the guests to
sit down before their chamber. The guests thus become
scattered through the house. First they are offered areca
nut and betel leaf smeared with lime to chew, for among
the Ibans this chewing takes the place of the smoking of
cigarettes, which is common to all the others; and they
are then fed and entertained individually, or by twos and
threes, in various rooms. Usually no pig is killed or rice-

spirit offered on such occasions, though possibly some fowls' eggs, a toasted bat, or bit of salted wild pig may be served as a relish.

At great feasts the Ibans and Muruts drink more freely than the other peoples. Men and women alike drink deeply, and many on festive occasions become intoxicated.

Among all the other tribes, however, strong drink is seldom or never abused, but is put only to its proper use, the promotion of good fellowship and social gaiety.

PART III

TRIBAL AND VILLAGE LIFE (*continued*)

CHAPTER I

RIVER LIFE

Boating—The paddle—Poling up rapids—The fluent cox—Camping
out—Fishing—The cast-net—A scoop-net used by women—Fish-
traps—The *Selambo*—A Kenyah hook—The *Bubu* and *Kilong*—
Fish-spearing—Crocodiles hunted by Malays only—A collective
vendetta—Spearing from boats—Catching Leviathan with a hook.

WITH the exception of the Punans, and some of the
Muruts who inhabit regions devoid of navigable streams,
all the peoples of Borneo make great use of the rivers.
It is only for hunting or the gathering of forest produce that
the rivers are abandoned. Occasionally rice is cultivated
at a distance of a mile or more from the nearest navigable
stream, and a rough pathway is then made between the
field and the nearest point of the river. Again, in the
flat country near the coast, where waterways are less
abundant than in the interior, forest tracks are used for
communication between villages. Otherwise the ordinary
jungle paths are only used when it is impossible to reach
the desired point by boat, or if the waterway is very
circuitous.

On the lower and deeper reaches of the rivers the paddle
is the universal instrument of propulsion. It is used in
the same manner, and with as much skill, as may be
observed on the Upper Thames, the right hand being
held a little above the blade, and the left pushing the
upper end forward. A small canoe may be propelled by

Poling up the rapids.

Travelling in the far interior of Borneo.

a single rower, who, sitting in the stern, steers in the orthodox way, with his paddle, using it on one side of the boat only. In a war-boat of the largest size, the two men occupying the bow-thwart and the four men on the two sternmost benches are responsible for the steering : the two bow-men use their paddles very much like a punt-pole.

During a day's journey the crew of a boat will occasionally lighten its labour with song, one man singing, the others joining in the chorus ; and if several boats are travelling in company, the crews will from time to time spurt and strive to pass one another in good-humoured rivalry. At such times each crew may break out into a deep-pitched and musical roar, a relic of the triumphal chorus of a victorious war party in days of old.

In the upper reaches of many of the large rivers there are numerous rapids, and here and there actual falls. The boat is usually propelled up a rapid by poling. Each member of the crew has beside him a strong light pole some eight or nine feet long ; and when the boat approaches a rapid, the crew at a shout from the captain, who is usually the chief steersman, springs to its feet, dropping its paddles and seizing its poles. Thrusting these against the stony bottom in perfect unison, the crew swings the boat up through the rushing water with a very pleasant motion. If the current proves too strong and the boat makes no progress, or if the water is too shallow, three or four men, or, if necessary, the whole crew, spring into the water and, seizing the boat by the gunwale, drag it up-stream till quieter water is reached. While rapids are being shot it is necessary for a man or a boy to bale out the water that constantly enters over the gunwale. During these exciting operations the captain directs and admonishes his men with a volubility and choice of invective that would astonish a crew on the waters of the Cam or Isis.

Sometimes, when much water is coming down after

H

heavy rains, the current is so swift in the deeper places that neither paddling, poling, nor wading is possible. Then three or four men are landed on the bank, or on the boughs of the trees, and haul on the boat with long rattans tied to both bow and stern.

The passage down-stream in the upper reaches of a river is even more exciting and pleasurable. The crew paddles just sufficiently to keep good steerage way on the boat; as it goes down the rapids, the steersman stands up to choose his path, the water leaps over the gunwale, and the men break out into song. The smaller waterfalls do not check its onward rush: as the boat approaches a fall, several men near the bow stand up to see if there is sufficient water for them to pass; then they resume their seats, and all paddle with might and main until the boat takes the leap.

When a long journey is made, the nights are passed, if possible, in friendly villages. When no such village can be reached, the crew camps either in the canoes or on the bank. In the former case palm-leaf mats, of which each man carries at least one in his basket, are used to roof the boat; in the latter case a rude hut is quickly built, a framework of saplings lashed together, roofed with the mats, and floored at a level of a foot or so above the ground with bamboos or slender saplings.

Fish, which form an important part of the diet of most of the peoples, are caught in various ways. Perhaps in the lower reaches of a river the cast-net is most commonly used. This is a net which, when fully extended in the water, is about twenty yards round. Its central part rises in a steep cone, to the peak of which a strong cord is tied, and the periphery is weighted with bits of metal or stone. This net is used both in deep and in shallow water. In the former case one man steers and paddles a boat, while the other stands in the bows with the cord of the net wound about the right hand. The bulk of the net is gathered up on his right arm, while the free end is held

McDougall Falls, Baram River.

Mount Dulit.

in the left hand. Choosing a still pool some two fathoms in depth, he throws a stone into the water a little ahead of the boat, in the expectation that the fish will congregate about the spot. As the boat approaches the spot he deftly flings the net so that it falls spread out in a circle upon the surface; its weighted edge then sinks rapidly to the bottom, enclosing any fish that may be beneath the net. If only small fish are enclosed, the net is twisted as it is drawn up, the fish becoming entangled in its meshes, and in pockets formed about its lower border. When large fish are enclosed, the steersman dives overboard and gathers the lower part of the net so as to secure them.

In other cases the boat is paddled to the foot of a small rapid, where the fisherman springs out and, running to the head of the rapid, casts his net in the still water immediately above the fall where fish are frequently found to congregate.

A third method is for a party to take a net to the mouth of a small tributary, and, while some hold the net open so as to block the mouth of the stream almost completely, others run through the forest to a point some hundred yards further up, and then drive down the fish by wading, splashing, shouting and beating the water with paddles. As soon as a number of fish come down against the net its upper border is let down so as to enclose them.

Another kind of net, made quite flat and some fifteen yards long by four feet in depth, is suspended by wooden floats across a small river so that the fish may become entangled in its meshes.

A scoop net, in shape like a deep basin, is used only by the women; its wide mouth is attached to a stout circle of rattan, and a wooden bar is tied across the mouth to serve as handle. With this the women catch the little sucker fish which adhere to the large pebbles in the shallow rapids, one turning up stones, the other catching in the net the fish that dart from beneath them.

Yet another mode of netting fish is to suspend a small

net, a few feet square, attached at its corners to the ends
of two crossed sticks. The net is suspended by cords
from its corners to the end of a long bamboo which moves
about an attached point about half-way down. The
fisherman lowers the net into the water, and when he sees
fish swimming above it, suddenly levers the net above
the surface.

Various kinds of fish-traps are in use. One of the most
ingenious is the *Selambo*, which is used in small streams
where fish are abundant. A fence of upright bamboos is
built out from each bank, converging down-stream to two
points near the middle of the stream, the stakes being six
or seven feet apart; where each terminates a stout pole is
driven firmly into the bed of the river. Between the two
up-stream points a net is loosely stretched. This lies
submerged until fish coming down-stream are directed to
the lower net by the convergent fences. Here the fisherman stands, and when he feels the fish in the net he jerks
it up with a lever, and so brings the net quickly above the
surface. Beside him he has a large cage of bamboo
standing in the water, into which the fish are allowed to
slide from the elevated net.

The Kenyahs use a hook made of rattan thorns. A
strip is cut from the surface of a rattan bearing two thorns
about an inch apart; this is bent at its middle so that the
cut surfaces of the two halves are brought into opposition,
and the thorns, facing outward opposite one another, form
the barbs. The line is tied to the bend, and the bait is
placed over the two tips projecting beyond the thorns.
When the fish takes the bait into his mouth and swallows
it, the two tips are released and the barbs spring outward
in the mouth and secure the fish.

Another commonly used trap is the *Bubu*. This varies
in length from eighteen inches to eight feet or even more.
The body of the trap is a conical cage of bamboo. From
the wide mouth of the cone a second smaller, flatter cone
passes upwards within the outer one; the slender bamboo

Camp on a gravel bed.

Limestone caves in Mount Mulu.

strips of which it is made come almost together in the centre, their inner ends being free and pliable. This is ·fixed beside the bank, its mouth turned down-stream, and a few stakes are driven into the bed of the river to guide the fish towards the mouth of the trap ; or it may be laid in shallow water, two barriers of stones converging to its mouth. The fish working up-stream pass in at the mouth, and, when they have passed the inner lips, cannot easily pass out again.

A still simpler trap consists merely of a long slender cone of bamboo strips. The fish entering the mouth and passing up to the confined space of the other end become wedged fast and cannot get back.

An Iban trap found in the South-west of Borneo is a cylindrical cage of bamboo attached to a pole driven vertically into the bed of the river. At one side of the cage is a circular aperture. Into this fits a section of bamboo, the end of which within the cage is cut into longitudinal strips that are made to converge, forming a cone, through the apex of which the fish can push his way into the cage, but cannot return.

A larger trap is the *Kilong*, which is used in the lower reaches of the rivers and also on the coast. It consists of a fence of stakes running out from the bank or shore into water some two fathoms in depth. The outer end of the fence is shaped in a spiral with about two turns. One or two openings are made between the outer and the inner chambers of the spiral on the side nearest to the bank or shore, and are left open when the trap is set. The fish, finding themselves confined by the fence, make for deeper water, and entering the central chamber do not readily return. The fisherman then closes the gate and takes out the fish with a landing-net.

A prawn-trap is very much like a lobster-pot, and consists of a cylinder of bark. One end is closed with a conical valve of bamboo strips like that of the two traps described above ; the other is hinged to open for the extraction of the catch. The trap is baited with decaying cocoanut and thrown into the river with a long rattan attached to it and tied to a stake.

Fish are speared on the largest scale by polluting the water with the milky-coloured juice which is beaten out from the root of the derris plant or *tuba*, which is cultivated in the paddy-fields. The sport takes place in the smaller rivers at times of slack water, all the people of a village co-operating. Pieces of the roots are cut off without destroying the plants. When a large quantity has been gathered in bundles, a fence is built across the river at the spot chosen, and big traps are let into it facing up-stream. Then all the available small boats are manned and brought into the reaches of the river for about a mile above the fence. Each boat carries a supply of the root, which is then pounded and rinsed in water stored in the bottom of the boat. The water in all the boats, which has become whitish from the juice, is emptied at a given signal into the stream, either by baling or by overturning the boats. Some twenty minutes later the fish begin to rise to the surface and rush wildly to and fro. In the meantime the boats have been put to rights, and pursue the fish, the men armed with fish-spears, the women with landing-nets. The sport goes on for several hours. Some men armed with clubs stand upon a platform sloping up at a low angle out of the water and resting upon the fence. Big fish come leaping upon this platform and are clubbed by the men, who have to exert their agility to avoid the spikes with which most of these fish are armed. Large quantities of fish are sometimes taken in this way; what cannot be eaten fresh is dried and smoked over the fires in the forest or in the houses.

While the fishing party is being arranged and the preparations are going forward, great care is taken to avoid mentioning the word *tuba*, and all references to the fish are made in indirect phrases. This precaution is observed because it is believed that birds and bats can

Ibans cock-fighting

Drawing up a captured crocodile.

understand human speech, and may, if they overhear remarks about the preparations, give warning to their friends the fish, whose magician (a bony fish called *Belira*) will then bring down rain, and, by swelling the river, prevent the successful polluting of the water.

Tickling fish is also practised with some success, the men stand along the edge of a lake among the grass and sedges, where the fish seek cooler water in the heat of the day, and capture the fish amongst the rushes and roots.

The crocodiles, which are numerous in the lower reaches of all the rivers, are not hunted, save on provocation, by any of the peoples of Borneo except the Malays. Occasionally a bather may be seized by one; and cases have been known of people being dragged out of boats. If men are at hand they turn out promptly to attack the crocodile when it rises to the surface; but there is small chance of rescue. Should the victim have sufficient presence of mind and strength to thrust his thumbs into the eyes of the reptile it is said that it may release him; but most attacks are fatal. In such a case the men of the village turn out to avenge the outrage, and, in the case of the seizure of an important person, those of neighbouring villages will join with them. All available boats are manned by men armed with spears, some of which are lashed to the ends of long poles. Congregating in their boats near the scene of the disaster, the men prod the bed of the river with their spears, working systematically up or down river and up the small side streams. In this way they succeed in stabbing some of the reptiles; and in such cases, though they usually do not rise to the surface, their bodies are found some days after in the creeks, death having ensued from the inflammation set up in the wounds. The wound caused by a spear-thrust would seldom be fatal to the crocodile, except that such a wound is liable to the perpetual assaults of smaller creatures—fish while he is in the water, flies when he lies on the bank. These irritate and extend the wound and torment the creature until he is worried to death. The stomachs of those crocodiles that are captured are opened in search of traces of the person taken, traces which usually remain there for some time in the shape of hair or metal ornaments. If no trace is found the people's vengeance is not satisfied, and they set baited hooks, or pay Malays to do so, partly because the Malays are experts, partly because a Kayan does not care to take upon himself the individual responsibility of catching a crocodile, though he does not shrink from the collective pursuit. A dead fowl, monkey, or other animal is bound to a strong bar of hardwood, sharpened at both ends and some fifteen inches in length. A number of small rattans connect this bar to a log. The whole arrangement is allowed to float down river; for if it does not float freely, the crocodile will seldom take the bait. When a crocodile rises to the bait and swallows it, the bar gets fixed cross-wise in his gullet as he pulls on the rattans. The hunters, having kept the log in sight, then attach the ends of the rattans to the boat, draw the infuriated crocodile to the surface of the water, thrust a spear attached to a strong rope into its body, tie its jaws and feet, and tow the reptile to the bank, and haul him up on dry land. They secure his tail and feet with nooses, which they lash to a pole laid along his back, and lash his jaws together. Throughout these operations the crocodile is addressed deferentially as *Laki* (grandfather). He is then left exposed to the sun, when he soon dies or is killed by a Malay; in this way the people avoid the risks attaching to slaying the crocodile with their own hands.

Charles Hose attends the Sarawak State Council.

Hunting scene on the Rejang river; deer driven by dogs into the river.

CHAPTER II

JUNGLE LIFE

Hunting on foot—River pig-sticking—The *Jaring*—Various traps—The *jerat*, a trap for small animals—An Iban device—How the Klemantans catch the ground-pigeon—Gathering jungle produce—Profit and pleasure combined on long expeditions—Gutta-percha—Wild rubber from a creeper—Para rubber—Honourable policy of Sarawak Government—Camphor: its collection an ancient pursuit marked by superstition—The rattan palm—Honey and beeswax—Wild honey from the *tapang* tree—Smoking out the bees—Vegetable tallow and wild sago—Edible nests.

MOST of the Bornean peoples are, at least partially, hunters, since they breed no animals, except the pig and fowl, for the table; while such tribes as the Punans rely almost exclusively on their powers as *shikaris*.

The wild pig is the principal object of the chase, but deer of several species are also hunted. The largest of these is rather bigger than the English fallow deer; the smallest is the mouse deer, standing only about thirteen inches at the shoulder; intermediate in size is the muntjac or barking deer. There are also small herds of wild cattle, a small rhinoceros, large lizards, various apes and monkeys, a large porcupine, and many small mammals, such as otters, bear-cats, civet-cats, and squirrels of various species, all of which are hunted for their flesh, as well as several birds. The tiger-cat and the honey-bear are hunted for their skins and teeth, and the dried gall-bladder of the bear is sold for medicine to the Chinese.

The pig and deer are hunted on foot by parties of men with a pack of four or five dogs. The dogs, having found the trail, chase the pig until he turns on them. They then surround the pig, barking and yelping, and keep it at bay till the men run up and despatch it with their spears. Both men and dogs sometimes get severely mauled by the boar's tusks.

River pig-sticking is another method. During the fruit season the pigs migrate in large herds and cross the rivers at certain known places. The people lie in wait for them in little huts built on the banks, and kill them from their boats as they swim across.

Kenyahs and Klemantans sometimes catch deer by driving them into what is called a *jaring*. This contrivance consists of a strong rope of plaited rattans stretched in a straight line across the forest, from tree to tree, some five feet above the ground. It is generally laid so as to complete the enclosure of an area that is almost surrounded by a bend of the river. Dependent from the whole length of the rattan rope is a series of running nooses also of rattan, each of which, overlapping its neighbours on both sides, forms a loop about two feet in diameter. Men armed with spears are stationed along the enclosed space at short intervals, and some of the watchers paddle their boat slowly along the bend of the river; the rest of the party with the dogs either beat the jungles, or patrol the river-bank, driving any deer in the enclosed space headlong towards the nooses. Some of the deer may escape, but one or more will usually run their heads into the nooses and fall victims to the spears of the watchers.

Wild cattle are sometimes killed in the rivers, when they have taken to water; but usually they are too dangerous to attack. The rhinoceros is hunted by the Punans, who lie in wait for him beside the track by which he comes down to his daily mud-bath, and drive a spear into his flank or shoulder; then, hastily retiring, they track him through the forest until they come on him again, when they drive in another spear or a poisoned dart.

Birds and monkeys are chiefly killed with the blow-pipe: parrots are sometimes caught with bird-lime made from the latex of a wild-rubber tree.

Traps of many varieties are made. For pig and deer traps are set in the fences about the rice-fields. They consist of a sort of trigger arrangement, the chief part being a bamboo spear, the point of which is sharpened and hardened in the fire. This is laid horizontally about two feet from the ground, resting on guides. Its butt end is lashed to one end of a horizontal springy pole at right angles to it. The other end of the pole is firmly fixed to a tree, while the part carrying the spear is bent forcibly backwards and held back by a loop of rattan. This spring is set by means of an ingenious trigger, in such a way that an animal passing through the gap must push against a piece of bark attached to the trigger, and so release the spring, which then drives the bamboo spear across the gap with great force. The only disadvantage of these traps is that villagers sometimes get killed by inadvertently walking into them.

Of many ingenious traps for small animals the *jerat* is the most widely used. A rude sort of fence several hundreds of yards in length, is made by filling up with sticks and brushwood the spaces between the trees and undergrowth of the jungle. At intervals of ten or twenty yards, and in the runs of animals, narrow gaps are left, through which various small creatures, finding their way barred by the fence, seek to pass. Such a gap is floored with a small platform of light sticks, six to eight inches long, laid across it parallel to one another in the line of the fence. The ends of these are supported at one side of the gap, about two inches above the ground, by a cross-stick lying at right angles to them. This stick in turn is supported about one inch above the ground in the following way : the two ends of a green pliable stick are thrust firmly into the ground, forming an arch over the end of the platform, and the extremities of the cross-stick are in contact with the pillars of the arch, and kept a little above the ground by being pulled against them by the spring trigger. This consists of a short stick attached by a cord

to a strong springy pole thrust vertically into the ground.
To set the trigger it is pulled down, bending the pole, and
passed under the arch from the platform side outwards;
the upper end of the trigger is then kept by the pull of
the cord against the curve of the arch, and its lower end
is pulled against the middle of the cross-stick. The
pressure being maintained by the tension of the cord, this
end of the platform is supported by the friction between
the trigger and the cross-stick. The cord is prolonged
beyond the trigger in a slip noose which lies open on the
platform completely across the gap, so that any small
animal entering the gap, and stepping upon the platform,
necessarily places its foot within the noose. A few dead
leaves are laid upon the platform and cord to disguise
them. Thus, if a medium-sized bird or animal steps on
to the platform, its weight causes the cross-stick to slip
down from the hold of the trigger, and this being released,
is violently jerked with the noose into the air by the elastic
reaction of the bent pole; in a large proportion of cases
the noose catches the victim's feet and jerks him into the
air, where he dangles by the feet till the arrival of the
trapper, who visits his traps twice a day, in the early
morning and the evening.

Another very curious and strikingly simple plan is
employed by the Ibans to secure the Argus pheasant,
whose beautiful wing feathers are highly valued. The
cock-birds have a habit of congregating at certain spots
in the jungle, where they display their feathers and fight
together. These spots the birds attempt to clear of all
small obstacles, pulling and pushing away sticks and
leaves with their beaks and necks, as well as scratching
with their feet and flapping their wings. The Ibans,
taking advantage of this habit, thrust vertically into the
ground slips of bamboo, the upper points and edges of
which are hardened in the fire and rendered very sharp.
In the course of their efforts to remove these obstructions,
the birds not infrequently inflict severe wounds about

Floods in the Rejang district.

Large fish speared by the Rajah.   From a photograph taken by himself.

their necks, and, weakened by loss of blood, are found at no great distance from the fighting ground.

The Klemantans and some of the Kenyahs catch a small ground-pigeon in large numbers by the aid of a pipe or whistle, on which the cooing notes of the birds are closely imitated. The instrument consists of a piece of bamboo closed at one end and having a small hole half-way along its length. The hunter, concealed behind a screen of leafy branches, blows across this hole through a long slender tube of bamboo; and when a bird approaches the whistle, he slips over its head a fine noose attached to the end of a light bamboo, and drawing the fluttering bird by the neck behind the screen, puts it alive into a cage without much disturbing the other birds.

The principal natural products gathered by the people in addition to the edible fruits are gutta-percha, rubber, camphor, various rattans, beeswax and honey, vegetable tallow, wild sago, gums from various trees, and the famous edible birds'-nests. To obtain these commodities, small parties of men and boys go out into the forest, sometimes travelling many days up-river before striking into the jungle; for it is only in the drier upland forests that such expeditions can be undertaken with advantage. The party may remain several weeks or months from home, but regard the enterprise as wholly enjoyable, if not always profitable. They carry with them a supply of rice, salt, and tobacco, cooking pots and matches, a change of clothes, spears, swords, shields, blow-pipes, and perhaps two or three dogs. On striking into the jungle they drag their boat on to the bank and leave it hidden in thick undergrowth. They live in rude shelters roofed with their leaf mats and with palm leaves, moving camp from time to time. Their labours are varied and their food-supply augmented by hunting and trapping. However, as with camping parties in other parts of the world, cooking is generally regarded as a nuisance, to be shirked if possible.

Valuable varieties of gutta-percha are obtained from trees of more than a score of species. The best is known as Kayan gutta, because, in its purest form, it is gathered and sent to the bazaars by that people. The trees are felled and the stem and branches are ringed at intervals of about two feet, a narrow strip of bark being removed at each ring. The milky viscid sap drips out into leaf cups, which are then emptied into a cylindrical vessel of bark. It is then poured into boiling water with a little salt added, when it rapidly congeals. Then, still in a semi-viscid state, it is kneaded with the feet and pressed into a shallow wooden frame, which in turn is compressed between two pieces of wood. In this way it is moulded into a small triangular slab. While the slab is still warm, a hole is pierced through the narrower end ; and it is then thrown into cold water, where it sets hard, and is ready for the market.

The best wild rubber, known to the Ibans as *kubal* and to the Kayans as *pulut*, is obtained from a creeper, the stem of which grows to a length of fifty to two hundred feet and has a diameter of six inches or more. It bears a brilliant red luscious fruit which is eaten by the people ; and as its seeds are swallowed whole, it becomes widely distributed. The Punans carefully transplant the young seedlings (which come up in clusters) to the most suitable positions. The latex of the creeper is gathered and treated in much the same way as the gutta. It is rolled up while it congeals into spherical lumps, each of which is pierced with a hole for convenient transportation.

The history of Para rubber in Sarawak is, naturally, recent ; but it affords a splendid example of the disinterested goodness of the late Rajah, and of the fatherly character of his Government. It is within the memory of all that between the years 1908 and 1911 occurred the great rubber " boom " in the markets of Europe. In hopes of profit, speculators hurried to any region where rubber might grow. Para seeds had been introduced to

Kayans working gutta percha in the forest.

A Kenyah woman dancing during the harvest festival.

Sarawak many years before; the suitability of the soil and climate for the production of Para rubber of the best quality had been abundantly demonstrated; and the natives had been encouraged to plant for their own profit the seeds and young plants which were distributed to them from the Government stations, so that when the boom came, many of them possessed small plantations of their own. The wily speculator calculated to buy these plantations at prices which to the owners might seem handsome, but were much more handsome to the buyers. To his great credit the Rajah caused warnings to be published, by which the natives were informed that they were at full liberty to appropriate forest land for the formation of rubber plantations, and that their tenure of such lands would be secured to them so long as they cared for the trees and worked the rubber properly. He likewise ordered that no sales of rubber plantations should be effected without the knowledge and approval of the Government.

Camphor is formed in the crevices of the stems of old trees of the species *Dryobalanops aromatica*, when the heart is decayed and a central hollow is left in the trunk. The tree can then be cut down, the stem split up, and the crystalline scales of pure camphor shaken out on to mats. It is then made up in little bundles wrapped in palm leaves. The large-flaked camphor worked locally fetches as much as £6 per lb. weight in the Chinese bazaars. Special precautions are observed by men in search of camphor. A party of Kayans, setting out to seek camphor, commonly gets the help of Punans, who are acknowledged experts in this business. Omens are taken before setting out, and until these are favourable the party will not start.

On entering a small river the party stretches a rattan across its mouth; and where they leave the river they erect on the bank a pole or frayed stick. Those who see such sticks set up understand and respect the desire for privacy. They then march through the forest to the place where they expect to find a group of camphor trees, marking their path by bending the ends of twigs at certain intervals in the direction in which the party is moving.

Having found a likely tree they cut into the stem with a small long-bladed axe, making a deep small hole. An expert, generally a Punan, then smells the hole and the chips and gives an opinion as to the chances of finding camphor within it. If he gives a favourable opinion, the tree is cut down and split in pieces as described above. On cutting down the camphor tree, a thick oil which smells strongly of the camphor sometimes pours out and is collected. From the ceremonies observed, it is probable that the collecting of camphor is a very ancient one, whereas the collection of gutta and rubber has been undertaken in comparatively recent years in response to the demand of the European market.

Many varieties of the rattan palm grow luxuriantly in the forests of Borneo, some attaining a length of 150 to 200 feet. The rattan is a creeping palm which makes its way towards the light, suspending itself to branches and twigs by means of the curved spines and hooks which prolong the midribs of the leaves. The cane is collected by cutting through the stem near its root, and hauling on it, several men combining their efforts. The piece cut down is dragged through the jungle to the river bank. Here it is cut into lengths of about fifteen feet and dried in the sun. If the sap is thoroughly dried out, the cane assumes a permanent yellow colour; but if any is left, it darkens when soaked in water. When a large number of bundles have been collected, they are bound together to form a raft. On this a hut is erected, and two or three men navigate the raft down river to the Chinese bazaars, which are to be found at the mouth of every large river.

The pretty yellow fruit of the rattan is gathered in large quantities and subjected to prolonged boiling. The fluid

The Residency bungalow at Sibu, some fifty miles from the sea.

Mrs. Hose and baby son in the Residency garden at Sibu, after meeting the rebel border chiefs Bantin and Kana who surrendered to the Government in 1906. The Rejang river is nearly a mile across at this point.

turns a bright crimson colour, and is boiled down till it has the consistency of beeswax. It is then known as dragon's blood, and is both used and exported as a colouring mordant.

Honey and beeswax are collected from combs built by the wild bee in the high branches of the large *tapang* trees; sometimes as many as fifty or sixty combs may be found on one tree. To reach the nest, which is usually attempted after nightfall, the men climb the trunk by an improvised ladder. A large number of sharpened pegs of ironwood having been driven into the softer bark and sapwood of the stem in a vertical row about two feet apart, long bamboos are lashed to them, and also to the stems of the lower branches. The ladder is thus built up until at some sixty or eighty feet from the ground it reaches a branch bearing two or three combs. A man now ascends the ladder, carrying in one hand a burning torch of bark, which gives off a pungent smoke, and on his back a large hollow cone of bark. Straddling out along the bough, he hangs his cone of bark beneath the honeycomb, smokes out the bees, and cuts it away from the bough with his knife, so that it falls into the cone of bark. Then, choosing a piece of comb containing grubs, he munches them with gusto, indicating in pantomime to his envious friends their delicious quality.

After thus gathering two or three nests he lets down the cone with a cord to his expectant partners, who then feast upon the remaining grubs and squeeze out the honey into jars. The tree having been cleared of nests in this way, the wax is melted by boiling in an iron pot and moulded into balls. The honey is eaten in the houses; the wax is sold to the Chinese traders.

Vegetable tallow is procured from the nuts or seeds of the Enkabong tree (*Shorea*). The nuts, which are known in the market as Ilippi nuts, are shipped in large quantities to Europe; locally they are crushed, the vegetable fat being melted out and gathered in bamboo receptacles.

I

It is used as a food, commonly in combination with hot rice; and for the Punans it often forms the principal feature of their diet.

To obtain wild sago (commonly used as a supplementary food), the sago tree is felled and cut into lengths, which are split into several pieces with wedges. The pith is knocked out with a bamboo mallet, and sago prepared from the pith by women, who stamp it on coarse mats, pouring water upon it. The finer grains are carried through on to a trough below. It is then washed and boiled in water, when it forms a viscid mass; this is eaten with a spoon or with a strip of bamboo bent double, the two ends of which are turned round in the sago and withdrawn with a sticky mass adherent to them; this is plunged in the gravy of pork and so carried to the mouth.

Resins and gums are exuded by many of the forest trees. They are collected in the forest and on the beach, and used in the houses for torches and for a number of purposes, such as repairing boats. A large quantity is brought to the bazaars, where the best kinds fetch good prices. Sometimes the gum is found in large masses on the ground where it has dripped from the trees.

The most important of the natural products gathered by the people are the well-known birds'-nests, from which soup is made, and which belong to three species of swift: *Collocalia fuciphaga*, whose nest is white; *C. lowii*, whose nest is blackish; and *C. linchii*, whose nest contains straw and moss as well as gelatine. All three kinds are collected, but those of the first kind are much more valuable than the others. The nest, which is shaped like that of our swallow, consists wholly of a tough, gelatinous, translucent substance, which exudes from the bill of the bird as it builds. The natives believe that the substance of the nest is dried sea-foam, which the birds bring from the sea on returning from their annual migration.

The nests are always built in the crevices of the roofs and walls of caves; but the white nests are usually found in low-roofed caves, generally in sandstone rock; the black in the immense lofty caves formed in the limestone rocks. The latter are reached by means of tall scaffoldings made from strong poles of bamboo, often more than a hundred feet in height. The nests are swept from the rock with a pole terminating in a small iron spatula, and carrying next to the extremity a wax candle; falling to the ground, which is covered with guano several feet deep, they are gathered up in baskets. The white nests are gathered three times a year and at intervals of about a month, the black nests usually only twice; as many as three tons of black nests are sometimes taken from one big cave in the course of the annual gathering. During the gathering of the nests in a large cave the people live in roofless huts built inside it. The nests are sold to the Chinese traders, the black for about a hundred dollars a hundredweight, and the white for as much as thirty or forty shillings per pound. The price at which " Birds'-nest Soup " is sold to the foreigner is not within the scope of this volume.

CHAPTER III

Rice the essential food—Preparation of the land—Rotation of fields—An
uneconomic system—Family plots—Clearing a patch—" Whistling
for the wind "—Seed-time—Watching the fields—Rattles—Fencing
—Weeding—The harvest—The rites of the rice-grain.

FOR all the peoples of the interior of Borneo, the Punans
and Melanos excepted, the rice grown by themselves is
the principal food-stuff. Throughout the year, except
during the few weeks when uncultivated products are
most abundant, rice forms the bulk of every meal. In
years of bad harvests, when the supply is deficient, the
place of rice has to be filled as well as may be with wild or
cultivated sago, maize, tapioca, and sweet potatoes; but
the basis of his food is, when he can get it, rice; just as
the basis of a Russian's or an Italian's is paste, and that of
the nations of Western Europe, bread. Anything else,
therefore, that is grown, is considered as merely an adjunct
to the rice. In a moist warm climate weeds grow apace,
and the essential fields, being near the virgin forest, are
subject to attacks of many kinds of pests, birds, monkeys,
and wild pigs. Hence all the efforts and care of a village
are directed towards the obtaining of an adequate supply
of rice.

The plough is unknown, except in parts of North
Borneo, where it was probably introduced by Chinese
immigrants. In some of the alluvial areas certain tribes
have learnt, perhaps from intercourse with Indo-China
and the Philippine Islands, to prepare the land by leading
buffaloes to and fro across it while it is covered with water.
With these exceptions the preparation of the land is every-

Pepper vines.

Rice irrigation.

where very crude, consisting in the felling of the timber and undergrowth, and in burning it off when dry as completely as possible, so that its ashes enrich the soil. After a single crop has been grown and gathered on land so cleared, weeds grow up very thickly, and there is, of course, in the following year no possibility of repeating the dressing of wood ashes in the same way. Hence it is the universal practice to allow the land to lie fallow for at least two years, while crops are raised from other lands. During this period young trees and plants grow up so rapidly and thickly that by the third year the smaller weeds and grass have almost died out, choked by the larger growths. The same land is then prepared again by felling the young trees and burning it as before, and a crop is again raised from it.

When a piece of land has been prepared and cropped in this way some three or four times, at intervals of two, three, or four years, the crop obtainable from it is found to be so inferior in quantity that the people usually prefer to undertake the severe labour of felling and burning a patch of virgin forest rather than continue to make use of the old areas. In this way a large village uses up in the course of some twelve or fifteen years all the land suitable for cultivation within a convenient distance, i.e. within a radius of some three or four miles. This is the chief reason for the wholesale migration of villages; although, very often, a village will often return to its original site, reclaiming some of its old land, and adding at least a small area of virgin soil.

Each family cultivates its own plot of land, selecting it by arrangement with other families, and works as large an area as the strength and number of its members permit. A hillside sloping down to the bank of a river or navigable stream is usually considered the choicest area for cultivation, partly because of the effective drainage, and also because felling is easier on the slope, and the stream, however small, affords easy access to the field.

When an area has been chosen, the men of the family first cut down the undergrowth of a **V**-shaped area, the apex pointing up the hill, and the base lying along the river bank. This done, they call in the help of other men of the house, usually relatives who are engaged in preparing adjacent areas, and all set to work to fell the larger trees. In the clearing of virgin forest, when a very large tree has to be felled, a platform of light poles is built around the trunk to the height of about twelve or fifteen feet. Two men standing upon this rude platform on opposite sides of the stem attack it with their small " whippy " axes. One man cuts a deep notch on the side facing up the hill, the other cuts a similar notch about a foot lower down on the opposite side, each cutting almost to the centre of the stem. This operation is accomplished in a surprisingly short time, perhaps thirty minutes to an hour in the case of a stem two to three feet in diameter.

When all the large trees within the **V**-shaped area have been cut in this way, all the workers and any women and children (or dogs) who may be present are called out of the patch, and one or two big trees, carefully selected to form the apex of the phalanx, are then cut so as to fall down the hill. The workers are skilled woodmen, and know how to cut a tree so as to ensure its falling in any desired manner. In their fall these giants throw down the trees standing immediately below them on the hillside ; these, falling in turn against their neighbours, bring them down. And so, like an avalanche, the huge disturbance propagates itself with a thunderous roar and increasing momentum downwards over the whole of the prepared area, the authors of this catastrophic display dancing and shouting in wild triumphant delight.

Before it can be burnt the fallen timber must lie some weeks. This period is mainly devoted to making and repairing the implements to be used in cultivating, harvesting, and storing the crop, and also in sowing at the earliest possible moment small fields of early or rapidly-growing paddy, together with maize, sugar-cane, sweet potatoes, and tapioca.

The time of the burning of the timber depends on the state of the weather : if the weather is fine, a month will suffice ; rain naturally delays operations. A " likely " day for burning is a windy one, and, after suitable warnings, the matter is put in hand. While the burning goes on, the men " whistle for the wind," or rather blow for it, rattling their tongues in their mouths. The older men deliver powerful orations adjuring the wind. The fire, if successful, burns furiously for a few hours and then smoulders for some days, after which little of the timber remains but ashes and the charred stumps of the bigger trees. If the burning is very incomplete, it is necessary to make stacks of the lighter timbers that remain, and to fire these again.

As soon as the ashes are cool, sowing begins. Men and women work together ; the men go in front with wooden dibbles, making shallow holes about six inches apart ; the women follow, carrying round their necks small baskets of paddy seed, which they throw into the holes, three or four seeds to each hole. No care is taken to fill in the holes with earth, for by this time the dry season, which is not really dry and lasts only some two months, is at an end, and copious rains cause the seed to shoot above the ground a few days after the sowing. Several varieties of rice are in common use, some more suitable for the hillsides, some for the marshy lands. As the rates of growth of the several kinds are different, the sowings are so timed that the whole area ripens as nearly as possible simultaneously.

When the rice is in the ear there is built on each field a small hut, which is occupied by most of the able-bodied members of the family until harvest is gathered in, some fourteen to twenty weeks after the sowing of the rice. The main object now is the scaring of birds, and for this purpose bamboos about eight or ten feet in length are stuck upright in the ground every twenty to thirty yards.

Between the upper ends of these, rattans are tied, connecting together all the bamboos on each area of about one acre. As the largest individual field is generally about four acres in extent, there will thus be four groups of bamboos, each of which can be agitated by pulling on a single rattan. Each group is connected with the watcher's hut, and some person, generally a woman or child, is told off to tug at these at short intervals. Upon the rattans between the bamboos are hung various articles, such as old kerosene oil tins in which a few pebbles are placed, calculated to make as much noise as possible. The watcher remains in the hut all day long, while his companions are at work in the field ; he varies the monotony of his task by shouting and beating with a pair of mallets on a hollow wooden cylinder. He is relieved from time to time, but the watch is maintained continuously day and night from the time that the rice is about two feet above the ground until it is all gathered in.

Further protection against wild pig and deer is made by running a rude fence round a number of closely adjacent patches of growing corn. The fence, some three to four feet high, is made by lashing to stout poles thrust vertically into the ground, and also to convenient trees and stumps, bamboos or saplings as horizontal bars. When this is completed the men take no further part until the harvest, except perhaps to lend a hand occasionally with the weeding. This is the time generally chosen by them for long excursions into the jungle in search of rattans, rubber, camphor, and, formerly, for warlike expeditions or the paying of distant visits.

Weeding is the duty of the women-folk. The women of each room go over each patch completely at least twice, at an interval of about a month, scraping down the weeds with a short-handled hoe. This is an implement much like one side of the ordinary English hoe, except that the blade is about half the size, and the shaft about a quarter the length of the familiar implement. A spade, manifestly, cannot be used by those who work with bare feet, and the Bornean hoe, taking its place, is worked in a dragging fashion with one hand. In the weeding process some three weeks are consumed. Meanwhile, the women gather the small crops of pumpkin, cucumbers, and other vegetables, spending several weeks together on the farm, sleeping in the hut. In a good season this is the happiest time of the year; for both men and women take the keenest interest and pleasure in the growth of the crop.

During the time when the rice is formed but not yet ripe, the people eat the unripe grain, which they prepare by gathering the green ears and beating them flat. These are not cooked, but merely dried in the sun, and though they need much mastication they are considered something of a delicacy.

During the time of the ripening of the corn a spirit of gaiety and joyful anticipation prevails. It is a favourite time for courtship and the arrangement of marriages.

To the Borneo peoples the harvest is certainly the most important event of the year. Men, women, and children all take part. As the grain begins to ripen the rice-sparrows congregate in thousands, and even the noisiest efforts fail to keep them at a distance. The gatherers walk carefully through the crop, gathering all ripe ears, using a small rude knife-blade mounted in a wooden handle along its whole length. This is held in the hollow of the right hand, the ends of a short cross-bar projecting so as to be held between the first and second fingers and between thumb and first finger. The thumb seizes and presses the head of each blade of corn against the edge of the knife, and the ears are thrown into a basket slung round the neck. As soon as enough has been collected by the reapers, it is spread out on mats on a platform before the hut. After an exposure of two or three days, the grain is separated from the ears by the bare feet. The separated grain passes through the meshes of a coarse mat on to a finer mat beneath. The grain is then further dried by exposure to the sun. When the whole crop has been gathered, threshed, and dried in this way, it is transported in large baskets to the barns adjoining the Long House, and the harvest festival, which is a celebration of the principle of fertility and vitality and which is described elsewhere, begins.

According to the Kayan view of life, a view shared by most of the cultivators of Borneo, science is not sufficient to produce a good rice-crop; but at every stage a variety of rites must be observed. The grain is held to have a peculiar life of its own, subject to influences both good and bad, and must therefore be cherished by some sort of spiritual means. In the first place the determination of the time for sowing is a matter of so great importance that in each village a special man is appointed who makes it his profession to observe the signs of the seasons. His importance is such that he is not expected to cultivate a crop for himself or for his family, but is furnished with all the rice he needs by contributions from all the other members of the village.

It is essential to determine the approach of the short dry season, in order that in the course of it the timber may be felled and completely burned. In Borneo, lying as it does upon the equator, the revolution of the year is marked by no very striking changes of weather, temperature, or of vegetation. In fact, the only constant and striking evidences of the passage of the months are the alternations of the north-east and the south-west monsoons. The former blows more or less regularly from October to March, the latter from April to September, the transitions being marked by variable winds. The relatively dry season sets in with the south-west monsoon, and lasts about two months; but occasionally in some years the rainfall during this season is hardly less abundant than during the rest of the year.

The observer of the weather in any village has no official

position, although his functions command general respect. He relies very little on any scientific observations, except the changes of the sun's altitude, which he notes by means of an instrument much like the Greek gnomon, known in Borneo as *tukar do* or *aso do*.

A straight cylindrical pole of hardwood is fixed vertically in the ground; this is carefully adjusted with the aid of plumb lines, and the possibility of its sinking deeper into the earth is prevented by passing its lower end through a hole in a piece of wood laid horizontally on the ground, its surface flush with the surface of the ground. The pole is provided with a shoulder which rests upon this board. The upper end of the pole is generally carved, sometimes elaborately, in the form of a human figure. The length of the pole from the collar to its upper extremity is usually made equal to the span from tip to tip of the outstretched arms of its maker, plus the length of his span from tip of the thumb to that of the first finger. This pole stands on a cleared space before or behind the house, and is surrounded by a strong fence; the area within the fence, some two or three yards in diameter, being made as level and smooth as possible. For observation, the weather prophet has a neatly worked flat stick, on which lengths are marked off by notches regularly laid off, the stick being placed along the radial side of the left arm, its butt end against the armpit. A notch is then cut at each of the following positions : one notch about one inch from the butt end, a second opposite the middle of the upper arm, one opposite the elbow, one opposite the bend of the wrist, one at the first interphalangeal joint, and one at the finger-tip. The other side of the rod bears a larger number of notches, of which the most distal marks the greatest length of the midday shadow, the next one the length of the midday shadow three days after it has begun to shorten, the next the length of the shadow after three more days' shortening, and so on. The midday shadow is, of course, the minimal length reached in the course of the day, and the marks denoting the changes in length of the shadow are arrived at, purely empirically, by marking off the length of the midday shadow every three days.

The shadow is naturally measured when the sun is unclouded. As it grows shorter after the reaching of its maximal length, it is observed with special care, and at that point the village is told that the time for preparing the land is near at hand. When the shadow reaches the notch made opposite the middle of the arm, the best time for sowing the grain is considered to have arrived; by this time the land must have been cleared, burnt, and made ready. Sowing at times when the shadow reaches other notches is held to render the land liable to more than the usual number of pests—monkeys, insects, rats, and sparrows. In the case of each successful harvest, the date of the sowing is recorded by driving a peg of ironwood into the ground at the point denoting the length of the midday shadow at that date. The weather prophet has, however, other marks and notches whose meaning is known only to himself; his procedures are surrounded with mystery and kept something of a secret, even from the chief as well as from all the rest of the village, and his advice is always followed.

The method of observing the sun described above is universal among the Kenyahs, but some of the Kayans practise a different method. Among them a hole is made in the roof of the weather prophet's chamber in the Long House, and the altitude of the midday sun and its direction, north or south of the meridian, are observed by measuring along a plank fixed on the floor the distance of a beam of sunlight (falling through the hole on to the plank) from the point vertically below the hole. The horizontal position of the plank is secured by placing upon it smooth spherical stones and noting any inclination to roll. The sunbeam which enters this hole is called *kleput toh.*

Some Klemantans practise a third method to determine when the time for sowing is at hand, using a bamboo some feet in length which bears a mark at a level determined empirically by filling it with water while in the vertical position, and then tilting it until it points towards a certain star, when of course some water escapes. After it has been restored to the vertical, the level of the surface of the remaining water is noted. The coincidence of this level with the mark mentioned above indicates that the time for sowing is come.

The appropriate season having been determined, it is necessary to secure good omens before the preparation of the land can be begun. The announcement of the nature of the omens observed is made to the chief in the presence of a deeply interested throng of both sexes. The observers usually go out for a period of two days, but if the omens observed are considered to be unfavourable, or of doubtful import, they go out for a second period. If they are now favourable, the women of each room perform the private rites over their stores of seed-rice, which are kept in their rooms. Finally, after considerable discussion, the date for the beginning of the clearing operations is arranged.

At the beginning of the sowing the house is again subject to *malan* for one day. During the growth of the rice various charms and superstitious practices are brought into use to promote its growth and health, and to keep it from pests. The rice charms are a miscellaneous collection or bundle of small articles, such as curious pebbles and bits of wood, pigs' tusks of unusual size or shape, beads, feathers, shells, and crystals of quartz. Such charms are generally acquired in the first instance through indications afforded by dreams, and are handed down from mother to daughter. They are kept in a basket in a rice-barn, from which they are taken to the field by the woman and waved over it, usually with a live fowl in the hand, while she addresses the seed in some such terms as the following : " May you have a good stem and a good top, let all parts of you grow in harmony." Then she rapidly repeats a long customary formula of exhortation to the pests, saying, " O rats, run away down the river, and do not trouble us ! O sparrows and noxious insects, feed on the rice of the peoples lower down ! " If the crop is very much infested the woman may kill a fowl and scatter its blood over the growing crops, while she charges the pests to disappear, and calls upon Laki Ivong (the god of harvests) to drive them out.

Women alone gather the first ears of the crop. Should they encounter on their way to the fields any one of the following creatures, they must at once return home, and stay there a day and a night, on pain of illness or early death : certain snakes, spiders, centipedes, millipedes, and birds of two species, *jeruit* (a small flycatcher), and *bubut* (a bird of the cuckoo species, but with none of its habits). Or, again, if the shoulder-straps of their large baskets should break on the way, if a stump should roll down or fall against them, or the note of the spider-hunter be heard, or if a woman should strike her foot by accident against any object, the party must return as before.

From this account it will be clear that the principal part in the rites and actual operations of the rice culture is taken by the women ; the men only being called in to clear the ground and to assist in some of the later stages. It is they who select and store the seed-grain, and they are the repositories of most of the lore connected with it. It seems to be felt that they have a natural affinity to the fruitful grain, which they speak of as becoming pregnant. Women sometimes sleep out in the rice-fields while the main crop is growing, probably for the purpose of increasing their own fertility or that of the rice ; but they are very reticent on this matter.

When the crop is all gathered in, the house is *malan* to all outsiders for some ten days, during which the grain is transported from the fields to the village and stored in the small barns. When this process is completed or well advanced, the festival begins with the preparation of the seed-grain for the following season. Some of the best of the new grain is carefully selected by the women of each room, enough for the sowing of the next season. This is mixed with a small quantity of the seed-grain of previous good seasons, which has been carefully preserved for this purpose in a special basket. This basket is never emptied, but a pinch of the old grain is mixed in with the new, and a small handful of the new mixture is added to the old stock. The idea, which is said to go back to the earliest times of rice-planting, is that the old grain, preserving continuity generation after generation with the original seed of mythical origin, ensures the presence in the grain of the soul or spirit or vital principle of rice. While mixing the old with the new seed-grain, the woman calls on the soul of the rice to cause the seed to be fruitful and to grow vigorously, and to favour her own fertility. The whole festival is, in fact, a celebration or cult of the principle of fertility and vitality—that of the women no less than that of the rice-grain.

Those women who have been delivered of children during the past year will make a number of toys, consisting of plaited basket-work, in the shapes of various animals, which are partially filled with grains of the rice and then boiled. These they throw to the children of the house, who scramble for them in the gallery and eat the contents. They seem to be of the nature of a thank-offering.

At this time also another interesting custom is observed. Four water-beetles, of the kind that " skates " about on the surface of the still water, are caught on the river and placed on water in a large gong. Some old man specially wise in this matter watches them, calling to them to direct their movements. The people crowd round deeply interested, while the old man interprets the movements of the beetles as forecasting good or ill luck with the crops of the following season, and invokes the goodwill of Laki Ivong, begging him to prevent the soul of the rice from leaving its home. Juice from a sugar cane is poured upon the water, which the women then drink, while the beetles are carefully returned to the river. The beetles are charged to carry messages from the people to Laki Ivong. When these observances have been duly honoured, there begins a scene of boisterous fun. The younger women and girls make pads of the sticky newly-boiled rice, and cover one side of it with soot from their cooking vessels. With these they approach the young men and dab the pads upon their faces and bodies, leaving round sooty marks that are not easily removed. The men thus challenged give chase, and playfully attempt to get possession of the rice pads and to return the compliment. For a short space of time a certain licence prevails among the young people; and irregularities, even on the part of married people, which would be gravely reprobated at all other times, are looked upon with toleration. Each room-hold has prepared a stock of spirit from the new rice, and this now circulates freely among both men and women, while large meals of rice and pork are eaten. All join in dancing, some of the girls dressed like men, others carrying rice-pestles; at one moment all form a long line marching up and down the gallery in step to the strains of the *keluri*. The women also dance together in a long line, each resting her hands on the shoulders of the one before her, and all keeping time to the music of the *keluri*. The carnival is kept up with much good-humour the whole day long. In the evening more rice-spirit is drunk and love-songs are sung, the women mingling readily with the men, instead of remaining in their rooms as on other festive occasions. Before midnight a good many of the men are more or less slightly intoxicated, although here, as always, they never become offensive or incapable.

The harvest festival is the time when everyone must dance or, at all events, try to do so. The dances fall into two chief classes, namely, solo dances by either sex and those in which many persons take part. Most of the solo

Klemantan women dressed as men at the harvest festival.

Kenyah women from the far interior of Sarawak.

dances take the form of comic imitations of the movements of animals, especially the big macaque monkey (*dok*), the hornbill, and big fish. These dances seem to have no connection with magic or religion, but to be purely æsthetic entertainments; the animals that are regarded with most awe are, however, never mimicked in this way. Of group dances, there are at least four, in which both men and women take part. The movements and evolutions of each are very simple. The *lupa* resembles the dance on return from war. In the *kayo*, a similar dance, the dancers are led by a woman holding one of the old dried heads taken down for the purpose; some young women, dressed as men in war-coats and waistcoats, pretend to take the head of an enemy. The *lakekut* is a musical drill in which the dancers stamp on the planks of the floor with their heels in time to the music. The *lupak* is a kind of slow polka. In none of these, however, do the dancers fall into couples or embrace one another. A fifth dance of a somewhat unusual kind is the dance of the departure of the spirit, a dramatic representation by three persons of the death of one of them, and of his or her restoration to life by means of the Water of Life—supposed to be brought from the country which is traversed on the journey to the land of shades. This dance is sometimes given with so much dramatic effect as to move the onlookers to tears.

K

CHAPTER IV

WAR

THE Kayans are, perhaps, the least aggressive of all
the interior peoples with the exception of the Punans.
Nevertheless, prowess in war has made them respected
or feared by all the peoples; and during the last century
or so they established themselves in the middle parts of
the basins of all the great rivers, driving out many of the
Klemantan communities, partly by actual warfare, partly
by the simpler but equally effective method of appro-
priating to their own use the tracts of forest most suitable
for the cultivation of rice.

The fighting quality of the individual Kayan, the
loyalty and obedience of each household to its chief,
the custom of planting Long Houses upon some spot
carefully chosen for its tactical advantages, and the strong
cohesion between the Kayans of different and even widely
separated villages—all these factors combine to render the
Kayans comparatively secure and their villages immune
from attack. But though a Kayan village is seldom
attacked, and though they do not wantonly engage in
bloodshed, yet they will always stoutly assert their rights,

and will not allow any injury done to any member of the tribe to go unavenged.

The avenging of injuries and the necessity of possessing heads for use in funeral rites are for them the principal grounds for warfare; and these are generally combined, the avenging of injuries being generally postponed, sometimes for many years, until the need for new heads arises. Though a borrowed old dried head of an enemy of the tribe will serve all purposes of the rites performed to terminate a period of mourning, yet occasionally, especially in the case of mourning for an important chief, it is felt that fresh heads are desirable.

War is generally undertaken by the Kayans very deliberately, after much preparation and in large well-organised parties, ranging in numbers from fifty to a thousand or more warriors, recruited in many cases from several neighbouring villages, and under the supreme command of one chief of acknowledged eminence.

They seldom or never wage war on other Kayans, and rarely attack any people merely to secure heads or in sheer vainglory, as the Ibans not infrequently do. Nor do they attack others merely in order to sustain their prestige, as is sometimes done by the Kenyahs, who in this respect carry to an extreme the principle that attack is the most effective mode of defence.

The weapons and war-dress are very similar among all the peoples. The principal weapon is the sword known as *parang ilang*, or *malat*, a heavy blade of steel mounted in a handle made from an antler of the Bornean deer or of hardwood. The blade, which is about twenty-two inches long, has its cutting edge slightly convex, and the back is convex; the two edges diverge gradually up to a point about five inches from the tip, the blade here being about two inches in breadth. At this point the back edge is turned sharply until it meets the cutting edge at the tip. The appearance is, so far, much that of a scimitar. One particular feature, however, is that the blade itself is hollow-ground, or laterally concave. This peculiar shape of the blade, which is found nearer home in the joiner's gouge, renders the *parang* peculiarly efficient in sinking into or through either limbs or wood, and easy to withdraw, because the " heel " prevents too durable an insertion. It is carried in a wooden sheath suspended by a plaited waist-strap, and is the constant companion of every man ; for it is used not only in warfare, but also for a variety of purposes, such as the hewing down of jungle undergrowth, cutting rattans and bamboos, and the rough shaping of wooden implements.

The weapon second in importance is the spear. This consists of a flat steel blade, about one foot in length, the widest part (between one and two inches) being about four inches from the tip. The tip and edges of the blade are sharp, and its haft is lashed with strips of rattan to the end of a wooden shaft, the end of the haft being bent back to prevent its being dragged off the shaft. The shaft is of tough wood and about seven feet in length ; its butt end is usually shod with iron. The spear is used not only for thrusting, but also as a javelin and to ward off the spears hurled by the foe. It is invariably carried in every kind of river or jungle excursion.

The only other weapons commonly used are heavy bars of ironwood, sharpened at both ends and flung so as to twirl rapidly in the air. These were formerly used mostly in defending houses from attack, a store of them being kept in the house. For the same purpose, short sharp stakes of split bamboo are thrust obliquely into the ground, so as to present the sharp tip towards the feet of the oncoming foe.

In addition to his weapons, the equipment of the fighting-man consists of a war-cap, a war-coat, and a shield. The former is a round closely-fitting cap woven of stout rattans split in halves longitudinally. It affords good protection to the skull against the stroke of the sword, and in the case of a man who has taken part in

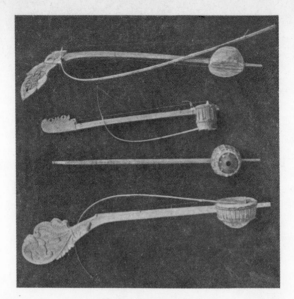

Musical instruments.

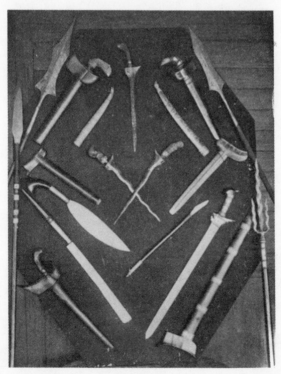

Weapons.

successful expeditions, is adorned with two of the long black-and-white tail-feathers of the hornbill.

The coat is made of the skin of the goat, deer, bear, or (in case of distinguished chiefs) tiger-cat. The whole of the skin is used in one piece, except that the skin of the belly and of the lower parts of the fore-limbs are cut away. A hole for the warrior's head is made in the mid-dorsal line a little behind the skin of the head, which is flattened out and hangs over the chest, descending to the level of the navel; while the skin of the back, flanks, and hind-limbs, in one large flap, covers the back down to the bend of the knees. A large mother-of-pearl shell usually adorns the breast of the warrior, while in the finest coats there is a patch of brightly coloured beadwork at the nape of the neck, and the back-flap is adorned with rows of loosely dangling hornbills' feathers; but these, as with the cap, are considered appropriate only for men of proved valour.

The shield used by most of the peoples is an oblong plate cut from a single piece of soft wood, about three to four feet long. The inner surface of the shield forms a flat hollow; the outer is formed by two flat surfaces meeting in a flat obtuse angle or ridge extending from top to bottom. The grain of the wood runs longitudinally, as a downward blow of a *parang* is liable to split the wood or become wedged fast in it. In order to prevent the shield becoming divided in this way, and to hold fast the blade of the sword, it is bound across with several stout strips of rattan which are laced closely to the wood with finer strips. The handle, carved out of the same solid block of wood as the body of the shield, is a simple vertical bar.

Many of these shields are elaborately decorated, except the Kayan, which is merely stained red with iron oxide, and touched up with black pigment. On the other hand, almost all Kenyah shields are covered, on either side, with elaborate designs in red and black. These designs are sketched out on the wood with the point of a knife, and the pigment is applied with the finger and a chisel-edged piece of wood. The principal feature of the designs on the outer surface is in all cases a large conventionalised outline of a face with large eyes, indicated by concentric circles in red and black, and a double row of teeth with two pairs of canines projecting like huge tusks. This face seems to be human, for in many cases it surmounts the highly conventional outline of a diminutive human body, the limbs of which are distorted and woven into a more or less intricate design. Each extremity of the outer surface is covered by a similarly conventionalised face-pattern on a smaller scale. On the inner side each longitudinal half is covered with an elaborate scroll-pattern, generally symmetrical in two halves, with occasionally the " Dog " or " Prawn " pattern and the head of the hornbill in the corners of either side ; the centre of this pattern is generally a human figure more or less easily recognisable ; the two halves sometimes bear male and female figures respectively.

The Kenyahs have certain shields, very much prized, which are decorated with tufts of human hair taken from the heads of slain enemies. The hair is put on in many rows so as roughly to frame the large face with locks three or four inches in length on scalp, cheeks, chin, and upper lip ; and the smaller faces at the ends are similarly surrounded with shorter hair. It is attached by forcing the ends of the tufts into narrow slits in the soft wood and securing it with fresh gum from forest trees.

Klemantan shields are, in the main, mere varieties of the Kenyah patterns. Those of the Muruts closely resemble those of the Kayans, while the Dusuns, who have domesticated the buffalo, use a shield of buffalo-hide attached to the forearm by a strap—a feature unknown in all the other types, which are borne by a handle only. The Ibans nowadays make a great variety of shields, copying those of the other tribes with variations of their own. The shield originally used by them before

Coat, Cap, Sword, Knife, and Shield of a Kenyah Warrior

coming into contact with other tribes, but now discarded, was made of strips of bamboo plaited together and stiffened with a longitudinal strip of wood. It was of two shapes, one with rounded, the other with pointed ends.

The Land Dayaks still use a shield made of tough bark, of a type which not improbably was used by other tribes also at no distant date.

Boats are, naturally, essential to war, and every Kayan household possesses one or more boats specially designed for this purpose. A typical war-boat is one made from a single tree-trunk, and is in length from 100 to 150 feet; its breadth varies from about three and a half feet at bow and stern, to six or seven feet amidships. It carries from sixty to seventy men seated two abreast. The speed which these boats attain is considerable : the writer, on one occasion, when a race between twenty-two of them was rowed at Marudi (Claudetown) on the Baram River, timed the winning boat over the downstream course of four and a half miles. The time was twenty-two minutes and thirteen seconds, which would be a reasonable time, over a similar distance, for the University Boat Race.

War is only undertaken after long and formal consultation (which may last for some days) between the chiefs and the leading men. If the village primarily concerned does not feel itself strong enough to achieve its ends alone, it will seek the help of some neighbouring village, usually, but not always, one of its own tribe.

The first step is to seek favourable omens, for which purpose two men are specially selected. They repair to some spot in the jungle, usually on the bank of a river, where they build a small hut ; this they adorn by fraying the poles of its framework, to secure themselves against the interruptions of passing acquaintances. Here they take the omens : of which more is said elsewhere.

From the moment of leaving the village the men of the war-party must observe many taboos until their return home. They may not eat the head of a fish; they must use only their home-made earthen cooking pots; fire must be made only by friction; they must not smoke; boys and youths may not lie down, but must sleep sitting.

If the object of the attack is a village on their own river, the expedition paddles steadily day after day until it reaches the mouth of some small stream at a convenient distance from the enemy's village. Forcing their boats a short way up this stream, they make a camp. Here two solid platforms are built about twenty feet apart, and a large beam is laid from one to the other. The chiefs and principal men take their seats on the platforms, and then every man of the party in turn approaches the beam, the fighting leader, who is usually not one of the chiefs, coming first. If he is willing to go through with the business, he slashes a chip from the beam with his sword and passes under it. On the far side of the beam stands a chief holding a large frond of fern, and, as each man passes under, he gives him a bit of the leaf, while an assistant cuts a notch on a tally-stick for each ten of the volunteers. If for any reason a man is reluctant to go farther, he states his excuse (such as a bad dream, or sore feet) and returns to the boats, often amid the jeers of those who have "joined up," to form one of a party to be left in charge of the camp and boats.

Next, all the left-handed men are sorted out to form a squad whose special duty is to ambush the enemy if possible at some favourable spot. These are known as the hornets. If any swampy ground or other obstruction intervenes between their camp and the enemy's village, a very rough path of poles is made through it to facilitate retreat to the boats. A password is agreed upon, which serves as a means of making members of the attacking party known to one another upon any chance meeting in the dark.

At dusk scouts are sent out, and, if their reports are favourable, the attack is made just before dawn. About a third of the warriors take with them large bundles of

Kayan woman dancing with a recently taken head.

War boats.

dry wood shavings, which they place under the Long House to be attacked; others carry torches. When the house has been completely surrounded, these heaps of shavings are ignited. Then ensues a scene of wild confusion. The calm stillness of the tropical dawn is broken by the deep war-chorus of the attacking party, the shouts and screams of the people of the house suddenly roused from sleep, the cries and squeals of the frightened animals beneath the house, and the rapid beating of the alarm signal inside. If the building is set on fire, the encircling assailants strive to intercept the fleeing inhabitants. These, if the flames do not drive them out before they have time to take any concerted measures, hurl their javelins and discharge any fire-arms that they have at their assailants; they then descend the ladders, bringing the women and children with them, and make a desperate attempt to cut their way through and escape to the jungle or to their boats.

Kayans conducting a successful attack of this kind make as many prisoners as possible, and as a rule kill only those men who make desperate resistance, though occasionally others, even women and children, are killed in the excitement of the moment. It is not unusual in the case of an able-bodied man who has surrendered, but shown signs of attempting to escape or of renewing his resistance, to deal him a heavy blow on the knee-cap, and so render him temporarily lame. Those who escape into the jungle are not pursued far, if the victors have secured a few heads and sufficient prisoners. In the case of those who die fighting, the head is hacked off at once, while the trunk is left lying where it fell. In the case of Ibans, if any of the attackers are killed, their heads are taken away and buried by their friends : the corpses, in the case of Kayans, are usually left where they fell; with other peoples, they are roughly and quickly buried. If any of the enemy are found to be so badly wounded that they are not likely to recover, they are killed and their heads taken; and should no heads have been secured in the fight, the head of one of the more seriously wounded captives is taken, or of one who is deformed or incapacitated in any way. Should a captive die of his wounds during the fight, his head is taken; but it is a rare exception for Kayans to kill any of their captives after the actual battle.

The attacking party, even though it has gained a decisive victory, usually returns with all speed, but in good order, to its boats, carrying with it through the jungle all the loot that is not too cumbersome for rapid portage, especially old beads, gongs, and brass-ware; for they are always in danger of being cut off by a party of their enemies, rallied and reinforced by friends. This danger is, naturally, increased if the attack on the village has failed through the defenders having been warned; in fact an expected attack has little chance of success. The pursuit of the retreating party may be kept up throughout one or two days, and frequently a brisk and bloody battle is the outcome. But here again it is seldom that any large proportion of either party is slain; for the dense jungle everywhere offers abundant opportunities of concealment, and there are few, even among the Kayans and Kenyahs, who will fight to the bitter end if the alternative of flight is open to them.

A successful war-party returning home makes no secret of its success. The boats are decorated with palm leaves, and a triumphal chorus is raised from time to time, especially when villages are passed. As the villagers come out to gaze on them, those who have taken heads stand up in the boats. The heads, slightly dried with fire, are wrapped up in palm leaves and placed in baskets in the stern of the boat. If the return home involves a journey of several days, the victors, when possible, pass the nights in the houses of friendly villages, where they are made much of, especially those who have taken heads; and on these occasions the glamour of victory is apt to break down the

Chinese shops in Kuching, the capital of Sarawak.

Annual boat races.

reserve that modesty normally imposes upon the women-folk.

On approaching their own village, whither the rumour of their success usually precedes them, the war-party is received with loud acclamations, the people coming down to the river-side to receive them. Before they ascend to the house, the heads have to be safely lodged in a small hut hastily built for that purpose, and the young boys are brought down to go through their first initiation in the arts of war, as already described.

The victorious warriors usually spend the first night after their return encamped before the house. A strip of green palm leaf is tied about the left wrist of each man who has taken part in the expedition. Those who have taken heads adorn their war-caps with the same leaf and with feather-like sticks. On the following day a tall post of bamboo (*balawing*) is erected near the wooden figure of the war-god. It is covered with frayed palm leaves, and from its tip a single head, also wrapped in palm leaves, is suspended by a long cord. Before the altar-post several shorter and thicker posts are erected, and to each of these two or three small pieces of human flesh, brought home from the corpses of the slain enemies for this purpose, are fastened with skewers. These pieces of flesh, which appear to be a sort of thank-offering to the omen-birds, are partly dried over a fire before being so exposed; and to this act I attribute certain cases of alleged cannibalism.

As soon as the news of the taking of heads reaches the house, the people go out of mourning, *i.e.* they shave the parts of the scalp surrounding the crown and pull out eyebrows and eyelashes (which have been allowed to grow); they put off their bark-cloth garments and resume their cotton-cloths and ornaments. If, as is usually the case on the return of a war-party, mourning for a chief is to be terminated, one of the heads is carried down-river to his tomb, followed by most of the men, while the women wail in the house. The head is first brought to a spot near the house, but not actually into it. One of the old men now shoots a dart into the air in the direction of the enemy, and then, with a tedious and conventional ritual slaughters a fowl and puts a part of the carcase upon a short stick thrust into the earth. The men of the party then march past, each touching the carcase with his knee, with the words, " Cast out all sickness, make me strong and healthy, and exalt me above my enemies." Beside the tomb the tall pole is set up, and the head, dressed in leaves, suspended by a cord from the upper end. A number of pigs have already been slain in preparation for the feast, and their lower jaws are also hung about the tomb on poles. The deep war-chorus is shouted by the party as it travels to and from the tomb. On its return the whole party bathes in the river, and while they are in the water an old man waves over them some of the palm leaves with which the head has been decorated, wishing them health and long life.

Within three or four days from the return of the war-party, the heads, with much rejoicing and ceremony, are brought into the house. Each family kills and roasts a pig, brings out stores of rice-spirit, and prepares cakes of rice-flour. The pigs' livers are examined, and their blood is smeared upon the altar-post of the war-god with a sort of brush elaborately made from the end of a frayed stick. Each head, adorned with a large bunch of palm leaves, is carried by an elderly man or woman into the house, and is followed in long procession by all the people of the village. The party marches up and down the whole length of the gallery many times, the people shouting, singing, stamping, and pounding on the floor with rice pestles, or playing the *keluri*. There follows a general celebration, each family preparing its feast in its own chamber, and entertaining friends and neighbours, who come to take part in the general rejoicing. The heads are usually temporarily commandeered by the women, who perform with them a wild, uncouth dance,

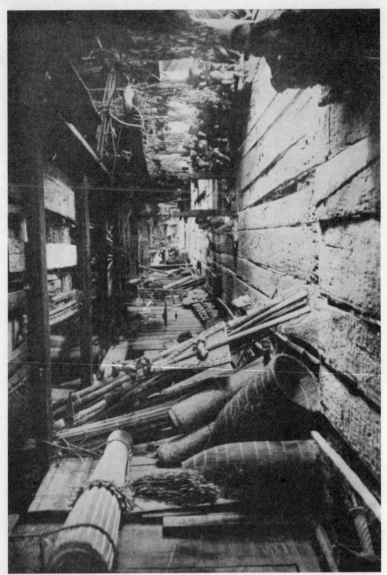

Gallery of a Kayan Long House.

waving them to and fro, and chanting in imitation of the men's war-song. The procession is resumed at intervals until the heads are finally suspended beside the old ones over the principal hearth of the gallery.

Heads are usually prepared for preservation as follows : the brain is removed through the great foramen, after being dried over a fire : the lower jaw is lashed to the skull with strips of rattan. The suspension of the skull is effected by piercing a round hole in the crown, and passing through it from below, by way of the great foramen, a rattan knotted at the end. The free end of the rattan is passed through and tied in a hole in the lower edge of a long beam suspended parallel to the length of the gallery from the beams of the roof, and out of reach of the dogs.

The defence of a Bornean Long House is in exact proportion to the science of the attack. Usually a fence of vertical stakes is raised around it, some three yards outside the posts on which it is supported and some six to eight feet in height. This fence is rendered unclimbable by a *frise* consisting of a multitude of slips of bamboo, each of which is bent round circularly, so that its two sharpened ends point outwards. These form an obstacle not easily to be overcome ; for the loosely fitting bamboo slips can neither be hacked away nor removed separately without a great loss of time, during which the attackers are exposed to a shower of missiles from the house. A double ladder in the form of a stile is often placed across the fence to permit any passage from the house.

The attacked party, on its side, arranges traps for the invaders, choosing ordinarily a part of the river where there are rocks or rapids. A large tree overhanging the river is selected, and half cut through : it is then secured to a tree further from the bank by rattans. A watchman is in charge, and when the opposing war-canoe comes up the stream, the rattan is cut, and, with any luck, the half-felled tree demolishes it.

It will be understood that the presence of a party " on the war-path " is not a matter of indifference to such peaceful villages as it may pass. Among such peoples an alarm is given, and handed on from village to village, by the beating of the national *tawaks*, or gongs. The signal is a standardised one, and consists of a rapidly accelerated series of strokes on the boss of the instrument, followed by one deep note, and then two shorter notes on the body of the gong, once repeated. This suffices to call in field and forest workers and to put the village in a state of defence, so that the invaders are usually able to do little more than cut off stragglers. If the invading party is very strong, they may surround a Long House and starve the inhabitants into submission, or allow themselves to be " bought off."

Some features of the tactics adopted by both Kayans and Kenyahs are worthy of more detailed description. If a strong party determines to attack a house in face of an alert defence, they very often attempt to storm it in broad daylight by forming several compact bodies of about twenty-five men. Each body protects itself with a roof of shields held closely together, and the several parties move quickly in upon the house simultaneously from different points, and attempt to carry it by assault. The defenders of the village attempt to repel the attack by hurling heavy bars of ironwood, sharpened at both ends, in such a way that the bar twirls in the air as it hurtles through it ; and, moreover, this is one of the few occasions on which the blow-pipe is used as a weapon of defence.

On the other hand, a village that has been warned may send out a party to attempt to ambush attacks at some difficult passage of the river or the jungle. Scouts, sent out to locate the enemy, climb to the tops of tall trees to look for the smoke of the enemy's fires. Having located the enemy, they approach at night so closely as to be able to count their numbers and observe all their movements ; and, keeping in touch with the party, send

Interior of a Klemantan house.

The end of a Long House, showing how it is protected against attack.

messages to headquarters, where suitable steps are taken. Should, however, the defending party come upon the enemy struggling against a rapid, and especially if he is in difficulties through the upsetting of the boats, they may fall upon him on the open gravel-bed of the river, and then ensues that comparatively rare event, a stand-up fight in the open.

This resolves itself, in the main, into hand-to-hand duels between pairs of combatants. The warriors selecting their opponents approach warily; they call upon one another sometimes by name, hurling taunts and swaggering in the correct Homeric manner. Each roundly abuses the other's parents, and threatens to use his opponent's skin as a war-coat, or make use of other portions of his anatomy for menial or degrading purposes : doubts as to his opponent's sex are more than insinuated. While this exchange of compliments goes on, the warriors are manœuvring for favourable positions; each crouches, thrusting himself forward with little jumps and covering himself as completely as possible with his long shield, and dodging to and fro continually. Short javelins and spears are first hurled, and skilfully parried with spear and shield. When a man has expended his stock of javelins and even perhaps hurled his spear, he closes in with his sword. If one succeeds in catching his enemy's sword in his wooden shield, he throws down the shield and dashes upon his now weaponless foe, who takes to his heels, throwing away his shield and relying merely on his swiftness of foot. When one of a pair of combatants is struck down, the other springs upon him and, seizing the long hair of the scalp and yelling in triumph, severs the neck with one or two blows of the sword. The warrior who has drawn first blood of the slain foe claims the credit of having taken his head.

Such a free fight seldom lasts more than a few minutes. Unless one party quite overwhelms the other in the first few minutes, both draw off, and the fight is seldom renewed.

Such wanton raiding has, since the establishment of European Governments, become rarer : the Kayans and Kenyahs have been found rarely to give trouble, when once they have placed themselves under an established power ; the chief offenders have been the Ibans and some of the Klemantans.

In organising such an expedition, the European governments, especially that of Sarawak, have usually relied in the main on the services of loyal chiefs and their followers, acting under the control of a European magistrate, or District Officer, and supported by a small body of native police or soldiers armed with rifles. There is usually no difficulty in securing the co-operation of any desired number of native allies or volunteers, especially in the case of the Kayans ; for in this way alone can the people now find a legitimate outlet for their innate and traditional pugnacity.

The real head-hunters are the Ibans, who conduct their warfare less systematically, and with far less discipline than the Kayans and Kenyahs. An attack upon a house or village by Ibans is usually made in very large force ; but the party is more of the nature of a rabble than of an army, each man acting independently. They seek above all things to take heads, to which they attach an extravagant value ; and they have been known not infrequently to attack a house and kill a large number of its inmates for no other motive than the desire to obtain them.

So strong is this morbid desire that a war-party sometimes has been known to rob the tombs of the villages of other tribes and, after smoking the stolen heads of the corpses, bring them home in triumph. Their attitude in this matter is well expressed by a saying current among them, namely, " Why should we eat the hard caked rice from the edge of the pot when there is plenty of soft rice in the centre ? "

The Iban women urge on the men to the taking of

Iban women dancing with the heads of enemies at a festival.

A Klemantan chief pays a visit to a chief of another tribe.

heads; they make much of those who bring them home, and often a girl will taunt her suitor by saying that he has not been brave enough to take a head; and in some cases of wilful murder of an individual by Ibans, the murderer has no doubt been egged on in this way.

Like other tribesmen, Ibans do not bring home the heads of their companions who have fallen in battle, but frequently cut off the heads and bury them at a distance from the scene of battle, in order to prevent them from getting into the hands of the enemy.

The Ibans are, perhaps, the only people who can really be called head-hunters; but, curiously, it is probable that they adopted the practice not more than a few generations ago, and then in imitation of Kayans or other tribes among whom it had been established earlier. Later, however, when the Ibans became associated in piratical matters with the Malays of the coast, these latter assigned to their allies the heads of their enemies, as a sort of perquisite. This state of affairs lasted until well into the nineteenth century; and it is from their association with the Malays of the coast in their piratical expeditions that the Iban became known to Europeans as a Sea Dayak.

It seems not impossible that the practice of taking the heads of fallen enemies arose by extension of the custom of taking the hair for the ornamentation of the shield and sword-hilt common among all the Bornean tribes.

Another plausible view is that it arose out of the custom of slaying dependents on the death of a chief, in order that their spirits might accompany and serve him on the journey to the other world. It is obvious that since the soul of the dead man is regarded as hovering in the neighbourhood of the body for some little time after its death, the despatch of a companion soul would hardly be considered immediately urgent; and considerations of economy might well lead the mourners to prefer capturing and killing a member of some hostile community to slaying one of their own people. The next step might be to

L

supplant the practice of capturing a member of a hostile community, and bringing him home to be slain, by the simpler, less troublesome, and more merciful one of slaying the enemy on the field of combat and bringing home only his head. This second suggestion is strongly supported by the fact that Kayans, Kenyahs, and Klemantans occasionally, on returning home from a successful raid, carry one of the newly-taken heads to the tomb of the chief for whom they are mourning, and will hang it upon, or deposit it within, the tomb beside the coffin. The head used for this purpose is thickly covered with palm leaves tied tightly about it. It is possible that this thick covering was first applied in order to disguise the fact that the head is that of an enemy, and that the sacrifice of the life of a domestic slave, originally demanded by custom and piety, has been avoided by this substitution.

The story that it is the practice of Kayans to torture the captives taken in battle is, no doubt, largely due to the fact that very few Europeans have acquired any intimate first-hand acquaintance with the Kayans or Kenyahs, and that too often the stories told by Ibans have been uncritically accepted. The Ibans have been bitterly hostile to the Kayans ever since the tribes have been in contact, and the Iban is a great romancer. It will be found that many of the alleged instances of torture by Kayans have been described by Ibans, but if some of these accounts have been founded on fact, the Iban victims, or their companions, have in all probability provoked the Kayans to severe reprisals by their atrocious behaviour, and may often be fairly said to have deserved anything they got.

It is true that on one authenticated occasion Kayans have been guilty of leaving a captive bound upon a tomb until he died of starvation and exposure to the sun. But such occurrences as this (which is almost isolated) by no means justify the statement that it is the practice of Kayans to torture their captives. They commonly treat their captives so kindly that they soon become content to remain in the households of their captors. Their general feeling about torture is well illustrated by the fact that the Kayan village responsible for the exposure of the slave mentioned above was looked at askance by other Kayans. The spot was looked upon with horror, and to-day they regard as a consequence of this act the failure of the line of the chief of that village to perpetuate itself.

Some of the Klemantans cannot be so whole-heartedly defended against the charge. It is not, however, regularly practised by any Klemantan tribe, but rather only on occasions which in some way evoke an exceptional degree of emotional excitement. Thus, the Orang Bukits of the Brunei territory, having lost the most highly respected of their chiefs, purchased a slave in the town of Brunei to serve as the funereal victim, and, having shut him in a strong wicker cage for some days, killed him with a multitude of stabs, some eight hundred persons from the surrounding neighbourhood taking part. Even this act was, it must be observed, of the nature of a pious and religious rite rather than of wanton cruelty. And the history of Christianity cannot be said to be entirely free from accusations of cold-blooded brutality.

CHAPTER V

A PEACE CONFERENCE

A local Henley—Waiting for the parties—A sham fight . . . followed by
one which was nearly serious—Tama Bulan : his presence of mind—
The race : the best boat wins—The peace-making—The omens—
A happy ending.

SOME thirty years ago it was my privilege to be present
at a meeting at Marudi (Claudetown) in the Baram
district, and in the presence of an overwhelming force of
the tribes loyal to the Government of Sarawak, of all
those tribes whose allegiance was still doubtful, and all
those who were still at variance with each other. The
object was to abolish old blood-feuds and to persuade the
tribes to aid the Government in keeping the peace. In
calling this conference, I felt that in order to suppress
fighting and head-hunting, the normal young Bornean's
natural outlet, it would be well to replace them by some
other equally violent, but less disastrous, activity; and I
therefore suggested to the tribes a sort of local Henley,
the chief feature of which would be an annual race between
the war-canoes of all the villages. The proposal was
taken up eagerly by the people, and months before the
appointed day they were felling the giants of the forest
and carving out from them the great war-canoes that
were to be put to this novel use, and reports were passing
from village to village of the stupendous dimensions of
this or that canoe, and the fineness of the timber and
workmanship of another.

Between the peoples living on the banks of the two
rivers, the Baram and the Tinjar, and their tributaries,
there is a traditional hostility which just at this time had

Kayan family group.

Dayak feast.

Klemantan girls.

Cooking on the bank of a river.

been accentuated by the occurrence of a blood-feud between the Kenyahs, a leading tribe of the Baram, and the Lirongs, a powerful tribe of the Tinjar. In addition to these two groups was a large party of Madangs, a famous tribe of fighting men of the central highlands whose hand had hitherto been against every other tribe; and also a large number of Ibans, who more than all the rest are always spoiling for a fight.

The place of meeting was the headquarters of the government of the district. There the river, still nearly a hundred miles from the sea, winds round the foot of a low flat-topped hill, on which stand the strongly built wooden fort and court-house and the Resident's bungalow. On the appointed day some five thousand of the Baram people and the Madangs were encamped very comfortably in leaf and mat shelters on the open ground between bungalow and fort, while the Ibans had taken up their quarters in the long row of Chinamen's shops that form the local Oxford Street. As yet no Tinjar folk had put in an appearance, and men began to wonder what had kept them. Were the tokens sent them at fault? or had they received friendly warnings from one of the omen-birds? Had they, perhaps, taken the opportunity to ascend the Baram and sack and burn the Kenyah houses now well-nigh empty of defenders? One had to "wait and see."

At last, one evening, the Lirongs, with the main mass of the Tinjar people, came down the broad straight reach. It was that glorious half-hour of the tropical day between the setting of the sun and the fall of darkness; the great forest stood black and formless, while the sky and the smooth river were luminous with delicate green and golden light. The Lirongs were in full war-dress, with feathered coats of leopard skin and plumed caps plaited of tough rattan; and very effective they were as they came swiftly on over the shining water, sixty to seventy warriors in each canoe, raising their tremendous battle-cry, a deep-chested chorus of rising and falling cadences. The mass of men on the bank and on the hill took up the cry, answering shout for shout; and the forest across the river echoed it, until the whole place was filled with a hoarse roar. The Kenyahs ran hastily to their huts for their weapons, and by the time they had grouped themselves on the crest of the hill, armed with sword, shield, spear, and blow-pipe, the Lirongs had landed on the bank below and were rushing up the hill to the attack. A few seconds more and they met with clash of sword and shield and a great shouting, and in the semi-darkness a noisy battle raged. After some minutes the Lirongs drew off and rushed back to their boats as wildly as they had come; yet, strange to say, no blood was flowing, no heads were rolling on the ground, no ghastly wounds were gaping. The attack was merely a well-understood formality, a put-up job. When two tribes, between whom there is a blood-feud not formally settled, meet together to make peace, it is the custom for the injured party, that is, the tribe which has last suffered a loss of heads, to make an attack on the other party, using only the butt ends of their spears and the blunt edges of their swords. This act achieves two useful ends—it lets off those high spirits which, if too much bottled up, would be dangerous; and it saves the face of the injured party by showing how really bellicose its feelings are. When this ceremony had been duly performed, the public seemed to feel that matters were going on well; everyone settled down quietly for the night, and the great peace conference was announced for the following morning.

Soon after daybreak the people began to assemble beneath the great roof of the palm leaves that had been built for a conference hall. The Baram chiefs sat on a low platform along one side of the hall, prominent among them Tama Bulan, the most famous of them all, a really great man who made his name and influence felt throughout a very large part of Borneo. When all except

Tama Bulan Wang : a great Kenyah
chief of the Baram district.

An Iban man in full dress.

the Tinjar men were assembled (of course without arms), the latter, also unarmed, came up the hill in a compact mass, to take their places in the hall. As they entered, the sight of their old enemies, the chiefs of the Baram, all sitting quietly together, was too much for their self-control; with one accord they made a mad rush at them and attempted to drag them from the platform. Fortunately the white men had placed themselves with a few of the more reliable Dayak fort-men between the two parties, and by force or eloquence succeeded in beating off the attack, which probably was made in the spirit of a school " rag " rather than with serious intent. But just as peace seemed restored, a great shout went up from the Baram men, " Tama Bulan is wounded ! " and sure enough there he stood with blood flowing freely over his face. The sight of blood seemed to send them all mad together; the Tinjar people turned as one man and tore furiously down the hill to seize their weapons, while the Baram men ran to their huts and in a few seconds were prancing madly to and fro on the crest of the hill, thirsting for a bloody battle that now seemed a matter of a few seconds only. At the same time the Ibans were swarming out of the bazaar seeking something to kill, but not knowing which side to take. The Resident hastened after the Tinjars, threw himself before them, and appealed and threatened, pointing to the two guns at the fort now trained upon them; and Tama Bulan showed his true greatness by haranguing his people, saying that his wound was purely accidental and un-intended, that it was a mere scratch, and commanding them to stand their ground. Several of the older and steadier chiefs followed his example and ran to and fro, holding back their men. So the crisis passed, the sudden gust of passion slowly died away, and peace was patched up with interchange of messages and presents between the two camps. The great boat race was announced to take place on the morrow, and the rest of the day was spent in making ready the war-canoes, stripping them of their leaf roofs and other superfluous gear.

At daybreak the racing-boats set off for the starting-post four miles up-river. Strict orders had been given that no spears or other weapons were to be carried in the racing-boats; but as they started the boats were inspected in turn, and in one or two cases were relieved of contraband. There was a score of entries, and since each boat carried from sixty to seventy men sitting two abreast, more than a thousand men were taking part in the race. Getting the boats into line across the broad river was a noisy and exciting piece of work. At last something like a line was assumed, and at the sound of the gun the twenty boats leaped through the water, almost lost to sight in a cloud of spray as every one of those twelve hundred men struck the water for all he was worth. The rate of striking was at least ninety to the minute, and tended constantly to increase. Very soon two boats drew out in front, and the rest, drawing together as they neared the first bend, followed hotly after like a pack of hounds. The same order was kept throughout the course. It was a grand neck-and-neck race all through between the two leading boats, and every man rowed it out to the end.

The winners were a crew of peaceful down-river folk, who had learnt the art of boat-making from the Malays of the coast; and they owed their victory to the superior build of their ship rather than to superior strength. When they passed the post it was an anxious moment. How would the losers take their beating? Would the winners play the fool, openly exulting and swagger-ing? If so, they would probably get their heads broken, or perhaps lose them. But they behaved with modesty and discretion. The excitement of the crowds on the bank was great, but it was entirely good-humoured; in the interest of the racing they seemed to have for-gotten their feuds. This opportunity was naturally seized

to summon everyone to the conference hall. This time
they settled down with great decorum, the chiefs all in
one group at one side of a central space, and the common
people in serried ranks all round about it. In the centre
was a huge, gaily-painted effigy of the sacred hornbill,
on which were hung thousands of cigarettes of home-
grown tobacco wrapped in dried banana leaf. Three
enormous pigs were now brought in and laid, bound as
to their feet, before the chiefs, one for each of the main
divisions of the people, the Barams, the Tinjars, and the
Madangs (hill-country folk). The greatest chiefs of each
of these parties then approached the pigs, and each in
turn, standing beside the pig assigned to his party, addressed
the attentive multitude with a great flow of words and
many violent gestures ; for many of these people are
great orators. The purport of their speeches was their
desire for peace, their devotion to the Resident (myself),
(" If harm come to him, then may I fall too," said Tama
Bulan), and their appreciation of the security to trade,
life, and property brought them by the Rajah's Government ; and they hurled threats and exhortations against
unlicensed warfare and bloodshed.

As each chief ended his speech to the people he turned
to the pig at his feet, and, stooping over it, gently prodded
it with a smouldering fire-brand, while he addressed to it
a prayer for protection and guidance—a prayer that the
spirit of the pig, soon to be set free by a skilful thrust of
a spear into the beast's heart, should carry up to the
Supreme Being. The answer to these prayers might then
be read in the form and markings of the livers. The pigs
were despatched, and their livers hastily dragged forth
and placed on platters before the group of chiefs. Then
was there much anxious peering over shoulders, and
much shaking of wise old heads, and the learned elders
discussed the omens : ultimately I myself, as Resident,
was called on to give a verdict, as a noted augur. It was
not difficult to show that the only true and rational reading

of the livers was a guarantee of peace and prosperity to all
the tribes of the district; and the public, accepting this
interpretation, showed its approbation most vociferously.
These fortunate circumstances led to a speech, in which
the advantages of peace and trade were pointed out,
and how it is good that a man should sleep without
fear that his house be burnt or his people slain. Of
this effort the peroration consisted in the seizing of the
nearest chief by the hair of his head (as is their own
fashion), to show how, if a man breaks the peace, he
shall lose his head. Which is the " practical syllogism "
of German Philosophy.

This concluded the serious part of the conference, and
it only remained to smoke the cigarettes of good-fellow-
ship, taken from the hornbill effigy, and to drink long life
and happiness to one another. Great jars of rice-spirit
were brought in, and each chief in turn, standing before
an ex-enemy, sang his praises in musical recitative before
giving him the cup; and after each phrase of the song
the multitude joined in with a long-drawn sonorous
shout, which, as the drink flowed freer, rose to a
mighty roar. This is quite the most effective way of
drinking a man's health, since it combines the advantages
of making a speech in his honour with the allotment of
the drink to the right party, who, in this country, loses
an advantage.

When this state of affairs was reached, our work seemed
to be accomplished, and the white men retired to lunch,
leaving one chief in the midst of a long-winded speech.
As soon as the restraint of the Resident's presence was
removed, the orator began to utter remarks of a nature
to stir up the dying embers of resentment; at least so it
seemed to one wily old chief, a firm supporter of the
Government, who bethought him to send one of his men
to pull away the palm-leaf mats from above the indiscreet
orator, and so leave him and his verbosity exposed to the
rays of the mid-day sun. This was the beginning of the

end ; for others following suit made a rush for the mats
that are so useful in making camps and boats rain-proof.
There was a mighty uproar that brought ourselves headlong to the scene, only to see the big hall melt away like
a snowflake as hundreds of hands seized upon the mats
and bore them away in triumph. Thus the great peace
conference was brought to an end amid much laughter
and fun.

On the following morning all important business was
got through, and then the various parties set out one after
another in the great war-canoes on their long up-stream
journey ; some of them to battle for many days against
the constant power of the river, and thereafter to pole their
boats through the masterful rapids and through the
quietudes of the upper reaches and the dimness of the
over-arching forest, until, coming to their own upland
country, they could spread even in the remotest highlands
the news of the White Man's big boat that goes of itself
against the stream, of the great boat race, and of how they
came well-nigh to a fearful slaughtering : how they swore
peace and goodwill to all men, and how there should be
now peace and prosperity through all the land, since those
who had come to rule them had so pronounced it, and
the gods had approved their words.

NOTE.—Dr. McDougall attended to the wound of
Tama Bulan while I was engaged in quieting the other
section of the people. This Savage Peace Conference
took place in 1898, during the sojourn of Dr. McDougall
and the other members of the Cambridge Anthropological
Expedition who were invited to Sarawak by me. Dr.
McDougall first described this conference in the " Eagle "
XVI. pp. 70-82, the magazine of St. John's College,
Cambridge, in 1899.

PART IV

ARTS AND CRAFTS

CHAPTER I

METAL-WORK AND BUILDING

The Kayans skilled iron-workers—Smelting—Forging and tempering a
sword-blade—Brass-work—The fire-piston—Boat-building : every
boat a single piece of timber—Firing and opening out the stem—
Fitting the benches, gunwale, etc.—Smaller boats—Ford and Rolls-
Royce—The Long House—Use of old material—Sinking the main
supports—The roof-plate and floor—Co-operation of the whole
household—Omens : driving off inauspicious birds.

In any account of the arts and crafts of the Kayans, the
working of iron should claim the first place by reason of
its high importance of them and of the fine skill and
knowledge displayed by them in the manufacture of their
excellent swords. Where they obtained their knowledge
of the working of iron is utterly unknown, but there can
be little doubt that they were familiar with the processes
before they entered Borneo. They were the first workers
in iron, and they still remain the best.

To-day the Kayans, like all the other peoples, obtain
their iron in the form of bars of iron and steel imported
from Europe and distributed by Chinese and Malay
traders. But forty or fifty years ago nearly all the iron
worked by the tribes of the interior was from ore found in
the river-beds, and possibly from masses of meteoric iron.
Even at the present day ore is still smelted in the far
interior, and swords made from it by the Kenyahs are
valued above all others.

Kenyah sun-dial.

Kalabit smithy : working with stone hammers.

Smelting and forging demand a specialised skill which is attained by relatively few. But in every Kayan village there are to be found two or three skilled smiths, who, for a small fee, work up the metal brought them by their friends, the finishing touches being generally given by the owner of the implement.

The smelting is performed by mixing the ore with charcoal in a clay crucible, which is embedded in a pile of charcoal. The charcoal is blown to a white heat by the aid of four piston-bellows. These bellows consist of wooden cylinders (generally made from the stem of a wild sago palm) about four feet in length and six inches in diameter, fixed vertically in pairs, and connected with each other by a bamboo tube. The common tube thus formed in turn converges with the tube common to the other pair of cylinders, and with it opens, by way of a clay junction, into a final common tube of clay, which leads to the base of the fire. The piston consists of a stout stick bearing at its lower end a bunch of feathers just large enough to fill tightly the bore of the cylinder. When the piston is thrust downwards, it drives the air before it to the furnace; as it is drawn upwards, the feathers collapsing allow the entrance of air from above. By this ingenious device, the use of valves is avoided. The upper end of each of the piston-rods is attached by a cord to one end of a stout pliable stick, which at its other end is firmly fixed in a horizontal position. By the side of each pair of pistons is seated a man, who pushes down the piston-rods, allowing the reaction of the supporting rods above to draw them up again. The crucible, having been brought to white heat in the furnace, is allowed to cool, when a mass of metallic iron or steel is found within it.

The forging of implements from the metal is effected by the aid of a charcoal furnace to which a blast is supplied by the bellows described above. Formerly stone anvils and hammers were used, and may still be seen in use in the far interior, but the Kayans make iron hammers and an anvil consisting of a short thick bar of iron, the lower end of which is fixed vertically in a large block of wood.

The highest product of the Kayan blacksmith is a peculiarly shaped and finely tempered sword-blade. The smith begins his operations on a bar of steel some eight inches in length. One end is either grasped with pincers or thrust firmly into a block of wood to serve for a handle. The other end is heated in the furnace and gradually beaten out until the required shape of the blade is achieved, with the characteristic hollow on the one side and convexity on the other. If the blade is to be a simple and unadorned weapon, there follow only the tempering, grinding, and polishing. But many blades are ornamented with curled ridges along the back edge. These are cut and turned up with an iron chisel while the metal is hot and before tempering.

Two methods of tempering are in use. One is to heat the blade in the fire and to plunge it at a dull heat into water. The other is to lay the cold blade upon a flat bar of red-hot iron. This has the advantage that the degree of the effect upon the blade can be judged from the change of its colour as it absorbs the heat. The Kayan smiths are expert in judging by the varying colour of the surface the degree and kind of temper produced. They aim at producing a very tough steel, for the weapon has to serve not only in battle, but also for hacking paths through the jungle, and for many other purposes.

Many such blades are elaborately decorated with scroll designs along the posterior border and inlaid with brass. The inlaid brass commonly takes the form of a number of small discs let into the metal near the thick edge; small holes are punched through the hot metal, and brass wire is passed through each hole, cut off flush with the surface, and hammered flat. The designs are chased on the cold metal with a chisel, hammer, and file. The polishing and sharpening are done in several stages; at the first stage, usually by rubbing the blade upon a block of sandstone;

at the second, by the use of a hone of finer grain ; while the highest polish is attained by rubbing with the leaf of a plant (*Emplas*) whose surface is hard and probably contains siliceous particles. At the present time imported files are much used.

Other implements fashioned by the smiths are the small knives, spear-heads, hoes, small adzes, rods for boring the blow-pipe, the anvil, and the various hammers and chisels.

The sheaths for these Kayan swords are made from two thin slips of hardwood, cut to fit exactly together, and leaving a space accurately shaped for the lodgment of the blade. The slips are lashed together with rattan, and are frequently carved in elaborate patterns of a conventional design. Another sample of minor wood-work, now entirely superseded by vessels of European manufacture, was the ironwood dish. This was a well-shaped and beautifully adorned object, being decorated with carved designs in shell or pottery inlay-work, and usually distinguished by two " ears " or flanges for holding purposes.

Although brass-work is highly valued by all the peoples of the interior, the only brazen articles made by them are the heavy ear-rings of the women. The common form is a simple ring of solid metal interrupted at one point by a gap about an eighth of an inch wide, through which is pulled the thin band of skin formed by stretching the lobule of the ear. Other rings occasionally seen are of a spiral form. These rings are cast in moulds of clay, or in some cases in moulds hollowed in two blocks of stone which are nicely opposed.

The Malohs, a Klemantan sub-tribe in the upper basin of the Kapuas River, are well known as brass-workers ; their wares are bartered throughout the country, and a few Maloh brass-workers may be found temporarily settled in many of the larger villages of all tribes. They make the brass corsets of the Iban women, tweezers for pulling out the hair of the face, brass ear-rings, and a variety of small articles. They commonly use " scrap " brass of Malay or Chinese origin as their material.

One of the most ingenious instruments is a fire-piston for the making of fire, cast in metal by the Ibans. It consists of a hollow brass or leaden cylinder about five inches in length and one inch in diameter, the bore being about one-quarter of an inch in diameter and closed at one end. A wooden piston, closely fitting the bore, and ending in a rounded knob, is driven down the cylinder by a sharp blow of the palm and is quickly withdrawn. The heat generated by the compression of the air ignites a bit of tinder (made by scraping the fibrous surface of the leaf-stem of the Arenga palm) at the bottom of the piston. The cylinder is cast by pouring the molten metal into a section of bamboo, while a polished iron rod is held vertically in the centre to form the bore. When the cylinder is cold the iron rod is extracted, and the outer surface is trimmed and shaped with knife or file.

Two " key industries " of Borneo are naturally those of the Boat-builder and of the House-builder. All the peoples, especially the Kayans, make much use of the rivers, and boats are a necessity of life. Of these, naturally, the most important are the great war-canoes, some of which attain the length of 150 feet. In every case, however, the foundation is a single piece of timber, shaped and hollowed by fire and adze. Several kinds of timber are used, the best being the kinds known as *Aroh* and *Ngelai*. When a suitable stem is found (which usually means considerable search, unless Fortune sends one down the river), its branches are lopped away, it is cut to the required length, and roughly hewn into shape, not much more than a quarter of the original trunk being left.

The centre is roughly chopped out and the shell reduced to a thickness of some five inches. The trunk must now be brought down to the river. A track is laid through the jungle consisting of smooth poles laid across the direction of progress ; the hollowed stem is pulled endwise over this track with the aid of rattans, perhaps a hundred or more men combining their strength. If at any point of the journey the stem proves too heavy to be moved, a rough windlass is constructed by fixing the stem of a small tree across two standing trees and winding the rattans upon it, the trimmed branches of the tree serving as arms of the windlass. The Kayans are specially skilled in this kind of transport of heavy timber.

Arrived at the river bank, the hollowed stem is launched and towed down-stream to the village at a time when the water is high. It is made fast to the bank before the village at as high a point as the water will allow, so that when the river subsides it is left high and dry. A leaf shelter is then built over it to protect it and the workers from the sun. The shell is then further hollowed by being fired with shavings inside and out, and then cleared of the charred surfaces. The inside is fired first; when the outside is fired, the hollow is filled with water.

When in this way the shell has been reduced to a thickness of a few inches, and is still hot from firing and filled with water, it is opened out laterally : stout sticks some six to seven feet in length are wedged between the lateral walls, so that the hollow stem, which hitherto has only been some three or four feet in diameter, becomes a shallow trough six to seven feet wide. During the hollowing, small buttresses are left along each side at intervals of about two feet to form supports for benches.

The shell is now left lying covered with branches for some days, until the wood " sets." The outer surface is then adzed down to approximately the required degree, all irregularities are removed, and holes about a quarter of an inch in diameter are bored in the shell at intervals of some twenty inches. Wooden pegs are then hammered into these holes, each peg bearing two marks or grooves at an interval equal to the thickness of the shell desired at each part; the peg is driven in from the outside until the outer groove is flush with the outer surface of the shell.

M

The projecting part is now cut away, and the inner surface chipped and scraped at each point until it is level with the inner groove of the peg. The outer surface, which is now in shape about a third of a cylinder, is then finally smoothed and the foundation is complete.

The cross-benches are now lashed to their supports, the sides are raised by a lashed-on gunwale, and wedge-shaped blocks are fitted at bow and stern. The gunwale consists of a tough plank some ten inches wide overlapping the outer edge of the shell, and lashed firmly to it by rattan strips piercing both shell and planks at intervals of about six inches. In some cases the gunwale is further raised amidships by a second smaller plank lashed to the upper edge of the first. The block fitted in at the bow presents to the water a flat surface inclined at a low angle ; and a similar block completes the shell at the stern. The prow is often ornamented with a crocodile's or conventional dog's head carved in hardwood and painted red and black.

The whole operation, like every other important undertaking, is preceded by the finding of favourable omens, and may be postponed by unpropitious signs, bad dreams, or domestic calamities. Each house has certain men specially skilled in boat-making, and by them the work is directed and all the finer part of the work executed. In the case of a war-boat which is to be the property of the household, these special workers are paid a fee out of the wealth accumulated by way of fines and confiscations.

The war-boats are House property ; but the smaller craft, ranging from a small canoe suitable for one or two paddlers only, to one capable of carrying a score or more, are generally privately owned. These, like the war-boats, are made from a single stem. The larger ones are made in the same way as the war-boats. A craftsman who makes a boat for another is helped by his customer, and is paid by him a fee in brass-ware or dollars, the usual fee being a *tawak* varying in size according to the dimensions of the boat.

Of the interior tribes the Kayans are probably the best boat-makers; and most of the others follow their example. There are, however, a few of the Klemantan tribes who never attempt to make anything more than a very rough small canoe of soft wood, and who buy from others what boats they need. This is a curious instance of a persistent indifference to a craft which, one would have expected, would have been acquired from neighbours. In the same way, the Ibans, although seafarers, are quite content with a makeshift arrangement: these "light-hearted masters of the waves" content themselves, sometimes, with a canoe made by the simple process of stripping the bark from a big tree. The two ends of the sheet of bark are lashed with rattan to form bow and stern : the middle part is wedged open with cross-pieces to serve as thwarts, and the shell is reinforced with transverse ribs and longitudinal strips. Such a boat can be produced in about two hours; but it is a Ford against the Rolls-Royce of the Kayan.

To propel these craft, a rough paddle made from durable wood is generally used; the blade and shaft are of one piece; the flat blade, nearly two feet in length, is widest about six inches below its junction with the shaft, and from this point tapers slightly to its extremity; the shaft is about three feet in length and carries, mortised to its upper end, a cross-piece for the grip of the upper hand.

A few of the paddles, especially those made for women, are very finely shaped and finished, and have their shafts ornamented with carving of a variety of designs, generally one band of carving immediately above the blade and a second below the cross-piece. Some of the Klemantans excel the Kayans in this work, producing very beautiful women's paddles, sometimes with designs of inlaid lead.

The Long House, that most typical Kayan product, is built on piles, and the timbers that support it are usually floated down-river from an old house so as to be used in the construction of the new. The great planks of the floor, the main cross-beams, and the wooden shingles of the roof are also commonly used. If a house has been partially destroyed by fire, no part of the materials of the old house is used in the construction of the new ; for it is felt in some indefinable way that the use of the old material would render the new house liable, by a perpetuation of ill-fortune, to the same fate. In such cases, or upon migration to a different river, the whole of the timbers for the house have to be procured, shaped, and erected—a laborious process. But when once the timber has been collected, the work goes on so rapidly that a whole Long House may be substantially completed within a fortnight.

The main supports of the structure are four rows of massive columns of ironwood. These are driven down into the soil to a depth of about four feet, and so arranged that a single row supports the front of the house, another the back, and a double row the middle. The intervals between the columns of each row are about twenty feet. To sink a pile in its required position, rattans are tied round it a little above its middle, and then passed over a tall tripod of stout poles. A number of men haul on to these, while others shove up the top end of the pile with their shoulders. The pile is thus suspended with its butt end resting so lightly on the ground that it can easily be guided into the hole prepared for its reception. Smaller accessory piles, to serve as additional supports, are also put under the main cross-beams of the floor. The columns of the double row in the middle line are about six feet taller than those of the front and back rows. For the support of the floor a massive squared transverse tie is mortised through each set of four columns at a height of some fifteen to twenty feet from the ground, and secured by a wooden pin through each extremity.

A squared roof-plate, still more massive than the floor-ties, is now laid upon the crowns of the columns of the front row, along its whole length, and a second one upon the back row. This is dowelled upon the columns (*i.e.*

the top of the column is cut to form a pin which is let into the longitudinal beam); and the beams which make up the roof-plate are spliced, generally in such a way that the top of a column serves as the pin of the splice. Each of these heavy beams is generally lifted into its place by tiers of men standing on poles lashed at different heights across the columns, their efforts being seconded by others pulling on rattans which run from the beam over the topmost cross-pole. The framework of the roof is then completed by laying stout roof-ties across the crowns of the double row of columns of the middle line, and lashing their extremities to stout purlins (longitudinal beams for the support of the rafters in the middle of their length), and by laying the ridge-timber upon a line of perpendicular struts. The ridge-timber and purlins, though less heavy than the roof-plates, consist also of stout squared timbers, spliced to form beams continuous throughout the whole length of the house. The rafters are laid at an angle of about forty degrees and at intervals of eighteen inches, they are lashed to the ridge-timber and to the purlins, and lipped on to the roof-plates, beyond which they project about four feet to form an eave. Strong flat strips or laths are laid along the rafters parallel to the length of the house at intervals of about sixteen inches. On these are laid the shingles or slats of ironwood in regular rows, just as roof-tiles are laid in this country. Each slat is a slab about 1 × 30 × 12 inches, and is lashed by a strip of rattan, which pierces its upper end, to one of the laths.

The floor is built of stout longitudinal joists lying across the main floor-ties, and notched to grip the ties. Upon, and transversely to them, are laid a number of flat strips which immediately support the floor planks; these are kept in place by their own weight.

In a well-built house these planks are between thirty and forty feet in length, two or three feet in breadth, and three or four inches thick. They are made from tough strong timber, and are moved from house to house, some of them being, probably, hundreds of years old. A single tree is generally made to yield two such planks. After being felled it is split into halves longitudinally in the following way. A deep groove is cut along one side, into which wedges of hardwood are driven with heavy mallets. When the trunk is split, each half is fined down by cutting deep transverse grooves at an interval of from three to four feet, when the intervening masses of wood can be split off. In this way each half is whittled down until it is only some six inches thick. The plank is then trimmed down to the desired thickness by blows of the adze struck across the grain. The two ends are generally left untrimmed until the plank has been transported to the site of the house and has lain there for some time. This prevents its splitting during the journey to the house and during the period of seasoning.

When the floor has been laid it only remains to make (1) the main partition wall which separates the gallery from the rooms, and (2) the walls between the several rooms. These walls are made only some eight or nine feet in height. The wall of the gallery is made of vertical planks lashed to horizontal rails, the extremities of which are let into the columns of the front set of the two middle rows.

The work of construction is carried on by all the men of the house; the women and children lend what aid they can in the way of fetching and carrying, and in preparing strips of rattans for tying. The ownership of each section is arranged beforehand; the section of the chief being generally in the middle, and those of his near relatives on either side of it. Each man pays special attention to the construction of his own section, and carries out the lighter work of that part, such as laying the shingles, with the help of his own household. If the head of a household is a widow, her section is constructed by her male neighbours or relatives without payment.

Before beginning the building of a new house favourable

Carved door of a Klemantan chief.

Ornamented wall of a chief's room in a Klemantan village—dog and prawn designs.

omens must be obtained ; and the Kayans would be much
troubled if bad omens were observed during the building,
especially during the first few days.   At this time, therefore, children are told off to beat upon gongs so as to
prevent the appearance or the hearing of bad omen-birds.
Unfavourable omens combined with ill luck, such as death,
bad dreams, or an attack by enemies during building
(even if this were successfully repelled), would lead to
the desertion of a partially built house and the choice of
another site.

All the interior peoples construct their houses on
principles similar to those described above, but with considerable diversity in detail.   The greatest diversity of
plan is exhibited by the houses of Ibans.   An Iban
community seldom remains in the same house more than
three or four years ; and, no doubt for this reason, their
houses are built in a less solid style than those of most
other tribes.   The timbers used are lighter ; the house
is not raised so high above the ground, and the floor is
usually made of split bamboo in place of the heavy planks
used by Kayans and others.

The houses of the Klemantans are generally very
inferior to those of the Kayans in respect to size, solidity,
and regularity of construction ; lashed bamboos largely
replace the strongly mortised timber-work of the better
houses ; but the worst houses of all are made by those few
Punans who from being nomads have only recently
adopted the settled habits of the other peoples.

CHAPTER II

ALL the tribes of Borneo practise a number of decorative
arts. Some of the Klemantans, notably the Melanos,
attain a high level of various achievement in many arts ;
but every tribe preserves the tradition of some one or
two decorative arts in which it is especially skilled. Thus
some of the Klemantan tribes excel in the finer kinds
of wood-carving (*e.g.* the decoration of paddles) ; the
Kayans in tattooing and in chasing designs on steel ; the
Kenyahs in the painting of shields and the production of
large designs carved in low relief on wood and used for
adorning houses and tombs ; both Kayans and Kenyahs
excel in the carving of sword-handles from the antlers
of deer ; the Barawans and Sebops in bead-work ; the
Kalabits and Ibans in tracing designs on the surface of
bamboo ; Punans in decorative mat-work ; Kanowits
and Tanjongs in basket-work.

The most generally practised, and on the whole the most
important, of these arts, is wood-carving. Much of this
is done on very hard wood ; and the principal tools are the
curved sword or *parang*, the small knife carried in the
sword-sheath, and adzes and axes of various sizes. The
blade of the knife is some three inches in length, and
resembles in general shape the blade of the sword ; it is
wider in proportion, but has the same peculiar convexity
of the one side and concavity of the other in transverse

Valuable old Kayan beads.

Kayan women farmers.

Iban girls.

section. The shaft is sunk into the end of a handle of hardwood about one foot long, and half an inch in diameter, and secured with gutta and fine rattan lashing. The butt end of the handle is cunningly carved in the shape of a crocodile's head, or prolonged by a piece of carved deer's antler. The blade of the knife is held between the thumb and finger of the right hand, the cutting edge directed forwards, and the long handle is gripped between the forearm and the lower ribs; the weight of the body can thus be brought to the assistance of the arm in cutting hard material. With this knife most of the finer carving is done, the adze and sword being used chiefly for rough shaping.

The adze consists of two parts, a haft and a flat blade. The haft is made from a small branch of springy wood, to which is attached a portion of the main stem, usually at an angle of from 70° to 80° to it. The other end fits into a handle made of soft root-wood, so as to form a grip. The blade is in the shape of a very narrow isosceles triangle, the cutting edge (which is convex) being the base : this is firmly lashed with rattans to the distal surface of the transverse piece, a strip of skin being often placed between the metal and the lashings to facilitate removal and to enable the worker to alter the angle between the cutting edge and the haft. When the edge is in the plane of the shaft the implement is a small axe; but, by turning it round through an angle of 90°, it becomes an adze.

Carved wood-work is commonly painted with black and red colours, prepared respectively from soot and iron oxide mixed with sugar-cane juice or with lime ; the moist pigment is applied with the finger to the larger surfaces, and the finer lines and edges are marked out with the aid of a chisel-edged stick of wood.

Old beads are much valued and sought after by all the tribes but especially so by the Kayans. There are few families of the upper class that do not possess a certain number of them.

Many varieties are well known, and some of the Kayan women are very expert in recognising the genuine old specimens, and in distinguishing these varieties from one another and from modern imitations.

The fondness of the women for beads has already been remarked; but beside their use as personal ornaments, strips of them are often put to decorative uses, for the adornment of sword-sheaths, women's head-bands, cigarette-boxes. The designs worked in this way are but few, and most of them are common to all the tribes. The thread used is prepared by rolling on the thigh fibres drawn from the leaf of the pine-apple, or other fibrous plants; it is very strong and durable. The design to be reproduced is drawn or carved in low relief on a board. A thread is fixed across the end of the board and others are tied to it at short intervals; on these the beads are threaded, neighbouring threads being tied together at short intervals; the colours of the beads are selected according to the demands of the pattern over which they are worked.

Besides these designs on the flat, tassels, girdles, neck-laces, ear-rings, and cigarette rings are also made of these beads. Modern imported beads are used for these purposes, and are sometimes improved by being ground flat on the two surfaces that adjoin their neighbours; this is done by fixing a number of them into the cut end of a piece of sugar-cane, which is then rubbed against a smooth sharpening stone. This treatment of the beads gives to the articles made of them a very neat and highly finished appearance.

Not unlike this bead-decoration is the shell-work with which the Iban women decorate their woven coats. The Kalabits wear shells in concentric circles on their hats; and, more rarely, among other tribes, baskets, cradles, and armlets are so decorated.

Another effective form of decorative art is the working of designs on the surface of pieces of bamboo. Among

An Iban jacket.

Ear ornaments.

Bead baskets.

the articles generally so decorated are the native drinking-cup, the tobacco-box, and tubes for carrying a flint and steel.

The design to be produced is first outlined by the point of the knife and then made to stand out boldly from the ground by darkening the latter. This is achieved in two ways : (1) the ground is covered with close-set scratches, grouped in sets of parallel lines some few millimetres in length, the various sets meeting at angles of all degrees ; or (2) the hard surface of the bamboo is wholly scraped away from the ground areas to a depth of about half a millimetre. In either case black or red paint is then smeared over the whole surface with the finger, and when it dries the surface is rubbed with a piece of cloth (Kayan), or scraped lightly with a knife (Iban). The pigment is thus removed from the intact parts and remains adherent to the lines and areas from which the hard surface layer has been removed. The design is thus left in very low relief, and is of the natural colour of the bamboo upon a black or dark red ground, or on a ground merely darkened by the parallel scratches.

The designs themselves are usually traditional and conventional, the artist working from his memory of an old pattern, but adapting it to suit his material. Iban workers allow themselves much more latitude, planning each section of the whole as he proceeds ; others usually make a general scheme for the whole. This greater freedom makes for greater originality ; and, also, the Iban is more ready to embody and modify patterns used by other tribes. It should be observed that much Iban work has a great deal in common with Malay craftsman-ship ; this is to be seen in their preference for flower and leaf patterns, for the Malays, by their religion, may not represent living creatures.

The use of rivets, nails, and screws is almost unknown to the Bornean. In its place we find lashing with strips of rattan and with coarse fibres from the leaf-stem of palms and ferns. This is carried out extremely neatly and commonly has a decorative effect, which is in some cases enhanced by combining blackened threads with those of the natural pale yellow colour; and the finer varieties of this work deserve to be classed with the decorative arts. The finest lashing-work is done by the Kalabits, who cover small bamboo boxes with a layer of close-set lashing, producing pleasing geometrical designs by the combination of yellow and black threads. The surface of the bamboo to which the lashing is applied is generally counter-sunk to a depth of about one-sixteenth of an inch; it is thus rendered less slippery than the natural surface, and can be gripped more firmly by the lashing, and the surface of the lashing is brought flush with the natural surface. Not only is the effect highly ornamental, but also a greatly increased durability is given to the article, the natural tendency of the bamboo to split longitudinally being very effectively counteracted.

Similar fine decorative lashing is used by all the tribes for binding together the two halves of the sword-sheath, and for binding the haft of knife or sword where it grips the metal blade, though fine brass wire is sometimes used for this purpose.

Closely allied to this lashing is the production of decorative knots. A considerable variety of knots is in common use; they are always well tied and practically effective, but some are elaborated for decorative purposes to form rosettes, especially by Kayans in making their sword-sheaths.

Painting with black, red, and white pigments is commonly applied to carved wood-work. Wooden surfaces are often painted on the flat, especially shields, the outer surfaces of walls of rice-barns and tombs, the gunwales of boats, and decorative planks in the inner walls of the long gallery of the house. The Kenyahs and some of the Klemantans, especially the Sekapans and Barawans, are most skilled in the work, and make more use than

Beautifully carved Kenyah sword handles made from the antlers of the Bornean deer.

Kayan and Klemantan workmanship. The patterns and carvings are fashioned in very hard wood on these plates.

others of this form of decoration; but it is practised in some degree by all the peoples of Borneo.

The three pigments mentioned above—black, red, and white, made respectively from soot, iron oxide, and lime—are, so far as I know, the only native varieties; but at the present day these are sometimes supplemented with indigo and yellow pigments obtained from traders.

As regards the general application of design, the Kayans make use of a large number of conventional patterns, especially in tattoo bead-work, the production of panels of wood for the adornment of houses, tombs, boats, and rice-barns, the decoration of bamboo boxes, and the painting of hats, and the carving of highly ornate doors for the rooms. All these applications involve the covering of flat or curved surfaces with patterns either in low relief only or without relief. The most numerous and most widely applied are conventionalised derivatives from animal forms. Of these animal forms the human figure, the dog, and the prawn have been the originals of the largest number of patterns; the macaque monkey and the large lizard are also traceable. A few seem to be derived from vegetable forms; while some, for example the hook-pattern, seem to be derived from no animal or vegetable form, but to be purely symbolic.

Of all the designs, variants of the dog-pattern are the most numerous and the most frequently applied. The name itself (*kalingai asu*) is given to a very large number of designs, some of which obviously reproduce the form of the dog, while others retain merely a hazy memory of the animal, or of anything else; and the term ordinarily means simply an appropriate pattern. Some Kayans habitually speak of most of these dog-patterns by the term *usang orang* (which possibly means the prawn-pattern). This use probably indicates some gradual substitution of designs of the one origin for those of the other.

Animal forms are used chiefly as the figure-heads of war-boats and at the ends of the main roof-beams of the houses; and some of these are executed with an artistry that must win admiration. The animals most frequently represented are the dog, crocodile, monkey, hornbill, and bear. Carved dogs, comparatively little conventionalised, are sometimes used as the supports of the low platforms upon which chiefs sit on ceremonious occasions.

Sword-handles, generally of deer's antlers, but sometimes of wood, exhibit a group of highly peculiar, closely allied designs. All these seem to be derived from the human form, but in the most elaborate examples all obvious trace of the human figure is lost in a profusion of detail.

The patterns reproduced in fretwork are in the main adaptations of some of those used in decorating surfaces, but they are always highly conventionalised. The human form is seldom or never traceable in work of this kind. Fretwork is chiefly used to adorn the tombs of chiefs.

A very distinctive group is formed by the designs chased on the surfaces of the blades of swords, knives, and spear-heads. They are flowing scroll patterns containing many spirals and curves in which no animal or plant forms can be with certainty traced, though suggestions of the dog-pattern may be found. The lack of affinity between these patterns and those applied to other surfaces suggests that they may have been taken over from some other people together with the craft of the smith, but possibly the distinctive character is due only to the exigencies of the material.

A remarkable point about nearly all the Art work of these peoples is that it is nearly all of a public character. The work is done in public, by voluntary co-operation, on the big galleries, and rarely in the private rooms; while, as regards their display, most ornamentation is for public objects, such as the village war-canoes, or the local gods; and the most elaborate shields and war-hats are communal, rather than of private ownership.

All these forms of Art work are distinctly amateur

Spoons and ladles used by Klemantans made of hard wood.

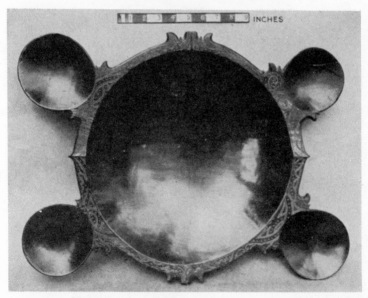

Kayan family rice-dish, the four smaller plates attached to the rim of the rice-dish are for pork, fish, and condiments, or relishes.

efforts; that is to say, although certain individuals attain special skill and reputation in particular forms of art, they do not make their living by the practice of them, but rather, like everyone else, rely in the main upon the cultivation of rice for the family support. They will exchange services of this kind, and definite payments are sometimes agreed upon, but the great amount of such work is done for one another without any material reward.

CHAPTER III

RATTAN-WORK : THE BLOW-PIPE

Basket-weaving: various kinds of basket—Dying black with *tarum*—
Punan basket-ware—Hat-making—*The sumpitan*—The boring and
sighting of the pipe—Poisoned darts—The quiver—Pottery—Bark-
cloth—Spinning and weaving—Dyeing before weaving—The loom.

A MOST characteristic craft is the weaving of baskets,
mats, and caps. It is chiefly practised by the women,
though the men help in collecting and preparing the
rattans, from which they are made. A rattan about one-
third of an inch in diameter is the usual material, but
other jungle-plants also are used ; it is split into five strips,
and the inner surface of each strip is smoothed with a knife.
This is then used to make baskets, of which the chief are
(1) the large one used for carrying rice from the farms to
the house ; (2) the small basket hung on the back by a
pair of shoulder-straps, and always carried by the men
on going far from home ; (3) fish-baskets ; (4) large
baskets provided with lids for storing clothing and other
personal valuables ; and (5) winnowing trays, and the
large rough basket used for carrying water-vessels or any
other heavy objects.

Rattan-mats also are common, such as that worn round
the waist for sitting upon ; the large mats spread for seat-
ing several persons in the gallery of private chambers ;
mats for the drying of rice, and mats to sleep upon.

The weaving of these baskets and mats, which are made
of narrow strips of rattan varying from one-sixteenth to
one-eighth of an inch according to the size and use of the
article, is usually for two sets of strips to cross one another
at right angles, each strip passing over and under two of

2. Drilling the bore.

1. Preparing the shaft.

the opposed set. Methods naturally vary. The Kayans are generally content to make strong serviceable basketware without ornamentation ; but in the basket-ware made by the other peoples, strips of rattan dyed black are combined with those of the natural pale yellow colour, and very effective patterns are worked in. The strips are dyed by beating out in water the soft stem and leaves of a plant known as *Tarum*. The dark stain is rendered still blacker by subsequently burying the strips in the mud of the river for some ten days, or by washing them in lime. The dyed strips are then jet-black with a fine polished surface, and the dye is quite permanent.

A form of mat-work deserving notice is the *lampit*, the mat used largely for sleeping and sitting upon. It is made of stout strips of rattan sega lying parallel to one another, and held together by strings threaded through them at intervals of four or five inches. This mat has an extremely neat appearance and can be easily rolled up.

The most elaborately decorated and finely plaited basketware is made by the Punans and some of the Klemantan sub-tribes, who use, as well as the black dye, a red dye. This is made by boiling the seeds of the rattan in water and evaporating the product until it has the consistency of a thick paste. These adepts barter much of their handiwork in this kind with the people of communities less skilled in it. This fact is yet another proof that the various specialised handicrafts are traditional in certain tribes and sub-tribes, and are practised hardly at all or in an inferior manner only by the other tribes, who seem to find it impossible to achieve an equal degree of mastery in them.

An interesting craft is the manufacture (practised by women only) of the large, flat, circular hats worn by the Kayans and made of palm-leaves. The hard, tough, fluted leaves are pressed flat and dried, when the flutes form ribs diverging from the stem. Triangular pieces of the length of the radius of the hat (*i.e.* from twelve to eighteen inches) are cut and then sewn together in a double layer ; those

N

of the upper layer radiate from the centre; those of the under layer are disposed in the reverse direction. This arrangement gives great rigidity to the whole structure. The two layers are stitched together by threads carried round the hat in concentric circles at intervals of about an inch. The peripheral edges are sewn to a slender strip of rattan bent to form a circle, the two ends overlapping. The centre is generally finished with a disc of metal or strong cloth on the apex. The hats hung upon tombs are decorated on the upper surface with bold designs painted in black and red.

Most of the other tribes make similar hats, and the Melanos and Land Dayaks are especially skilled in this craft. The former make very large hats of similar shape, the upper surface being of strips of rattan dyed red and black, and woven to form elaborate patterns.

Besides these sun-hats, the Kayans and Kenyahs and some of the Klemantans weave with fine strips of rattan close-fitting skull-caps and head-bands. The ends of the strips, some three or four inches in length, are sometimes left projecting from the centre or forming a fringe round the lower edge.

The close-fitting, hemispherical war-cap is made of rattans about half an inch thick split in halves.

One of the most typical and at the same time the finest products of Bornean craftsmanship is the blow-pipe : it is made by Kayans, Kenyahs, Punans, and occasionally by Ibans and Klemantans.

The best *sumpitans* are made from the hard straight-grained wood of the *Jagang* tree. The trunk is split into long pieces about eight feet in length, which are then shaved with the adze until they are roughly cylindrical and three to four inches in diameter. Such a piece may be carried home to be worked at leisure, or the boring may be done upon the spot. A platform is erected about seven feet above the ground, and the prepared rod is fixed vertically with the upper end projecting through the plat-

3. Lashing on the spear-head.

4. Making the darts.

form, its lower end resting on the ground. The upper end is lashed to the platform, the lower to a pair of stout poles lashed horizontally to trees, and the middle to another pair of poles similarly fixed. The actual boring is done by a straight rod of iron about nine feet long, of slightly smaller diameter than the bore desired for the pipe, and having one end chisel-shaped and sharpened. The worker, standing on the platform, brings down the chisel edge upon the flat surface, slightly turning the rod after each blow. The rod soon bites its way into the wood. An assistant, squatting on the platform with a bark-bucket of water beside him, ladles water into the hole after every two or three strokes, and thus causes the chips to float out. The boring rod is kept vertical by means of forks of wood at different levels, which act as guides. The total operation takes from six to ten hours.

In boring the lower part, the craftsman aims at producing a slight curvature of the tube in order to allow for the bending of the blow-pipe, when in use, by the weight of the spear-blade which is lashed on, bayonet-fashion, to the muzzle end. If the desired degree of curvature is not produced in this way, the wooden pipe, still in the rough state as regards its outer surface, is suspended horizontally on loops, and weights are hung upon the muzzle end until, on sighting through the bore, only a half-circle of daylight is visible—this being the degree of curvature of the bore desired. The wood is then heated with torches, and on cooling retains the curvature thus impressed on it.

The remaining processes are the whittling down of the rough surface to a smooth cylinder slightly tapering towards the muzzle; polishing the pipe inside and out; lashing the spear-blade with strips of rattan; and attaching a small wooden sight to the muzzle end opposite the spear-blade. The polishing of the bore is effected by working to and fro within it a long piece of closely fitting rattan; that of the outer surface, by rubbing it first with the skin of a sting-ray (which, although a marine fish, sometimes ascends to the upper reaches of the rivers), and afterwards with a certain leaf (*Emplas*), which is the local substitute for emery paper.

The poisoned darts used with the *sumpitan* are about nine inches in length and one-sixteenth to one-eighth of an inch in diameter, and are made from splinters of the *Nibong* and sago palms. At one end is fitted a small tapering cylinder of tough pith, about one inch in length, its greatest diameter at the butt end being exactly equal to the bore of the pipe. The pith is shaved to the required diameter by the aid of a small wooden cylinder of the standard size; this is prolonged in a pin of the same diameter as the shaft of the dart. A piece of pith transfixed by the pin is shaved with a sharp knife until its surface is flush with that of the wooden gauge.

The poison is prepared from the sap of the *Ipoh* tree (*Antiaris toxicaria*). When the bark is incised, a milky sap runs out and is collected in a bamboo cup. It is then heated slowly over a fire in a trough made from the leaf-stem of a palm, until it becomes a thick paste of a dark purple colour. Before it is applied it is worked into a thinner paste on a palette with a wooden spatula. A circular groove is cut round the shaft of the dart about two inches from its tip, and the part so marked off is rolled in the paste and then dried before a fire. For use against large game, such as pig, deer, or men, a larger dose of poison is required than can be carried on the tip of the shaft. The tip is therefore split, and a narrow triangular piece of metal inserted and secured with a fine thread of rattan or fern-stem, and then coated with the poison.

The quiver for carrying the darts is a section of bamboo about three inches in diameter and ten inches in length, fitted with a cap of the same material. A wooden hook lashed to the quiver enables it to be hung from the belt. The darts, mostly without piths, are wrapped in a squirrel skin and thrust tip downwards into the quiver. A small

5. Collecting the poison.

6. Drying the poison.

7. Shooting a bird.

8. The hunter's return.

gourd tied to the quiver carries a supply of piths ready
to be placed on the darts.

The art of the Potter has nowadays been killed by the
importation of earthenware, and of cooking pots of brass
and iron ; but in former times simple earthenware vessels
for boiling rice were made by Kayans, Kenyahs, Ibans,
and some of the Klemantans. Those who made no pots
boiled their rice and sago in bamboos. The earthenware
cooking pot is a simple egg-shaped vessel, one end of which
is open and surrounded by a low everted lip or collar.
It is built on a hollowed base by squeezing the clay between
a smooth rounded stone held by one hand within the vessel
and a flat piece of wood, with which the clay is beaten from
without. The roughly shaped vessel is first allowed to
dry in the sun and then baked in the fire. In some cases
the surface is smoothed and glazed by rubbing resin over
its surface while it is hot. The potter's wheel is unknown,
and only this one shape of pot is made, although in various
sizes. The commonest size holds about a quart ; the largest
about two gallons. It is carried in a basket made of fine
unsplit rattans loosely woven in the form of interlaced rings.

As regards textiles, and similar fabrics, one notes a native
cloth, which was in universal use among the tribes of the
interior until supplanted in recent years by imported
articles, and which is made from the bark of trees of several
species (principally the *Kumut*, the *Ipoh*, and the wild fig).
The material used is the fibrous layer beneath the outer
bark, and the manufacture is pleasantly simple. A large
sheet of it is laid on a wooden block and beaten with a heavy
wooden club until it is soft and pliable. A piece of the
required size and shape is then cut from the sheet, and
sewn across the grain with needle and thread at intervals
of about an inch, in order to prevent the material from splitting longitudinally. Before European needles were introduced, the stitching was done by piercing holes with a
small awl and pushing the thread through the hole after
withdrawing the awl.

The only tribes which to-day practise spinning and weaving are the Ibans, the Muruts, and a few of the Klemantans, although the Kayans claim to have been weavers in the past. The Iban methods are similar to those of the Malays, and have probably been learnt from them. The weaving is done entirely by women, though the men make the machinery employed by them. The fibre used is cotton, which is obtained from shrubs cultivated for the purpose. The seed is extracted from the mass of fibre by squeezing the pods between a pair of rollers arranged like a rude mangle, while the fibre is pulled away by hand. The thread is spun from the fibre by the aid of a simple wheel, turned by the right hand while the left hand twists the fibres. When the thread is thus obtained, if a pattern is to be produced, the dyeing is done before the weaving. The web is first stretched on a wooden frame about six feet long and twenty inches in width, a long thread being wound round it from end to end. The parts of the web corresponding to the parts of the cloth that are to remain undyed and of the natural pale brown colour of the thread are tied round with dried strips of a fibrous leaf (*Lemba*), the upper and lower set of threads being wrapped up together in the same bundles. If only one colour is to be applied, the web is then slipped off the frame. The threads are held in their relative positions by the wrappings, but are further secured by a string tied tightly round the whole bundle at each end. The web thus prepared is soaked in the dye for some two or three days, and then dried in a shady spot. The wrappings upon the threads are waterproof and protect the wrapped parts, so that, when the web is stretched upon the loom, it presents the desired pattern in colour upon the undyed ground. When the actual weaving is done the threads of the weft do not appear on the surface, and so the dyed parts of the web present a uniformly coloured surface.

In most cloths, however, two colours, as well as the natural colour of the thread, appear on the surface—the

Iban woman extracting cotton seeds before spinning.

Iban woman weaving.

Iban woman tying up strands which are to form the pattern of the
cloth before dipping the threads in the dye.

Back view of a Klemantan jacket, the pattern known as pigeon's eye.

Blankets showing various patterns commonly woven into Iban cloths.

commonest colour being a warm brick red (obtained from the bark of the *Samak* tree) and a dark purple or black (obtained from the leaves of the *Tarum* plant).   Lime and gypsum are sometimes mixed with the watery extracts as mordants, but these are probably modern refinements. When two colours are to appear, those parts of the web which are to be of one colour are wrapped up during the immersion in the red dye together with the parts that are to appear uncoloured.   When this first dyeing is completed the web is prepared for the purple dye by uncovering the undyed parts which are to be purple, and wrapping up in bundles the threads which have already been dyed red. After being soaked in the purple dye and dried, all the wrappings are removed from the web, and the desired pattern in the three colours appears upon it when it is stretched.   Perhaps the most noteworthy feature of the operation is that the woman generally requires no guidance in the wrapping up of the threads, but judges the length and number of the threads to be included in each bundle purely by memory of the design aimed at.

As regards the looms, their only peculiarity is their extreme simplicity.   The upper ends of the web are looped over a stout bar which is fixed to a pair of uprights about a yard above the floor.   The lower ends of the web are looped over a stout rod, to the ends of which a loop of cord is tied.   The woman sits on the ground with this loop around her waist, and thus maintains the necessary tension on the web.   The manipulation of the shuttle and of the threads of the web is accomplished without other mechanical aids than the rods to which the one set of web-threads is tied by short threads.

CHAPTER IV

TATTOO

An Iban legend—Men's tattoo—The *Lukut* bead—Tattooing of women—
Class shown by pattern of tattoo—An elaborate ceremonial—
Hereditary artists in tattoo—The tools used—The actual operation—
Presents and fees—*Lasat mata* : *selivit*.

OF the origin of tattoo the Ibans relate the following
story :—

Long ago, when the plumage of birds was dull and
sombre, the coucal (or crow pheasant) and the argus
pheasant agreed to tattoo each other. The coucal began on
the pheasant first, and succeeded admirably, as the plumage
of the pheasant testifies to the present day. The pheasant
then tried his hand on the coucal, but being a stupid bird
was soon in difficulties. Fearing that he would fail miserably, he told the coucal to sit in a bowl of tan, and then
poured the dye over him, and flew off, remarking that the
country was full of enemies and he could not stop. That is
why the coucal to this day has a black head and neck with a
tan-coloured body.

Tattooing is extensively practised among the Pagan
folk, though a few tribes who have come under Mohammedan influence have almost abandoned it, while the Land
Dayaks aver they never indulged in it. The Kayans are
the most and best tattooed tribe in Borneo, and it is to
them that most of the other tribes owe their knowledge of
tattoo and the majority of designs.

The men tattoo chiefly for ornament, and there is now
little or no special significance in the designs used, nor is
there any particular ceremonial. There is no longer a
fixed time of life for the tattooing of a man, but in most

184

cases it starts in boyhood. A great variety of pattern is used and the parts of the body tattooed are usually the outside of the wrist, the surface of the forearm, high up on the outside of the thigh, on the breasts, and, in the case of warriors, on the backs of the hands and fingers. Amongst the Sarawak Kayans, if a man has taken the head of an enemy he can have the backs of his hands and fingers covered with tattoo : if he has only had a share in the slaughter, one finger only, generally the thumb, can be tattooed. The Mendalam Kayan braves are tattooed on the left thumb only, the thigh being reserved for head-taking heroes.

Lukut, an antique bead much valued by the Kayans, is the name given to a design tattooed on the wrist. When a man is ill it is supposed that his soul escapes from his body until he recovers. To prevent its departure on some future occasion the man will " tie it in " by fastening round his wrist a piece of string on which is sometimes threaded one of these beads. Since, however, the string may get broken and the bead lost, it is held safer to tattoo a representation of the bead on the part of the wrist which it would cover if actually worn. The *Lukut* bead, from having been a charm to prevent the second escape of the soul, has come to be regarded as a charm to ward off all disease, and the same quality is ascribed to its tattooed representation.

Amongst Kayan women tattooing is universal ; they believe that the designs act as torches in the next world, and that without these to light them they would remain for ever in total darkness. They also believe that after death the completely tattooed women will be allowed to bathe in the mythical river Telang Julan, and that consequently they will be able to pick up the precious articles that are found in its bed ; incompletely tattooed women can only stand on the river bank, whilst the untattooed are not allowed even to approach its shores.

Kayan women are tattooed in complicated serial designs over the whole forearm, the backs of the hands, on the whole of the thighs to below the knees, and on the feet. A Kayan chief of the Mendalam River told me that in his youth only the wives and daughters of chiefs were permitted the thigh tattoo, women of lower rank having to be content with tattoo on the lower part of the shin and of the instep. Amongst the Uma Tau Kenyahs the daughter of a chief must be tattooed before any of the other untattooed females of the house; should such a one die before she had been tattooed, all the other women of her age in the house are debarred from this embellishment.

Nowadays the class restrictions as regards tattoo are not so closely observed, but it is always possible to distinguish between a chief's daughter, an ordinary free-woman, and a dependent, by the fineness and number of the lines composing the patterns. Moreover, the designs of the lower-class women are not nearly so complex as those of the higher class, and they are generally tattooed freehand.

The tattooing of a Kayan girl is a serious operation, not only because of the pain and inconvenience caused, but also on account of the elaborate ceremonial required. The process is a long one, lasting sometimes as long as three or four years, since only a small piece can be done at a sitting, and several long intervals elapse between the various stages of the work. A girl when about ten years old has probably had her fingers and feet tattooed, and about a year later her forearms should be completed. The thighs are partially tattooed during the next year, and in the third or fourth year from the commencement the whole operation is, normally, completed. It is considered immodest to be tattooed after motherhood. A narrow strip of untattooed flesh down the back of the thigh is always left, as it is said that were this strip not left open mortification would probably set in.

The times and seasons for tattooing are considered of great importance. The appropriate period of the month is about the ninth day of the new moon—the lunar period

A Klemantan girl of the Tinjar river with
heavy copper rings in her ears.

A Klemantan woman of the Tuto river,
a rather handsome type.

Kalabit woman showing tattoo on legs, a large sub-tribe of the Muruts.   It is the custom
of these women to make proposals of marriage to the men of their tribe.

is known by the term *Butit Halap*, the belly of the *Halap* fish (*Barbus bramoides*). If, owing to tenderness of the skin, the operation has to be temporarily stopped, it may be resumed at any time, provided it was started at *Butit Halap*. As regards seasons, tattooing is considered *lali* during sowing-time and if a dead body is lying in the house unburied; bad dreams also, supposed to signify undue bleeding, may cause a cessation.

Other rites connected with tattoo are the forbidding of the eating of the monitor-lizard by a girl's parents until the tattooing is complete; while in the case of a girl who has brothers but no sisters, certain of the lines in the pattern are not joined together, as would be the case if she had sisters. Among the Bolongan Kenyahs a special hut has to be built for the tattooing ceremony; and the males of the family are confined to the Long House while the actual process is going on.

Among the Kayans tattooing is always done by a woman, and the office of tattooer is to a certain extent hereditary: the artists, like smiths and carvers, are under the protection of a tutelary spirit, who must be propitiated with sacrifices before each operation. The greater the number of sacrifices offered, or, in other words, the greater the skill and experience of the artist, the higher is the fee demanded. The tattooist must have no children of tender age, and is also debarred from eating certain food; it being supposed that, if an artist disregards the prohibitions imposed upon her profession, the designs that she tattoos will not appear clearly, and she herself may sicken and die.

The tools used by a tattoo artist are simple, consisting of two or three prickers and an iron striker which are kept in a wooden case. The pricker is a wooden rod with a short pointed head fastened at right angles at one end; to the point of the head is attached a lump of wax in which are embedded three or four short steel needles, their points alone projecting. The striker is merely a short iron rod, half of which is covered with a string lashing. The pigment is a mixture of soot, water, or sugar-cane juice, and it is kept in a double shallow cup of wood ; it is supposed that the best soot is obtained from the bottom of a metal cooking-pot, but that derived from burning resin or dammar is also used. The designs are carved in high relief on blocks of wood, which are smeared with the ink and then carefully pressed on the part of the body to be tattooed, leaving a clear impression of the designs.

For the actual operation, the subject lies on the floor, the artist and an assistant squatting on either side of her ; the artist first dips a piece of sugar-palm fibre into the pigment and, pressing this on to the limb to be tattooed, plots out the arrangement of the rows or bands of the design ; along these straight lines the artist tattoos the zig-zag lines, then, taking a tattoo block carved with the required design, she smears it with pigment and presses it on to the limb between two lines. Then either she or her assistant stretches with her feet the skin of the part to be tattooed, and, dipping a pricker into the pigment, taps its handle gently with the striker, driving the needle points into the skin at each tap. The operation is usually painful, and the subject can rarely restrain her cries of anguish ; but the artist is quite unmoved, and proceeds methodically with her task. As no antiseptic precautions are taken, a newly tattooed part often festers, much to the detriment of the tattoo ; but taking all things into consideration, it is wonderful how seldom one meets with a tattoo pattern spoilt by scars.

It is against custom to draw the blood of a friend, and therefore, when first blood is drawn in tattooing, it is customary to give a small present to the patient. This takes the form of four beads, or of some other object worth about one dollar. It is termed *lasat mata*, for it is supposed that if it were omitted the artist would go blind, and some misfortune would happen to the parents and relations of the girl.

When the half of one set of these lines has been completed the tattooer stops and asks for *selivit*; this is a present of a few beads, well-to-do people paying eight yellow beads of the variety known as *lavang*, valued at one dollar apiece, whilst poorer people give two only. It is supposed that if *selivit* were not paid the artist would be so worried by the household dogs and fowls that the work would not be satisfactorily done; however, to make assurance doubly sure, a curtain is hung round the operator and her subject to keep off unwelcome intruders. After *selivit* has been paid a cigarette is smoked, and then work recommences in earnest, there being no further interruptions for the rest of the day except for the purpose of taking food.

The food of the artist must be cooked and brought to her, as she must not stop to do any other work; her tools are indeed only laid aside for a few minutes while she consumes a hurried meal (pork or fowl), provided by the parents of the girl.

The fees which should be paid to the artist are more or less fixed; it is supposed, however, if her charges are excessive, that the artist will sicken and die within a year. For tattooing the fingers the operator receives a *malat* or short sword. For the forearms a gong worth from eight to twenty dollars is required, though on the Baram River a gong can only be demanded by an artist of about twenty years' experience, and lesser artists have to be content with beads and cloth. For the thighs a large brass *tawak* worth from six to sixty dollars according to workmanship is demanded. The fees may be paid by instalments; but, before the knee-cap, the last part to be tattooed, is touched, the artist must be paid the full amount. As this part of the design is the keynote of the whole, defalcations are unknown.

PART V

CREEDS AND SUPERSTITIONS

CHAPTER I

RELIGION AND BELIEFS

Belief in various powers, anthropomorphic and other—No belief in " devils " in inanimate objects—The gods : Laki Tenangan, the Supreme Being of the Kayans—A Creation myth—Lesser gods— The origin of Laki Tenangan—Bali Penyalong of the Kenyahs— *Toh* : objects of fear—Heads animated by *Toh*—Deserting the unwanted *Toh*—Young children and *Toh*—A benign *Toh*—Regulators of conduct—*Ngarong*, the Unknown Helper—When the dream comes true—Desired by all, yet found by few—Animal guardians— Some credible stories : gibbon, python, porcupine.

THE Kayans believe themselves to be surrounded by many intelligent powers capable of influencing their welfare for good or ill. Some of these are embodied in animals or plants, or are closely connected with other natural objects, such as mountains, rocks, rivers, and caves ; others manifest themselves in such processes as thunder, storm, and disease, the growth of the crops and disasters of various kinds. Some of these powers are, undoubtedly, conceived anthropomorphically : for they are frequently addressed by human titles, are represented by carvings in human form, and enjoy, in the opinion of the Kayans, most of the characteristically human attributes.

Others are conceived more vaguely, the bodily and mental characters of man being attributed to them less definitely ; and it is probably true to say that these powers range from the anthropomorphic being to (say) the power which resides in the seed-grain and manifests itself in its

growth and multiplication, and which seems to be conceived merely as a vital principle, or virtue inherent in the
grain, rather than as an intelligent and individual soul.

It has been said of some peoples of lowly culture that they
have no conception of merely mechanical causation, and
that every material object is regarded by them as animated
in the same sense as we ourselves regard the higher animals
as dynamically " alive." Such a statement cannot be
truthfully made about any of the peoples of Borneo. It
would be absurd to deny the recognition of mechanical
causation to people who show so much ingenuity in operations involving the intelligent application of mechanical
principles. These operations show that, though they may
be incapable of describing in general terms the principles
involved, they nevertheless have a nice appreciation of
them. If, for instance, a trap fails to work owing to its
faulty construction, the trapper treats it purely as a
mechanical contrivance, and proceeds to discover and
rectify the faulty part. He is under no illusion as to
possible sentient " devils " residing in the trap.

These spiritual powers are of three principal classes :—

(1) Anthropomorphic spirits thought of as dwelling in
remote and vaguely conceived regions and as very powerful
to intervene in human life. Towards these the attitude of
the Kayans is one of supplication and awe, gratitude and
hope, an attitude which is properly called reverential and
is the specifically religious attitude. These spirits must be
admitted to be gods in a very full sense of the word, and
the practices, doctrines, and emotions centred about them
must be regarded as constituting a system of religion.

(2) A second class consists of the spirits of living and
deceased persons, and of other spirits which, in the nature
and extent of their powers, are more nearly on a level with
human spirits than those of the first class. Such are those
embodied in the omen-animals and in the domestic pig,
fowl, and dog, in the crocodile, and possibly in the tiger-
cat and a few other animals.

(3) The third class is more varied, and comprises all the spirits or impalpable intelligent powers that do not fall into one or other of the two preceding classes; such are the spirits indefinitely conceived as always at hand, some malevolent, some good; such also are the spirits which are vaguely attached to the heads hung up in the houses. The dominant emotion in the presence of these is fear; the attitude that of avoidance and propitiation.

The Kayans recognise a number of gods that preside over great departments of their lives and interests. The more important of these are the god of war, *Toh Bulu*; three gods of life, *Laki Ju Urip*, *Laki Makatan Urip*, and *Laki Kalisai Urip*, of whom the first is the most important; the god of thunder and storms, *Laki Balari* and his wife *Obeng Doh*; the god of fire, *Laki Pesong*; gods of the harvest, *Anyi Lawang* and *Laki Ivong*; a god of the lakes and rivers, *Urai Uka*; *Balanan*, the god of madness; *Toh Kiho*, the god of fear; *Laki Katira Murei* and *Laki Jup Urip*, who conduct the souls of the dead to the Other World.

Beside or above all these is *Laki Tenangan*, a god more powerful than all the rest, and to whom are assigned no special or departmental functions, but who is a sort of President, or, so to say, Chairman of Directors.

About these gods the Kayans seem to have no very clear or generally accepted dogmas. Some assert that they dwell in the skies, but others regard them as dwelling below the surface of the earth. The former opinion is in harmony with the practice, when prayers are offered on behalf of a Long House, of erecting a tree with its branches buried in the ground and the root upturned; the tree seems to be regarded as in some sense forming a ladder of communication with the superior powers. The same opinion seems to be expressed in the importance attached to fire and smoke in prayer and ritual. Fire, if only in the form of a lighted cigarette, is always made when prayers are offered; it seems to be felt that the ascending smoke in some way facilitates communication with the gods.

While some gods, those of war and life, of harvest and of fire, are distinctly friendly, others, namely, the gods of madness and fear, are terrible and malevolent; while the god of thunder and those that conduct the souls to the world beyond the grave do not seem to be predominantly beneficent or malevolent.

Laki Tenangan seems to be the supreme being of the Kayan universe. He is conceived as beneficent and, as his title *Laki* (Grandfather) implies, as a fatherly god who protects mankind. He is not a strictly tribal god, for the Kayan admits his identity with *Pa Silong* and with *Bali Penyalong*, the supreme gods of the Klemantans and Kenyahs respectively. He is represented as an old man with long white hair, and speaking the Kayan language. He is sometimes to be seen in dreams, usually his back only, but, in cases of great fortune, his face. In the past privileged people are supposed to have spoken with him; but to-day the " age of miracles is passed." He dwells, far away, in a Kayan house with his wife, *Doh Tenangan*, who, though of less importance than himself, is specially addressed by the women. The god is addressed by name in terms of praise and supplication; the prayers seem to be transmitted to him by means of the souls of domestic pigs or fowls; for one of these is always killed and charged to carry the prayer to the god. The supplicant, having killed a pig and called the messengers of the god, addresses the god : " Grant my child life that I may instruct him in my own occupations. Thy powers are above our powers, and thou canst protect us from evil. I hold thee above my head, that men may look to me as to a high cliff."

Similar rites are observed on addressing *Doh Tenangan*. " Have pity upon me, Doh Tenangan. Turn my weakness to strength, that to-morrow I may find my food."

The Kayans have no opinions as to the creator of the

o

earth. Their creation-myth, in which *Laki Tenangan* does not figure, runs as follows :—

In the beginning there was a barren rock. On this the rains fell and gave rise to moss, and the worms, aided by the dung-beetles, made soil by their castings. On this a sword handle came down from the sun and became a large tree.

Next there came a creeper from the moon, and embracing the tree became mated with it through the action of the wind. From this union were born *Kaluban Gai* and *Kalubi Angai*, the first human beings, male and female. These were incomplete, lacking the legs and lower half of their trunks. These incomplete human beings produced various descendants who became the progenitors of the various existing peoples, such as *Oding Lahang*, claimed as ancestor by the Kayans, the Kenyahs, and some of the Klemantans.

As regards the minor departmental gods, it is difficult to draw the line between them and the spirits of the third class mentioned above. All of them are approached at times with prayers and with rites similar to those used in addressing *Laki Tenangan*. Before every Kayan house there stand several wooden posts, very roughly carved to indicate the head and limbs of a human form. Before these, when the gods are addressed on behalf of the household (as before or after an important expedition), the chief ceremony usually takes place. But the posts cannot be called idols : they are more of the nature of an altar. No importance attaches to them intrinsically, for they are often allowed to fall away and are renewed as required. Indeed if a party at a distance from home needs supernatural assistance, an improvised post may be set up *ad hoc*.

As yet we have little information bearing upon the origin and history of these Kayan gods. There is, however, some small amount of evidence indicating that the minor gods are deified ancestors, whose kinship with their worshippers has been, in some cases completely, in others partially, forgotten. If this hypothesis could be shown to be true, it would afford a strong presumption in favour of the view that *Laki Tenangan* also has had a similar history, and that he is merely *primus inter pares*. For among the Kayans, as we have seen, a large village acknowledges a supreme chief as well as the chiefs of the several houses of the village; and in the operations of war on a large scale a supreme war chief presides over a council of lesser chiefs. It is only to be expected that the theocracy should exhibit features commonly found in the village polity; for Man makes God after his own image.

On the other hand, none of the facts noted in connection with the minor gods as indicating their ancestral origin are found to be true of *Laki Tenangan*, except only his bearing the title *Laki*, which, as we have seen, is the title by which a man is addressed as soon as he becomes a grandfather. The name *Tenangan* is not a proper name borne by any Kayans, nor, so far as I know, does it occur amongst any other peoples. It is possibly connected with the Kayan word *tenang*, which means correct, or genuine. The termination *an* is used in several instances in Malay (though not in Kayan) to make a substantive of an adjective. The name then possibly means, "he who is correct or all-knowing"; but this is a very speculative suggestion.

It is just possible that the Kayans owe their conception of a supreme god to their contact with the Mohammedans. But this is rendered very improbable by the facts : first, that the Kayans have had such intercourse during but a short period in Borneo, probably not more than 300 years (though they may have had such intercourse at an earlier period before entering Borneo); secondly, that among the Ibans, who have had for at least 200 years much more abundant intercourse with the Mohammedans of Borneo than the Kayans have had, the conception has not taken root and has not been assimilated.

Among the Kenyahs similar beliefs to those of the

Kayans prevail. They also recognise a principal god or Supreme Being, whose name is *Bali Penyalong*, and a number of minor deities presiding over special departments of nature and human life. These minor gods are not uninteresting. *Bali Atap* protects the house against sickness and attack, and is called upon in cases of madness to expel the evil spirit possessing the patient. His image, a rude, wooden effigy, stands beside the gangway leading to the house from the river's brink; he holds a spear in the right hand, a shield in the left; about his neck he bears a fringed collar made up of knotted strips of rattan, one of each being tied on by the head of each room, and a knot being made for each member of his roomhold. Generally a wooden image of a hawk, *Bali Flaki*, stands beside him on the top of a tall pole.

The Kenyahs carve such images more elaborately than the Kayans, who are often content merely to indicate the eyes, mouth, and four limbs, by slashing away with the sword chips of wood from the surface of the log, leaving gashes at the points roughly corresponding in position to these organs. The Kenyahs treat these rude images with rather more care, and they associate them more strictly with particular deities. The children of the house are not allowed to touch one after it has been once used as an altar-post; it is only when it is so used, and blood of fowls or pigs sprinkled upon it, that it seems to acquire a malign influence.

Bali Utong brings prosperity to the house. *Bali Urip* is the god of life; he too has a carved altar-post, generally crowned with a brass gong. *Balinggo* is the god of thunder.

Bali Sungei is the name given to a being which perhaps cannot properly be called a god. He is thought of as a sort of glorified crocodile living at the bottom of the river, and the cause of the violent swirls and uprushes of water that appear on the surface in times of flood. He is regarded with great fear, for he is held to be responsible

Bali Atap: Kenyah god who protects the people of
the village from harm.

View of a Long House.

for the upsetting of boats. It does not seem that he is the spirit of the river itself, since floods and the various changes of the river are not attributed to him.

The altar-posts outside Kenyah houses are commonly surmounted by a carved crocodile, and adorned by a *Dracæna* plant, the deep red leaves of which are often seen growing close by, and a number of large spherical stones, known as *Batu Tuloi*. These stones, of unknown origin, are perpetual possessions of this house : they are supposed to grow gradually larger and to move spontaneously when danger threatens the house. When the people of a village decide to move to another site, stones, plants, and crocodile are taken with it.

While the second of the three classes of spiritual beings includes the souls of men and of some animals, those of the third class are powers vaguely conceived, of minor importance, and not regularly envisaged in any visible forms or material objects. These powers, for which the generic Kayan name is *Toh*, seem to be objects of fear, and, if not malevolent, are easily offended and capable of bringing misfortunes of all kinds upon human beings. The most important of these *Toh* are perhaps those associated with the dried human heads characteristic of many houses. It seems that these spirits are not supposed to be actually those of the persons from whose shoulders the heads were taken. At the same time they seem to be resident in or about the heads, though not inseparable from them. They are said to cause the teeth of the heads to be ground together if they are offended or dissatisfied, as by neglect of the attentions customarily paid to the heads or by other infringement of custom. The heads are thus supposed to be animated by the *Toh* ; if a head falls, through the breaking of the rattan by which it is suspended, it is said to have thrown itself down, being dissatisfied owing to insufficient attention having been paid to it. This view of the animation of the heads by the *Toh* is illustrated by the treatment accorded to them from the time they are brought into the house. Having been dried and smoked in a small hut made for the purpose, they are brought up to the house with loud rejoicings and singing of the war chorus. For this ceremony all members of the village are summoned from the fields or the forest. When all are assembled in the houses, the heads are carried in procession adorned with dried and frayed palm-leaves before one of the altar-posts between the house and the river. Here fowls and pigs are sacrificed, and their blood is scattered upon the assembled men with a wisp of shredded palm-leaves.

At all times the heads hanging in the house are treated respectfully and somewhat fearfully. When it is necessary to handle them, some old man undertakes the task, and children especially are prevented from touching them; for it is felt that to touch them involves the risk of madness, brought on by the offended *Toh*, or spirits of the heads.

The fire beneath the heads is always kept alight in order that they may be warm, dry, and comfortable. On certain special occasions they are offered rice spirit and pork in the way mentioned above.

On moving to a new house the heads are temporarily lodged in a small shelter built for the purpose, and are brought up into the house with a ceremony similar to that of their first installation. The Kayans do not care to have in the house more than twenty or thirty heads, and are at some pains occasionally to get rid of some superfluous heads—a fact which shows clearly that the heads are not mere trophies of valour and success in war. The moving to a new house is the occasion chosen for reducing the number of heads. Those destined to be left are hung in a hut built at some distance from the house which is about to be deserted. A good fire is made in it and kept up during the demolition of the house, and when the people depart they make up in the little head-house a fire designed to last several days. It is supposed that, when the fire goes

out, the *Toh* of the heads will notice the fact, and begin
to suspect that they are deserted by the people; when the
rain begins to come in through the roof their suspicions are
confirmed, and they then set out to pursue their deserters,
but owing to the lapse of time and weather are unable to
track them. The people believe that in this way they
escape the madness which the anger of the deserted *Toh*
would bring upon them.

These precautions illustrate very well the power for
harm attributed to the *Toh* and the fear with which they
are regarded. Nevertheless, these beings are not wholly
malevolent. It is held that in some way they bring
prosperity to the household, especially in the form of good
crops; and the presence of heads is essential to the welfare
of the house.

The *Toh* of the heads are but a few among many that
are conceived as surrounding the houses and infesting the
tombs, the rivers, the forests, the mountains, the caves,
and, by those who live near the coast, the sea; in fact every
locality has its *Toh*, and, since they are easily offended and
stirred to malignance, the people are careful to avoid offence
and to practise every rite by which it is thought possible
to propitiate them. Death and sickness, especially madness, accidental bodily injuries, failure of crops, in fact
almost any trouble may be ascribed to the malevolent action
of *Toh*. A good example of this feeling may be found
among the rice cultivators. In clearing a patch of jungle
in preparation for sowing paddy, it is usual to leave a few
trees standing on some high point of the ground in order
not to offend the *Toh* of the locality by depriving them of
all the trees, which they are vaguely supposed to use as
resting-places. Such trees are sometimes stripped of all
their branches save a few at the top; and sometimes a
pole bearing bunches of palm-leaves is lashed across the
stem at a height from the ground; a " bull-roarer, which
is used by boys as a toy, is sometimes hung upon such a
cross-piece to dangle and flicker in the breeze.

To these influences young children are held to be peculiarly susceptible. It is for this reason that, as mentioned before, no name is given to a child until it is two years of age. For the same reason the parents dislike any touching of an infant; and if for any reason such contact has taken place, it is usual to give the mother a few beads, which she ties about the wrist or ankle of the child, " to preserve its homely smell," as they say, for if outside influence were suspected by the *Toh*, the results might be unpropitious. If for any reason it is suspected that the attention of some evil-disposed *Toh* has been drawn to a child (and the same practice is sometimes observed by adults under similar circumstances), a sooty mark is made upon the forehead, consisting of a vertical median line and a horizontal band just above the eyebrows, in order that the *Toh* may not be able to recognise his victim. In such circumstances the Ibans go even further. They place a new-born child in a small boat and allow it to float down-stream, and standing upon the bank call upon all the evil spirits to take the child at once, if they mean to take it, in order that the parents may be spared the greater bereavement of losing it some years later. If, after floating some distance down-stream, the child is found unhurt, it is carried home, the parents feeling some confidence that it will be spared to grow up.

The fear of the *Toh* is also shown when, on going to a friendly village, the people make a black mark across the forehead in order to disguise themselves from the *Toh* of the strange region. For in the main, although all regions are infested with *Toh*, the locality in which a man dwells is regarded by him as less dangerous than other parts; for experience has shown him that in the neighbourhood of his own village he may behave in certain ways with impunity, whereas in distant regions all is uncertain.

The more remote and inaccessible the region, the more are the *Toh* of it feared; rugged hill-tops, and especially mountain-tops, are the abodes of especially dangerous

Toh, and it is often only with difficulty that parties of men can be induced to go to the summits of any of the mountains.

The influence of the *Toh* is thus not always pernicious; certain spots indeed become credited with the presence of *Toh* of benign influence. A rumour attached to a streamlet falling over the rocky bank of the Baram River some little distance below the mouth of the Akar says that a wild pig which had been speared fell into it and was allowed to lie there, but after a little while jumped up and made off. This benevolent action has brought the streamlet a great reputation, and passing boats now stop in order that the crews may splash some of the water on their heads and faces, as a restorative of health.

In regulating conduct the *Toh* play a considerable part; for they are the powers that bring misfortunes upon a house or village when any member of it ignores taboos or otherwise breaks customs, without performing the propitiatory rites demanded by the occasion. Thus on them, rather than on the gods, are founded the effective sanctions of prohibitive rules of conduct. For the propitiation of offended *Toh* fowls' eggs and the blood of fowls and of young pigs are used, repentance being proffered by the chief or some other influential person, while the blood is sprinkled on the culprit or other source of offence.

One of the most extraordinary and rarest beliefs is that held by the Ibans in the Ngarong, or Tua, an Unknown Helper. It is one of the few subjects on which the Ibans display a reluctance to speak freely : such is their reserve, indeed, that one may live for many years on friendly terms with them without suspecting the importance of the superstition, or even understanding the meaning of the word. This secret helper seems to be usually, though not always, the spirit of some ancestor or dead relative; in fact it is hardly clear that it is always conceived as the soul of a deceased human being. This spirit becomes the special protector of some individual Iban, to whom in a dream he manifests himself, in the first place in human form, announcing that he will be his secret helper and perhaps informing the dreamer in what shape he will appear in future.

On the day after such a dream the Iban wanders through the forest looking for signs by which he may recognise his guardian; and if an animal behaves in a manner at all unusual, if a startled deer or monkey stops a moment to gaze at him before bounding away, if a gibbon gambols about persistently in the trees near him, if he comes upon a bright quartz crystal or a strangely contorted root or creeper, that animal or object is for him full of a mysterious significance and is the probable abode of his guardian. Sometimes in a dream the helper is said to assume the form of an Iban and even to speak with him, promising help and good fortune. If this occurs in the jungle, the seer almost certainly faints away, and when he comes to himself again the guardian spirit has disappeared. Alternatively, a man may be told in his dream that if he goes into the jungle he will meet his guardian spirit in the form of a wild boar. He will then, of course, go to seek it, and if by chance other men of his house should kill a wild boar on that particular day, he will go to them and beg for the wild boar's head, or if needs be buy it at a good price, carry it home to his house-room, offer it cooked rice and kill a fowl before it, smearing the blood on the head and on himself, and humbly beg for pardon. On the following night he hopes to dream of his guardian spirit, and perhaps he is told in his dream to take the tusks from the dead boar and that they will bring him good luck. Unless he dreams something of this sort, he feels that he has been mistaken, and that this particular boar was not really his secret helper.

Although desired by all, possibly not more than one in a hundred men is fortunate enough to have a secret helper. Many a young man goes to sleep on the grave of some distinguished person, or in some wild and lonely spot, and lives for several days on a very restricted diet, hoping that a secret helper will come to him in his dreams.

When, as is most commonly the case, the guardian takes on the form of some animal,[1] all individuals of that species become objects of especial regard to the fortunate Iban ; he will not kill or eat any such animal, and, as far as he can, restrains others from doing so. A guardian spirit may after a time manifest itself in some new form, but even then the Iban will continue to respect the first animal-form in which it appeared.

In some cases the cult of an unknown helper spreads through a whole family or household. The children and grandchildren usually respect the species of animal to which a man's guardian belongs, and, without hoping for any help, will perhaps sacrifice fowls or pigs to it occasionally ; but it is asserted that if the great-grand-children of a man behave well to his secret helper, it will often befriend them just as much as its original protégé.

Information on this matter is hard to obtain, but Anggus (an Ulu Ai Iban of the Batang Lupar) told me that every Iban who has no guardian hopes to get some bird or beast as his helper at the *Begawai*, the feast given to the *Petara*. One man who had none would not kill a gibbon because it was the guardian of his grandfather, who had died twenty years before. A man, he said, came to his grandfather in a dream and said, " Do not kill a gibbon," and then immediately turned into one. The gibbon helped his grandfather to become rich, and assisted him in all possible ways. On one occasion, when his grandfather was about to go on the war-path, his guardian spoke to him in a dream and said, " Go forward, for I will help you," and the next day the old man saw in the jungle a grey gibbon which was un-doubtedly his guardian. When he died he said to his

---

[1] Most usually, it would seem, a snake, a tiger-cat, a wild boar, or a gibbon.

sons, " Never harm or kill a gibbon," and his sons and grandsons have obeyed him in this ever since.

Another statement came from Payang, an old Katibas Iban, who said that he has been helped by a python ever since he was a youth. A man came to him in a dream and said, " Sometimes I shall become a python and some-times a cobra, but I will always help you." This guardian has certainly helped him very much, but he does not know whether it has helped his children ; nevertheless he has forbidden them to kill a python or cobra, and has advised them to treat all snakes with kindness.

A third case was when some years ago a community of Ibans were building a new house on the Dabai River. One day, while they were at work, a porcupine ran out of a hole in the ground near by. During the following night one of the party was told in a dream by the porcupine to join their new house with his (the porcupine's). So they completed their house ; and ever since that time they have made yearly feasts in honour of the porcupines that live beneath the house, and no one in the house would dare to injure one of them, though some members of the household will still kill and eat other porcupines met at a distance. They had no death in the house for seven or more years after the house had been built, and this they attributed to the protecting power of the porcupines ; and when anyone was sick, they offered food to them, and regarded their good offices as far more important than the ministrations of the medicine-man. A few years later some of their relatives who were living in another district moved into this village, and for three months the knowledge of the part played by the porcupines was hidden from them as a mysterious secret. At the end of that time the valuable secret was disclosed to the new-comers, and the porcupines were feasted with every variety of cooked rice, some of it being made into a rude image of the animal, and with rice-spirit and cakes of sugar and rice-flour, salt and dried fish, oil, betel-nut, and

tobacco.   Several fowls were slain, and their blood was
daubed on the chin of each person in the house.   The liver
of one fowl was carefully taken out and put with the food
offered to the porcupines, that they might read the omens
from it; and they were then informed of the arrival of
the new-comers.   The fowls were waved over the heads
of the people by the old men, while they prayed the
porcupines to give them protection, long life, and health.

CHAPTER II

DEATH AND THE HEREAFTER

Two kinds of soul distinguished—Lying in state—Burial—The village
cemetery—Rites of purification—Bequests—Klemantan and Iban
customs—Life after death—*Long Malan* and the Five Districts—
Further journeys of the soul—The bridge of *Maligang—Patan*, the
fish—The last stage—Returned souls—*Ungap* of the Punans—
Maiwiang, the two-headed dog—Death neither feared nor desired—
The *Petara* of the Ibans—*Singalang Burong*—A tedious Pantheon—
Scepticism and fatalism : "*Nusi jam?*"

ONE of the most striking features of Bornean folk-lore
is the attitude towards death, and the language used about
it. For (curiously enough, in view of the theory implied in the Soul-catching Ceremony) a man's soul is
regarded as remaining in the neighbourhood of the body
as long as it remains in the house. It would appear that
the Kayans vaguely distinguish two souls—on the one
hand, the ghost-soul, which in a live man wanders afar, in
dreams and abstractions; and, on the other, the vital
principle, which possesses the " conatus in suo esse perse-
verandi," which is Life. As long as the latter remains in
the body, the ghost-soul may return to it; but, when
death is complete, the vital principle departs and the ghost-
soul with it. This interpretation is borne out by the use
of the word *urip*, which in common speech means " to
be alive," but may be also applied to a person recently
dead, as if to mark the speaker's sense of the continuance
of the personality, in spite of the death of the body. A
slight analogy may be found in Europe, in the words
animus and *anima*, and πνεῦμα and ψυχή. This view of
death affects all the ceremonies connected therewith.

When a death occurs, a gong or drum is beaten loudly,

to announce the fact to departed relatives and friends, the number of strokes depending on the sex and social position of the deceased. The corpse is kept in the house during a period varying from one night for people of the lower class, to three nights for middle-class folk, and ten days for a chief. During this time the dead man lies in state. The corpse has a bead of some value under each eyelid for use by the ghost-soul in paying for its passage across the River of Death : he is dressed in his finest clothes and ornaments, and is enclosed within a coffin hollowed from a single log, the lid of which is sealed with resin and lashed round with rattans.

The coffin is covered with a particular design in red and black and white, and is placed in the house-gallery on a low platform, surrounded by the most valuable personal property of the dead man, whose family takes pains to make the display of property as imposing as possible. A fire is kept burning near the coffin, and small packets of cooked rice and of tobacco are placed upon it for the use of the dead man's soul. Hundreds of cigarettes are hung in bundles about the platform by people of the house, sent by them as tokens of kindly remembrance to their departed friends, who are believed to be able to recognise by smell the hands that made each bundle. During the whole period the dead man is attended continuously by at least two or three mourners, either relatives or, more rarely, hired mourners, who from time to time throughout both day and night wail loudly, renewing their wailing at the arrival of each party of friends or relatives.

These parties come in from neighbouring villages, to which the death has been announced by special messengers ; in the case of an influential chief several thousand men and women sometimes congregate to do him honour.

Upon the arrival of any person of importance, gongs and drums are beaten, and the dead man is informed of the fact by the *Dayong*,[1] or by a relative. The visitor is

---

[1] The " medicine-man."

led to a seat near the coffin, where he will sit silently or join in the wailing, until after a few minutes he enters into conversation with his hosts. When all the expected guests have arrived, pigs are slaughtered and a feast is made.

While the coffin lies in the house all noises other than the wailing are avoided in its immediate neighbourhood, and the children, dogs and fowls are kept away from it. The *Dayong* will sit beside the coffin, occasionally brandishing a sword above it in order to keep in check the *Toh*, who, attracted to the neighbourhood of the corpse, might grow too bold.

On the day appointed for the removal of the corpse it is the duty of the *Dayong* to instruct the dead man's soul how to find his way to the other world; this he does, sitting beside the coffin and chanting aloud in doleful tones. When he has completed his instructions, the rattan lashings about the head of the coffin are loosed. This is the moment at which the soul is believed to take its final departure from the body, and it is probable that the custom of unlashing the coffin is connected with the idea of facilitating its escape, although I have never obtained any definite statement to this effect. At the same time the fire that has been kept burning near the coffin is allowed to die out. To the coffin, which is shaped roughly like a boat, two small wooden figures are attached —a figure of a woman at the head, a male figure at its foot. These figures are, not improbably, a vestige of a bygone custom of killing slaves, whose souls would row the boat of the dead man on his journey to the other world; a custom which probably gave rise to head-taking. This view of the slaves is borne out by the fact that a live fowl is usually tied to one of these wooden figures. The coffin is then conveyed out of the house and lowered to the ground with rattans, either through the floor, planks being taken up for the purpose, or under the eaves at the side of the gallery. In this way they avoid carrying it down the house-ladder; for it seems to be felt that this precaution renders it more difficult for the ghost to find its way back to the house.   Among some of the peoples it is customary to beat a big gong while this operation is in progress (or, in the case of a woman, a drum) in order to announce to the inhabitants of the other world the approach of the recently deceased.   Thus, with great deliberation, the coffin is brought to the river bank.   Here it is laid in a large boat gaily decorated with bright-coloured cloths, and is paddled down-stream to the graveyard, followed by the boats of the mourning friends, who preserve the strictest silence.

The burial-ground is usually on the river bank some quarter of a mile below the house, generally on the opposite bank.   Here a great log of timber, proportionate in size to the social standing of the dead man, and in the case of a chief some three feet or more in diameter and some thirty feet in height, has been erected.   The upper end, which is always the root-end of the log, is cut in the form of a deep cleft, just wide enough to receive the coffin. Above the cleft a large slab of hardwood, often elaborately carved, forms a cover for the coffin.   On landing at the graveyard the mourners carry the coffin between the two parts of a cleft pole which are fixed in the ground so as to make a large **v** (this is called *Nyring*, the wall), and all the mourners are expected to pass through this cleft, each, in doing so, placing his foot upon a fowl which is laid bound upon the ground.   The coffin is then lifted to its final resting-place in the cleft on the end of the huge pillar, and the weapons, implements, and war clothes, the large hat, the cooking-pot, and in fact any articles of personal property which may be of use to the departing soul, are hung upon the tomb.   If a gong is hung up, it may be cracked or pierced beforehand, but it is not usual among Kayans to spoil other articles before hanging them on the tomb.

It now remains for the mourners to purify them- selves.   This is done with the help of the lower jaws of the pigs that were consumed at the funeral feast.   The jaws

P

are placed together with water in a gong or other basin, and the *Dayong*, taking a fowl's feather, sprinkles drops of water from the basin upon all the assembled mourners, pouring out the while a stream of words, the purport of which is—" May all evil, sickness, and other tribulation be kept from you." Then the mourners return in a single file through the V in the imaginary wall formed by the cleft pole, each one again placing his foot on the fowl (which is crushed to death long before the end of the ceremony), spitting as he goes through, and exclaiming, " Save us from evil." When all have passed through, the upper ends of the two parts of the V are brought together and lashed round with rattans ; and a small tree, pulled up by the roots, and having its branches cut away, is laid beside the pole with its roots turned towards the grave ; and on the other side of the pole is put another vertical pole with a cross-piece tied at its upper end. Beside these structures fire is left burning. In this way the Kayans symbolically prevent any of the untoward influences of the graveyard following the party back to the house ; though they do not seem to be clear as to whether it is the ghosts of the dead, or the *Toh* of the neighbourhood, or those which may have contributed to his death, against whom these precautions are taken. This done, the whole party returns as quickly as possible to the village, halting only to bathe on the way.

The whole household of which the dead man was a member continues in mourning for a period varying according to his social standing ; the mourning rules are observed most strictly by the nearest relatives. The signs of mourning are the wearing of bark-cloth or of clothes made yellow with clay, the growing of hair on the parts of the head and face usually kept shaved, and the putting aside of ornaments such as ear-rings and necklaces. All music, feasts, and merry-making are avoided. The period of mourning is, " properly," terminated by the obtaining of a human head.

In case of any dispute regarding the division of the property of a dead man, his ghost may be called upon by a *Dayong* and questioned as to the dead man's intentions; but this cannot be done until after the harvest following upon the death. This ceremony is known as *Janoi*. A small model of a house, perhaps a yard in width and length, is made and placed in the gallery beside the door of the dead man's chamber. In it are placed food and drink of various kinds, together with cigarettes. Beside this model-house the *Dayong* sits, calling upon the soul of the dead man to enter the Soul-house, and mentioning the names of the members of his family. From time to time he looks in to the family-room, and after some time announces that the food and drink have been consumed. The people accept this statement as evidence that the ghost has entered the Soul-house. The *Dayong* acts as though listening to the whispering of the soul within the house, starting and from time to time emitting strange vocables. Then he announces the will of the ghost in regard to the distribution of the property, speaking in the first person and reproducing the phraseology and any peculiarities of the dead man. The directions so obtained are usually followed, and any dispute is thus terminated. But in some cases the people apply a test to verify the alleged presence of the ghost. A shallow dish filled with water is placed near the Soul-house, and a ring-shaped armlet of shell is placed vertically in this basin, the water covering its lower half. A few fine fibres of cotton-seed are thrown on to the surface of the water, and are kept in movement by tapping on the planks. If the threads float through the ring it is conclusive evidence of the presence of the ghost; but so long as the threads cannot be got to pass through the ring, the people are not satisfied that the ghost is present.

The Kenyahs' disposal of their dead is very similar in all respects to the Kayan practice. But the burial customs of most of the Klemantan tribes are different. Their

usual practice is to keep the coffin containing the corpse
in the gallery of the house until the full period of mourning
is completed. The coffin itself is sealed closely with wax
and gums, and elaborately decorated with carved and
painted wood-work. After several months or even years
have elapsed a feast is prepared ; the coffin is opened and
the bones are taken out and cleaned. They are then
packed into a smaller coffin or a large egg-shaped jar, which
is carried to the village cemetery. There it is placed either
in the hollowed upper end of a massive post, or into a large
wooden chamber containing the remains of several persons,
generally near relatives. These tombs are in many cases
very elaborately decorated with painted wood-work.

The small wooden coffin is, probably, historically older
than the jar—which, it should be said, can only be afforded
by the rich—for the Klemantans, who mostly use jars,
are incapable of manufacturing them themselves, and buy
them from China or Indo-China.

Among the same Klemantans, a rather different
procedure is sometimes adopted, the corpse being placed
in a jar a few days after death. Since the mouth
of the jar is too small to admit the corpse, it is
broken horizontally into two parts by the following
ingenious procedure. The jar is sunk in the water of the
river until it is full of water and wholly submerged ; it is
held horizontally by two men, one at either end, just
beneath the surface of the water. A third man strikes a
sharp downward blow with an axe upon the widest circumference of the jar ; it is then turned over and he strikes
a second blow upon the same circumference at a spot
opposite to the first. At the second stroke the jar falls
in two, sometimes as cleanly and nicely broken as though
cut with a saw. The corpse is now packed in with its
knees bound closely under the chin ; the upper part of the
jar is replaced and sealed on with wax or resin. When the
time of the feast arrives, the jar is reopened, the bones
cleaned, and replaced in the same jar.

This mode of jar burial is practised by the Muruts also, and is commoner in the northern parts of the island than elsewhere.

The Klemantans put selected articles of the property of the deceased within the tomb, but do not generally hang such articles on it externally as the Kayans and Kenyahs do.

The Ibans bury their dead in the earth, generally in a village graveyard on the river banks not far from the house. The body, together with some personal property, is merely wrapped in mats and laid in a grave some three feet in depth. It is not usual to keep the corpse in the house for some days, as is done by the Kayans, and the burial is effected with comparatively little ceremony. The graves of these people are not marked with any monument, but by a *sungkup* which consists of two pairs of stout posts, at head and feet respectively; each pair being erected in the form of an oblique cross, the upper ends of which are carved in decorative fashion. Two broad planks laid between the lower parts of these crossed posts form a roof to the grave. In the case of a man noted for great success in farming or fighting, a bamboo tube may be sunk through the earth to a spot just above the root of the nose, through which his tribesmen speak to him or pour rice-spirit in order to strengthen their appeal.

The Land Dayaks of Sarawak, as well as some other allied Klemantan tribes in South Borneo, have the peculiar habit of burning the bodies of their dead, or the bones alone after the flesh has dropped away. The burning is in some tribes carried out by the richer families only, the bodies that are not burned being buried in the earth.

After death the soul of the departed is supposed to wander on foot through the forest until it reaches the crest of a mountain ridge. From this point it looks down upon the basin of a great river, the *Long Malan*, in which five districts are assigned as the dwelling-places of souls, the destination of each being determined by the mode of death. The ghosts of those who die through old age or disease go to *Apo Leggan*, the largest of these districts, where they live very much as we do in this life. Those who die a violent death, whether in battle or by accident, go to the basin of a tributary river, *Long Julan*, where is *Bawang Daha*, the Lake of Blood ; there they live in comfort, and, though doing no work, become rich : they have for wives the ghosts of women that have died in childbed. Those that have been drowned find a home beneath the rivers, and inherit all property lost in the water by their surviving friends ; such places bear the name of *Ling Yang*. The souls of stillborn children dwell in *Tenyu Lalu* ; they are believed to be very brave, owing to their having experienced no pain in this world. Finally, suicides have assigned to them a special district, *Tan Tekkan*, where they live miserably, eating only roots, berries, and other jungle produce.

Other districts of this great country are vaguely assigned to the souls of Malays and other aliens. It is generally said that the left bank of the river is the place of the tribes of Borneo, while the right bank is assigned to outsiders ; and the soul is especially warned by the *Dayong* to avoid the right bank lest it should find itself among foreigners. These beliefs seem to involve some faint rudiment of the doctrine of *post-mortem* retribution or, at least, compensation—a doctrine which does not appear, as far as I am aware, in the beliefs of the other peoples.

The departed soul standing on the mountain ridge surveys these regions ; and it is not until he stops here to rest that he becomes aware that he is finally separated from his body. This fact is brought home to him by the arrival of the ghost-souls of the various articles hung upon his tomb, which hurry after him, and only overtake him at this his first resting-place.

Among various tribes there are current several versions of the further journey of the soul. The ghost descends the mountain to the banks of *Long Malan*, which river he must cross to reach his final destination. The river must be crossed by a bridge consisting of a single large log suspended from bank to bank, which is constantly agitated by a guardian, *Maligang* by name. If the ghost has during his earthly life taken a head, or even merely taken part in a successful head-hunting raid—the tattooing of the hands will show this—he crosses this bridge without difficulty; otherwise he may fall below and be consumed by maggots or, according to another version, be devoured by a large fish, *Patan*, and make a bad end. When the ghost reaches the other bank he is greeted by those of his friends who have gone before, and who lead him to their village. Some part of the journey is generally supposed to be made by boat, a theory which does not seem to fit into the general scheme. An equally doubtful matter is the part played by *Laki Jup Urip*, a deity or spirit whose function it is to guide the souls to their proper destinations.

In many Kayan villages stories are told of persons who, having died, have returned to life. In every case these legends seem to have risen from the person having lain in a trance for some days, during which he or she was regarded as dead. The Kayans accept the cessation of respiration as evidence of death, and the cessation of normal breathing is taken as equivalent to death.

In a case which I personally experienced, the body was laid out in the gallery of the house, and preparations for the funeral were far advanced when I arrived. On glancing at the alleged corpse I suspected that life was not extinct, and succeeded, by the application of ammonia to the nostrils, in restoring the entranced man to animation, and shortly to a normal condition of health. Such persons, in giving an account of their experiences during the period in which they have deserted their bodies, usually allege that they have traversed a part of the road leading to the Land of Shades, and describe it in terms agreeing more or less closely with the traditional account current among the Kayans. Since in these cases the person is thought to be dead, no efforts are made by the *Dayong* to lead back his departing soul, and its return has to be explained in some other way. In some cases the returned soul describes how he was turned back by *Maligang*, the awful being who guards the bridge across the River of Death.

In this matter the beliefs and traditions of the various tribes are commonly similar, possibly because of mutual intercourse, so that it is rarely possible to mark off any one feature especially characteristic of a particular people. The Punans, however, add to the general mass of tradition some picturesque incidents. According to them, a huge helmeted hornbill sits by the far end of the bridge across the River of Death, and with its peculiar noises tries to terrify the ghost, so that it may fall from the bridge into the jaws of a great fish which is in league with the bird. On the other side of the river is *Ungap*, a woman with a cauldron and spear. *Ungap*, if appeased with a gift, aids the ghost to escape from the monstrous bird and fish. To propitiate this friendly witch, pebbles or beads are put in the nostrils of Punan corpses.

Some of the Melanos hold peculiar views about the soul. Each man is credited with two souls. After his death one of these goes to some region in the heavens where it becomes a good spirit that assists at the *Bayoh* ceremonies. The other makes a journey to a world of the dead much like the *Apo Leggan* of the Kayans; and the journey involves the crossing of the river on a single log, the passage of which is disputed by a malign being, who tries to shake the nerve of the ghost by flinging ashes at him as he crosses the bridge. Other Melanos describe this opposing power as a two-headed dog, *Maiwiang* by name, whom it is necessary to propitiate with the gift of a valuable bead. For this reason a bead of some value is fastened to the right arm of the corpse before the coffin is closed. It is said of the Melanos that they were formerly in the habit of killing several slaves at the tomb of a chief; and, since it was believed that, if the victims died a violent death, their

Melanc image representing the sea-god Gamiling.

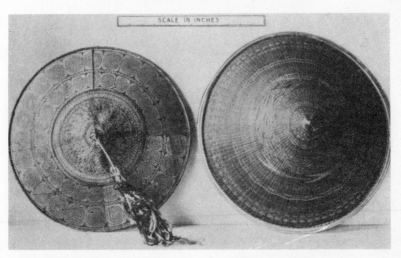

Land Dayak woman's hat.   Iban woman's hat (tangoi).

souls would not go to the same place as the dead chief, they were allowed to die from exposure to the sun while bound to the tomb. Now that homicide is prohibited, these people arrange a great cock-fight; and there can be little doubt that the death of the birds is felt to take the place of the human sacrifice.

The life after death is regarded as not in any way very different from this life, for better or for worse. Social distinction and consideration, especially such as are achieved by the taking of heads in war, are carried over into the life after death; and men are anxious that outward marks of such distinction should go with them. This is undoubtedly one of the grounds for tattooing the body. It follows that death is neither greatly feared nor desired; and often an old man, otherwise apparently cheerful and vigorous, will affirm that he is quite ready or even desirous to die.

The Ibans do not seem to have any conception corresponding to the Supreme Spirit of the races with which we have already dealt. Archdeacon Perham has given an account of the *Petara* of these people, showing how it is a conception of one God having very many manifestations and functions, each special function being conceived vaguely as that of an anthropomorphic deity. Among these are the mythical warrior-hero Klieng, and the God of War, Singalang Burong. As Archdeacon Perham has said, this last deity has a material animal form, namely, the white-headed hawk (*Bali Flaki* of the Kenyahs), and plays a somewhat similar part in their lives. Singalang Burong, on the other hand, is decidedly more anthropomorphic than Bali Flaki; he is probably generally conceived as a single being of human form living in a house such as the Ibans themselves inhabit; whereas Bali Flaki, even if sometimes conceived in the singular as the great Bali Flaki, is always a bird, although more human than the conceptions of the Kenyahs or Kayans. Corresponding with this increased importance of the anthropomorphic hawk-god, we find that for the

Ibans the virtue has departed out of individual hawks, and that they are no longer consulted for omens; for the Ibans say that Singalang Burong never leaves his house, and therefore they do not take omens from anyone but him. To the Ibans he is the chief or ruler over all the other omen-birds, who are merely his messengers. Thus he seems to have almost attained the supreme position accorded to Bali Penyalong by the Kenyahs.

Once a year a great feast is made for Singalang Burong, when the people sing for about ten or twelve hours, calling him and Klieng and all the *Petara* to the feast. (This is the ceremony known as *Gawai Burong*. After the first few hours it is a most tedious and monotonous performance.) In olden days Singalang Burong himself, it is said, used to come to these feasts, like an Iban in appearance and behaviour. At the end of the feast he would go out, take off his coat, and fly away in the form of a white-headed hawk. In recent years, however, he has not been seen. Singalang Burong is greater than Klieng, although it is Klieng that gives them heads in war. Singalang Burong married an Iban woman, Kachindai Lanai Pantak Girak, and he gave all his daughters in marriage to the omen-birds. Dara-Inchin-Tembaga-Monghok-Chelabok married the tiny woodpecker Katupong; Dara-Selaka-Utih - Nujut married Mambuas; Pingai - Tuai - Nadai - Mertas-Indu-Moa-Puchang-Penabas married the beautiful scarlet-breasted trogan Bragai; Indu-Langgu-Katubgsong-Ngumbai-Dayang-Katupang-Bunga-Nketai married the larger red-breasted trogan Papau; and lastly, Indu-Bantok-Tinchin-Mas-Ndu-Pungai-Lelatan-Pulas married the little brown woodpecker Kotok. He had also one son, Aji-Melieng (the names being carried on *ad inf.*), who married the daughter of Pulang Gana, the god of agriculture, her name being Indu-Kachanggut-Rumput-Melieng-Kapayan.

To hear an Iban unhesitatingly rattle off these sonorous names, while an accomplice confirms his accuracy by short vocables, is to learn much, and to be amused more.

The Kayans believe in the reincarnation of the soul, although this view hardly squares with their belief in the life in another world. It is generally held that the soul of a grandfather may pass into one of his grandchildren, and an old man will try to secure the passage of his soul to a favourite grandchild by holding it above his head from time to time. They, and most of the other peoples, believe that the human soul may be reincarnated in the body of almost any animal; but opinions in regard to this matter are very vague.

Among the Kayans and other peoples sceptics are to be found, and, as no inquisitorial methods are in vogue among them, such persons will on occasion give expression to their doubts about the accepted dogmas, although speech about such topics is generally repressed by some touch of awe. I myself actually heard a man argue that a man cannot continue to exist after death, for, said he, if men and women still lived after death, some of those who have been very fond of their children would surely return to see them, and would be in some way perceived by the living. Speculation, however, rarely goes beyond the fatalistic "*Nusi jam?*" ("Who knows?") with which such discussions commonly terminate.

CHAPTER III

THE HAWK, THE PIG, AND OTHERS

Bali Flaki—Taking omens and consulting the hawks—*Isit*, the spider-
hunter—The trogan and the woodpecker—*Laki Neho*, the brown
hawk—A witness and bearer of messages—The orang-utan and
gibbon—The domestic pig: a giver of information and omens on
many occasions—Similar use of the domestic fowl—An interesting
ceremony.

ANIMALS, both wild and domesticated, take an important place in a Bornean's life : those of greatest influence
are, it will be understood, the omen-birds, among whom
the common white-headed carrion kite (*Bali Flaki*) and
other hawks are by far the most important. The Kenyahs
especially respect this bird ; and not only do they take
omens from him, but on the return from a successful
warlike expedition they offer him pieces of the enemy's
flesh, which they fix on poles before each Long House,
as a thank-offering. In actual fact it seldom occurs that a
hawk eats these pieces of flesh, but that does not seem to be
expected.

Bali Flaki is also consulted before sowing and harvesting
the rice crop, but besides being appealed to publicly on
behalf of the whole community, his aid may be sought
privately by any man who wishes to injure another.
When a new Long House is built, a wooden image of
Bali Flaki with wings extended is put up before it, and an
offering of mixed food is put on a little shelf before the
image, and at times, especially if good omens have been
obtained, it is offered eggs, fowls, or small pigs or bits of
the flesh of fowls smeared with pig's blood. If the people
have good luck in their new house they renew the image ;
but if not, they usually allow it to fall into decay. Even

Kenyahs taking omens.

A Klemantan youth making an offering to the gods after recovery from sickness.

when a man is sitting down to a meal out of doors and he espies a hawk in the heavens, he will throw a morsel of food towards it, calling on the bird's name.

During a formal consultation of the hawks the women are sent to their rooms; but many women keep in the cubicles in which they sleep a wooden image of the bird with a few feathers stuck upon it. If the woman falls sick she takes one of these feathers and, waving it to and fro, says, " Tell the spirit that is making me sick that I have a feather of Bali Flaki." When she recovers her health the credit goes to Bali Flaki, and thank-offerings are made to him at the family altar.

Bali Flaki has a high standing among the Kenyahs: he is considered as a help and guide, but not exactly as one of the great Spirits, such as some other tribes hold him to be; he is rather considered as a messenger or intermediary between man and the Supreme Being. They would not themselves kill such a hawk, but they would not resent his death at the hands of an outsider, if, for instance, one stole a European's chickens. Such a bird would be regarded as one untrue to his class, a low fellow, an outsider, and a cad.

Certain secondary omen-birds also are observed by the Kenyahs. When favourable omens have been given by the hawks, a prominent man is always sent out to sit on the river bank beside a small fire and watch for these supplementary omens. Such are, especially, the movements and cries of the three species of the spider-hunter, known as *Isit*, and generally supposed to modify the omens given by the hawks. It is a particularly good omen to see such a bird on the left when a river is being crossed. In such a case each man of the party lights a cigarette (in order that he may have his own small fire) and murmurs a formula of imploration. After *Isit* has been seen on the left, it is propitious to see him once again cross the river on the right side.

Next in importance to the spider-hunters are the two

varieties of the trogan. The Borneans like to hear the melodious notes of this scarlet-breasted bird calling quietly while he sits on a tree to their left; if he is on their right, the omen is slightly less favourable. On hearing the trogan's call, they at once " adopt " it, as they say, by shouting friendly greetings to the bird, and by stopping to light a fire just as in the case of *Isit*.

Kieng, a small woodpecker, has two very distinct cries, one of which is of good, the other of bad omen. If good omens have been obtained from hawks or spider-catchers, this bird is to be avoided, lest he should utter a note of evil omen ; and he is commonly kept off by various sorts of noises.

Other omen-birds of less importance are *Asi*, who warns them of difficulties in their path, and *Ukang*, whose note means good luck. *Telajan*, the crested rain-bird, announces good luck by its call and warns of serious labour difficulties also, such as the harvesting of the rice-crop.

Kong, a white-headed hornbill, gives omens of minor importance by his strange deep cry.

Bali Flaki of the Kenyahs has his counterpart among the Kayans in the larger dark-brown hawk called *Laki Neho*. Since, however, it is not possible to distinguish these two kinds when seen at a distance, the Kayans address all large hawks by this term. The functions and powers of *Laki Neho* seem to be almost identical with those of Bali Flaki. He too is a giver of omens and a bringer of messages to *Laki Tenangan*. It is said that he has a house covered with palm leaves and message sticks, placed in the highest tree-top, and beside a river, and that it has a landing-place on the bank like every Kayan house. *Laki Neho* has certain powers of his own ; for example, if a large branch were likely to fall on a Kayan boat travelling on the river he would prevent it, for *Laki Tenangan* long ago taught him how to do such things. When a Kayan is sick, he will first appeal to *Laki Neho*, but if he does not get well he appeals to *Laki Tenangan* directly, killing a pig or fowl, the spirit of which goes first to the house of *Laki Neho*, and then on to the more distant house of *Laki Tenangan*. In other cases a man suffering from a chronic disease may himself pray to *Laki Tenangan*. He lights a fire and kills a fowl, and perhaps a pig also, and calls upon *Laki Neho* to be his witness and messenger. He holds an egg in one hand and says, " This is for you to eat ; carry my message direct to *Laki Tenangan* that I may get well and live and bring up my children, who shall be taught my occupations and the true customs of the people." A fire is then lighted (hawks being attracted by smoke) to make *Laki Neho* warm and energetic.

Certain other creatures are held in some sort of respect. The Kenyahs, for instance, like many other tribes, are more or less afraid of offending the orang-utan (*Maias*), or the long-nosed *Nasalis* monkey, and are very careful not to look one straight in the face, or to laugh at its antics. One of the Kenyah tribes takes the gibbon as a protector, and his effigy is carved on the cross-beams of the house. I was told by the chief of this house that when these beams are put up, it is customary to kill a pig, and divide its flesh among the workmen, no woman being allowed to come into the house until this has been done. This tribe will never kill a gibbon, although others kill and, probably, eat it.

Some other creatures are respected, certain snakes being avoided as unpropitious, and not even being killed ; while a certain kind of civet-cat is supposed to give warnings of danger.

From the sublime we pass to the ridiculous. All the people of the interior except the Punans keep numerous domestic pigs, which roam beneath and about the house, picking up what garbage they can find to eke out the scanty meals of rice-dust and chaff given them by the women. These creatures apparently never take to the jungle, although they are not confined in any way.

The domestic pig is not treated with any show of reverence, but rather with the greatest contumely, and yet it plays a part in almost all religious ceremonies, and before it is slaughtered explanations are always offered to it, and it is assured that it is a trusted messenger. It is probably true that Bali Penyalong is never addressed without the slaughter of one or more pigs, and also that no domestic pig is ever slaughtered without being charged beforehand with some message or prayer to Bali Penyalong, which its spirit may carry up to him. But the most important function of the pig is the giving of information as to the future course of events by means of the markings on its liver.

On particularly important occasions, such as the making of war or peace, when guidance as to the future is needed, a pig is caught by the young men of the house, and is brought and laid, with its feet lashed together, before the chief in the great gallery of the house. The more important the ceremony, the larger and the more numerous are the pigs selected as victims. An attendant hands a burning brand to the chief, and he, stooping over the pig, singes a few of its hairs, and then, addressing the pig as " Bali Bouin," and gently punching it behind the shoulder, pours out a rapid flow of words. The substance of his address is a prayer to Bali Penyalong for guidance as to the enterprise being undertaken, and an injunction to the soul of the pig to carry the prayer to Bali Penyalong.

Sometimes more than one chief will address one pig in this way; then, when the prayers are concluded, some follower plunges a spear into the heart or throat of the pig, and rapidly opens its belly in the middle line, drags out the liver and lays it on a leaf or platter with the underside uppermost, and so carries it to the chief or chiefs. The elders of the house now crowd round and consult as to the significance of the appearances presented by the underside of the liver. While spots, ulcers, and nodules in any part betoken future evils for the people of that part, a whole clean, healthy liver means good fortune and happiness for all concerned. The omens thus obtained are held to be the answer vouchsafed by Bali Penyalong to the prayers carried to him by the spirit of the pig.

It is obvious that this system of interpretation, which is common to nearly all the peoples, gives much room for the operation of prejudice, suggestion, and ingenuity; and the unanimity commonly reached is little less than surprising.

After any ordinary ceremony the body of the pig is usually divided among the people, and by them cooked and eaten without further ceremony. But when a war-expedition is contemplated, the bodies of the pigs are fixed upon tall stakes beside the altar-post of Bali Penyalong and there left; either as offerings to the hawks or to Bali Penyalong, or (perhaps) because they are very small and in some sense too holy to be used as food after being used in such rites. It is noticeable that Kenyahs never offer grown pigs, but only small ones.

Generally it may be said that Kenyahs do not kill domestic pigs simply and solely for the sake of food. The killing of a pig is always the occasion for, or occasioned by, some religious rite. It is true that on the arrival of honoured guests a pig is usually killed and given to them for food; but its spirit is then always charged with some message to Bali Penyalong, it being alleged that when a pig's spirit comes to Bali Penyalong, he is offended if it brings no message from those who killed the pig, and he sends it back to carry off their souls.

Pigs are killed on many other occasions; thus, on returning from a successful attack on enemies, one is usually killed for each family of the household, and a piece of its flesh is put up on a pole before the house; and in case of the severe illness of any person of high social standing, pigs are usually killed, and friendly chiefs come from distant parts, bringing with them sacrificial pigs and fowls to aid in restoring the sick person to health. On

Q

the death of a chief, too, a great feast is made, and many pigs are slaughtered, and their jaw-bones are hung up on the tomb. A pig is sometimes used in the ceremony by which a newly-made peace is sealed between tribes hitherto at blood-feuds, but a fowl is more commonly used.

The wild pig abounds in the forest and is hunted by the Kenyahs, and when brought to bay by the dogs is killed with spears, and is eaten without ceremony or compunction by all classes. It is never used as messenger to the gods, and its liver is never consulted. The lower jaws of all wild pigs that are killed are cleaned and hung up together in the house, for it is believed that if these should be lost or in any way destroyed the dogs would cease to hunt.

The domestic fowl is seldom killed for food, and its eggs can hardly be reckoned as a regular article of diet, though there is no prejudice against eating them. Fowls are kept in the main for ceremonial purposes, and their use as a food is of very secondary importance. They are killed also on many of the occasions on which pigs are sacrificed, and their blood may be poured upon the altar-posts of Bali Penyalong. It would seem, in fact, that fowls and pigs are to some extent interchangeable equivalents for sacrificial purposes. Perhaps the most important occasion on which the fowl plays a part is the performance of the rite by which a blood-feud is finally wiped away, but even in this case the life of a tiny chick will suffice.

It seems clear that the fowl, like the pig, is used as a messenger sent by man to the Supreme Spirit. In most cases when a fowl is slaughtered in the course of a ceremony, it is first waved over the heads of the people taking part in it, and its blood is afterwards sprinkled upon them.

In the blood-brotherhood ceremony, when each of the two men drinks or smokes in a cigarette a drop of the other's blood drawn with a bamboo-knife, a fowl is in many cases waved over them and then killed, and occasionally a pig also is killed. After going through this ceremony a man is safe from all the members of the household to which his blood-brother belongs; and in the case of two chiefs all the members of either household are bound to those of the other by a sacred tie.

When the belly of a fowl is opened there are prominent two curved portions of the gut. These are sometimes examined before the planting of rice, and also before attempting to " catch " the soul of a sick man. If the parts are much curved, it is a good omen; if straight or but slightly curved, the omen is unfavourable.

Some account of a ceremony which took place many years ago may be of interest. In the evening there was serious business on hand. Two chiefs, who had been burned out of their homes in the Rejang district by order of the Government, had settled themselves with their people in the Baram district. They had made a provisional peace with the Kayans some years before, but the final ceremony was to be performed that evening. The two chiefs of the immigrants, who had remained hitherto in a remote part of the house, seated themselves at one side, and the Kayan chiefs at the other, and Tama Bulan [1] and ourselves between the two parties. First, presents of iron were exchanged. In the old days costly presents of metal-work used to be given; but, as this led sometimes to renewed disputes, the Government had forbidden the giving, in such ceremony, of presents of a greater value than two dollars. So now old sword-blades were given, and the other essential part of the present was proportionately reduced from a full-grown fowl to a tiny chick. After much preliminary talking, two chicks were brought and a bundle of old sword-blades, which Tama Bulan, in his character of peacemaker, carries with him whenever he travels abroad. A chief of either party took a chick and a sword and presented them to the other. Then one led his men a little apart and began to rattle off an invocation beginning, " O sacred (Bali) Chick," snipped off its head with the sword, and with the bloody blade smeared

[1] See p. 151.

the right arm of his followers as they crowded round. The old fellow kept up the stream of words until every man was smeared ; and then they all stamped together on the floor, raising a great shout. Then the other party went through a similar performance ; and the peace being thus formally ratified, we sat down to cement it still further by a friendly drinking bout.

CHAPTER IV

THE CROCODILE AND OTHER FAMILIAR CREATURES

The crocodile treated with politeness—Not to be disturbed in his natural
state—Crocodile into man—The story of Silau—Klemantan ceremonies—A crocodile-charmer—The crocodile and the rice-crop—
The village dog—Deer and cattle—The tiger-cat—The name of a
dog as an oath—Superstitions as to deer.

THE crocodile, which can hardly be considered a
"friend of man," is yet regarded by all the races of
Sarawak with politeness and even a show of affability.
He is very much feared and is not mentioned by name,
especially if one be in sight, and is referred to as "*Laki*"
("old chief" or "grandfather"); but the fear is rather
a superstitious dread than the apprehension of being
seized by the creature. Local crocodiles are regarded as
more especially friendly, in spite of the fact that members
of their households are occasionally taken by crocodiles.

When Kenyahs go a journey into strange rivers or to
the lower part of their own river, they fear the strange
crocodiles of these waters, because they are unknown to
them, and any one of them might easily be mistaken by
the crocodiles for someone who has done them an injury.
Some Kenyahs tie the red leaves of the *Dracæna* below
the prow or stern of their boat whenever they go far from
home, believing that this protects them from all danger
of attack by crocodiles.

The attitude of the Kayan towards the crocodile is similar
to that of the Kenyahs. The creature is practically never
killed, except in revenge. In such cases, various attempts
are made to lure the offender to the shore, or the surface
of the water. One such method is rather of the "Dilly,
Dilly" order, the crocodile being invoked to come out,

because he has to be killed in any case : by another, he is conjured by charms and incantations : there is in either case a feeling that he must not be disturbed in his natural element.

Crocodiles were formerly considered as a sort of guardian-angel ; and clay images of him were set up to drive away evil spirits. But even to-day his affinity with man is very close. A crocodile may become a man ; and, *per contra*, a man (in a dream) may be asked by a crocodile to become his blood-brother : ceremonies are gone through, names are exchanged (still in the dream) and the man is immune from harm by crocodiles.

The most intimate relations with the crocodiles seem to be those of the Klemantans. One group, the Long Patas, claim the crocodile as a near relative. The story goes that a certain man named Silau became a crocodile. He was afflicted with itch, and he scratched himself till he bled and became rough all over. Then his feet began to look like a crocodile's tail ; as the change crept up from his feet to his body, he called out to his relatives that he was becoming a crocodile, and made them swear that they would never kill any crocodile. Many of the tribe about this period knew that Silau became a crocodile ; and stories are told how they saw him and spoke to him, and how his teeth and tongue were always like those of a man. On one occasion a man was roasting a pig on the river bank : he left it for a moment, and Silau seized it and divided it among the other crocodiles, who greatly enjoyed it. In return for this, Silau promised that he would give a sign to his human relatives by which the crocodiles might always be able to recognise them. He told them that they must tie leaves of the *Dracæna* on the bows of their boats, so that the crocodiles might know with whom they were dealing. This is done regularly by the tribe. If, as sometimes happens, one of them is taken by a crocodile, they attribute this breach of good faith to the fact that they have intermarried to some extent with Kayans and others. When they come upon a crocodile lying on the river bank, they say, " Be easy, grandfather, don't mind us, you are one of us." Some of the Klemantans will not knowingly eat anything that has been cooked in a vessel which previously may have come in contact with the flesh of a crocodile, and it is said that if a man should do so unwittingly his body would become covered with sores.

The Orang Kaya Tumonggong of the Tutu River [1] told me that in olden times the crocodiles used frequently to speak to his people, warning them of danger, but that now they never speak, and he supposes that their silence is due to the fact that his people have constantly inter-married with other tribes. The Long Pata tribe, who take omens from crocodiles, frequently carve a crocodile's head as the figure-head for a war-canoe.

The Batu Blah people (Klemantans) on returning from an expedition make a huge effigy of a crocodile out of cooked rice : they put fowls' eggs in its head for eyes and bananas for teeth, and cover it with scales made from the stem of the banana plant. When all is ready it is transfixed with a wooden spear, and the chief cuts off its head with a wooden sword. Then pigs and fowls are slaughtered and cooked, and eaten with the rice from the rice-crocodile, the chiefs eating the head and the common people the body. Tama Puit, the chief of these people, could give me no explanation as to the meaning of this ceremony : he merely says they do it because it is an old custom.

One community of Klemantans, the Lelak people, lived recently on the banks of a lake much infested with croco-diles. Their chief was reputed to be able to induce them to leave the lake, to achieve which he would stand in his boat waving a bundle of charms, including among other things a tiger's tooth and a misshapen wild boar's tusk, and then address the crocodiles politely in their own language. He would then allow his boat to float out of the lake into

[1] A chief.

the small river, and the crocodiles would follow him and pass on down into the main river.

Many, probably all, Klemantans put a wooden image of the crocodile over the altars which stand in front of their houses, and the Berawans carve the figure-head of their large boats in the form of a crocodile with gaping jaws.

Some of the Muruts make an effigy of the crocodile from clay for use on the celebration of a successful expedition.

Among the Ibans a special deity or spirit, Pulang Gana, presides over the rice-crops, but the crocodile also is intimately concerned with the planting of crops and the selection of suitable land. The Ibans say that *Klieng* (their War God) first advised them to make friends with Pulang Gana, a *Petara* who gave them the seed-grains of the rice. Pulang Gana first taught them to plant rice and instructed them in the following rites, which they follow to this day.

On going to a new district they make a life-size image of a crocodile in clay on the land chosen for the rice-farm. The image is made by some elder of good repute and known for his skill in farming. Then for seven days the house is under special restrictions—no one may enter the house or do anything in it except eat and sleep. At the end of the seven days they visit the clay crocodile and give it a cloth, food, and rice-spirit, and kill a fowl and a pig before it. The ground round about the image is kept carefully cleared and is held sacred for the next three years, for if this is not done the crops are likely to be poor. If the rites are duly performed, it is held that the crocodile will assist in driving away various pests; but since, simultaneously, portions of the jungle are burnt and cleared, the power of the image may not be the dominant factor.

An animal less spiritually but more intimately connected with the Borneans is the dog. In every Long House are large numbers of dogs, which vary a good deal in size and colour, but roughly resemble large, mongrel-bred, smooth-haired terriers or the dingo of Australia. Each family owns several, who, though they are fed with rice in the morning or evening, seem to be always hungry. The best of them are used for hunting; but besides these there is always to be seen in a Kenyah village a number of quite useless, ill-fed, ill-tempered curs; for no Kenyah dare kill a dog, however much he may wish to be rid of it. Still less, of course, will he eat the flesh. The dogs prowl about, in and around the house, much as they please, but are not treated with any particular respect. When a dog intrudes where he is not wanted it is usual to click with the tongue at him, and this is usually enough to make him pass on; but blows with a stick follow quickly if the animal does not obey. Except in the case of good hunting dogs, they display but little affection for them, and they do not like children to touch or play with dogs, but of course this cannot altogether be prevented.

One young Kenyah chief, on being questioned, said that the reason they will not destroy their dogs is that they are like children, and eat and sleep together with men in the same house; and he added that, should a man kill a dog, he would almost certainly go mad.

If a dog dies in a Kenyah house, the men push the carcase out of the house and into the river with long poles, and will on no account touch it with their hands. The spot on the floor on which the dog died is fenced round with mats for some few days in order to prevent the children walking over it.

Neither Kayans nor Kenyahs have any domestic cattle, and in their districts the buffalo is not found. Moreover, very few people of the upper class will eat the flesh of wild cattle or deer, believing that, if they did so, they would be violently ill and would spit blood. Some of the lower-class people of these tribes may eat deer or horned cattle, but to do so they must remove to a distance from the Long House. Restrictions in this matter are more strictly observed in the case of pregnant or ailing women, who are not even allowed to touch or be brought near articles made of leather or horn.

The war-coats of adults are usually made of the skin of goats or deer, because the skin is the most serviceable, and any man may wear such a war-coat. But when a man has a young son who has not yet been initiated, he is particularly careful to avoid contact with any part of a deer, lest through such contact he should transmit to his son in any degree the timidity of that animal.

The only large species of the *Felidæ* that occurs in Borneo is the tiger-cat. Kenyahs will not eat it, as men of other tribes do, but they will kill it; and they fashion its handsome spotted skin into war-coats. Such coats are worn only by men who have been on the war-path and are well-tried warriors. The upper canine teeth of this animal are much prized as ornaments; and the name *Kuleh*, which signifies this animal, is sometimes given to a boy, as also the name *Linjau* (the real tiger).

The true tiger does not occur in Borneo, and it is very doubtful whether it ever was a native of the island. Nevertheless the Kenyahs know it by name and by reputation, and a few skins are in the possession of chiefs. No ordinary man, but only a distinguished and elderly chief, would venture to wear such a skin as a war-coat, or even to touch it. These skins have been brought from other lands by Malay traders, and it is probable that whatever knowledge of the tiger the Kenyahs possess has come from the same source. Kayans will not allow a claw, tooth, or the skin of a tiger to come into their house.

The beliefs and customs of the Kayans with regard to deer, horned cattle, dogs, and the tiger-cat, are similar to those of the Kenyahs, save that they will not kill the last of these. They are perhaps more strict in the avoidance of deer and cattle. One old chief, who had been ailing for a long time, hesitated to enter the Resident's house because he saw a pair of antlers hanging up there. When he entered he asked for a piece of iron, and on returning home he killed a fowl and a pig, and submitted to the process of having his soul caught by a *Dayong*, lest it should have incurred some undefined injury in the neighbourhood of the antlers.

Like the Kenyahs, the Kayans entertain a superstitious dread of the Maias and the long-nosed monkey, but the *Dok* (*Macacus nemestrinus*), the cocoa-nut monkey of Malaya, has special relation to them. It is very common in their district, but the upper-class Kayans will kill it only when it is stealing their rice-crop; and they will never eat it as other peoples do. There is a vague belief that it is a blood relative.

Klemantans use the domestic pig and fowl as sacrificial animals just as the Kenyahs and Kayans do, but many of these widely scattered tribes have the same superstitious dread of killing a dog. One group of them, the Melanos, use a dog in taking their most solemn oath, and sometimes one is killed in the course of the ceremony. Nowadays, instead of the dog being killed, the end of its tail may be cut off, the man taking the oath licking the blood from the stump; this is considered a most binding and solemn form of oath, and is spoken of as *Koman asu*, i.e. " the eating of the dog."

Most Klemantans will kill and eat both deer and cattle. But there are exceptions to this rule. Thus Damong, the chief of a Melano household, together with all his people, will not kill or eat the barking deer (*Cervulus muntjac*), alleging that an ancestor of his became a deer of this kind, and that, since they cannot distinguish this incarnation of his ancestor from other individuals, they must abstain from killing all such deer. A similar superstition has been found among some of the Land Dayaks. I have also heard of an instance in which one of these people refused to use his cooking-pot because a Malay who had borrowed it had used it for cooking the flesh of deer of this species. This superstition is curious, because many of these people have been converted to Islam in recent years. On another occasion a chief resolutely refused to proceed on a journey through the jungle when a mouse-deer (*Plandok*) crossed his path; he will not eat this deer at any time, and seemed to consider it sacrosanct.

The people of Miri, who are Mohammedan Melanos, claim to be related to the large deer, *Cervus equinus*, and some of them to the muntjac deer also. These people live in a country in which deer of all kinds abound, and they always make a clearing of the jungle around a tomb. On such a clearing grass grows up rapidly, and so the spot becomes attractive to deer as a grazing ground; and it seems not improbable that it is through frequently seeing deer about the tombs that they have come to believe that their dead relatives become deer, or that they are in some other way closely related to the deer.

The Bakongs, another group of Melanos, hold a similar belief with regard to the bear-cat (*Arctictis*) and the various species of *Paradoxurus*; in this case the origin of the belief is admitted by them to be the fact that, on going to their graveyards, they often see one of these beasts coming out of a tomb. These tombs are roughly constructed wooden coffins raised a few feet only from the ground, and it is probable that these carnivores make their way into them, in the first place, to devour the corpse, and that they make use of them as lairs.

CHAPTER V

MEDICINE AND MAGIC

An interesting pharmacopœia—Crude surgery—The *Dayong*—" Soul-catching "—Extracting pain—The value of suggestion—Purification —Madness—Exorcism—The *Bayoh* ceremony—The invocation— The patient's part—A *Dayong's* explanation of the ceremony—The entry of the spirit " like a bright light "—Some elaborate rites— Iban medicine-men—*Tepang*—Black magic—The *Batang pra*—An Iban curse—Charms—The *Siap*, a household bunch—Personal *siap* —The *Empugau* of the Ibans—Love charms.

SEVERAL very different systems for the cure of sickness are practised among the Kayans, the number of which would seem to imply very different theories of the cause of disease ; but the various systems are held in honour by all the people, and one or the other is applied according to the indications of each case. Thus, bodily injuries received accidentally or in battle are treated surgically by cupping, splints, bandaging, and so forth. Familiar disorders, such as malarial fever, are treated medically, *i.e.* by rest and drugs. Cases of severe pain of unknown origin and madness are generally attributed to the malign influence of a *Toh*, and the method of treatment is usually that of extraction. Of herbs they have a certain knowledge, and use them commonly. They administer as an aperient a decoction of the leaves of a plant called *Orobong*, which is allowed to grow for this purpose on their farms. The root of the wild ginger plant is used both internally and for external application. As liniments a variety of vegetable products are used ; the basis most in request for these is the fat of the python and of other snakes, but wild boar's fat is more common, as it is easier to obtain.

The pharmacopœia of the Bornean is limited, but contains some interesting items. Kayan mothers, for instance, treat colic in their children by chewing the dried root of a creeper known as *pado tana* and areca nut, and then spitting out the juice on to the belly of the patient. A more scientific remedy is that used by the Punans of a portion of the *Ipoh* tree (the poison used on their darts) as an internal remedy for fever, and also to heal snake-bites and festering wounds. This may possibly be an example of unconscious homœopathy; on the other hand, it is quite possible that the Punans have acquired immunity from the poison through constantly handling it. It is at least certain that the Punans handle their poisoned darts with much more recklessness than the other peoples.

The surgery is even cruder. Broken limbs are bound round with neat splints made of thin parallel slips of bamboo, but hardly any effort is made to bring the broken ends of the bones into their proper positions or to reduce dislocations. Abscesses are not usually opened with the knife, but are rather encouraged to come to a head, and are then opened by pressure. A bad boil or superficial abscess is treated with a cold poultice of chopped leaves and gums from forest trees, and is protected from blows and friction by a small cage of basket-work made of slips of rattan. Festering wounds are usually dressed with the chewed leaves or the juice of the tobacco plant, or are washed with a solution of common salt. But a clean wound is merely bound up with a rag; or if there is much hæmorrhage, wood ashes are first applied, this being the only method they know to stop bleeding.

Headache is treated by tugging the hair of the scalp in small bundles in systematic order. Massage of the muscles is practised for the relief of pain, and is also used in cases of obstinate constipation. Bodily aches and fatigue are relieved by pulling and bending the parts of the limbs until all the joints crack in turn.

Cupping is, perhaps, the most frequently practised

surgical operation. Severe internal bruising from falls or heavy blows is the usual occasion. The operation consists in scratching the skin with the point of a knife, and then applying the open end of a bamboo-pipe previously heated over a fire. The pipe is a piece of bamboo some five or six inches in length and an inch or rather more in diameter, having a thin, smooth edge. In a case of extensive bruising several of these may be applied simultaneously. Since this operation, like tattooing, involves the shedding of blood, some small offering, such as a few beads, must be made to the patient by the operator.

In cases of severe maladies of mysterious origin which seem to threaten to end mortally, the theory generally adopted is that the patient's soul has left his body, and the treatment indicated is therefore an attempt to persuade the soul to return. This among the Kayans and Klemantans is the work of the professional soul-catcher, or *Dayong*, usually a woman who has served a considerable period of apprenticeship with some older member of the profession. Unlike the custom with regard to tattooing, the relatives of the sick person usually prefer to call in a *Dayong* from some other village. He, or she, is expected to make a diagnosis and to determine upon the line of treatment to be followed. If he decides that the soul of the patient has left his body, and has made some part of the journey towards the abode of departed souls, his task is to fall into a trance and to send his own soul to overtake that of his patient and to persuade it to return. This ceremony is usually performed by torchlight in the presence of a circle of interested relatives and friends, the patient being laid in the midst in the long public gallery of the house.

The *Dayong*, his face concealed by a formidable mask, struts to and fro, chanting a traditional form of words well known to the people, who join in the chorus at the close of each phrase, responding with the words " *Bali-Dayong*," *i.e.* " Oh, powerful *Dayong*," a sort of " Amen " added to the incantation. The chant with which the *Dayong* begins his operations is essentially a prayer for help addressed to *Laki Tenangan*, or, in case of a woman, to *Doh Tenangan* also.

The *Dayong* may or may not fall and lie inert upon the ground in the course of his trance; but throughout the greater part of the ceremony he continues, if not wearing a mask, to chant with closed eyes, describing with words and gestures the doings of his own soul as it follows and eventually overtakes that of the patient. When this point is reached his gestures generally express the difficulty required to induce the soul to return; at which point the anxious relatives usually bring out gongs or other articles of value and deposit them as possible additions to the *Dayong's* fee. Thus stimulated, he usually succeeds in leading back the soul towards the patient's body. One feature of the ceremony, not quite logically consistent with its general scheme, is that the *Dayong* takes in his hand a sword and, glancing at the polished blade with a startled air, seems, from time to time, to catch in it a glimpse of the wandering soul. The next step is to restore the soul to the body. The *Dayong* comes out of his trance with the air of one suddenly transported from distant scenes, and usually exhibits in his palm, or on the top of a short section of a wild ginger stem, some small living creature, or it may be a tiny piece of wax or a grain of rice, a small peeble or a bit of wood, in which the captured soul is in some sense contained. This he places on the top of the patient's head, and by rubbing causes the invisible soul to pass into the head, the small object which contained the soul being allowed to drop away out of sight. The soul having been thus restored to the body, it is necessary to prevent it from escaping again: this is done by tying a strip of palm-leaf about the patient's wrist.

A fowl is then killed, or, in very severe cases of sickness, a pig, and its blood is sprinkled or wiped by means of the sword or knife upon this confining bracelet. In mild cases the fowl may be merely waved over the head of the patient without being killed. The *Dayong* then gives directions as to the *malan* to be observed by the patient, especially in regard to articles of diet, and retires, leaving his fee to be sent after him.

This catching of souls is practised in very similar fashion among all the peoples of Borneo, even by the Punans, though the details of the procedure differ slightly from tribe to tribe.

No doubt ceremony does make strongly for the recovery of the patient, since it inspires him with hope and confidence. But it can hardly stave off death. If, therefore, in spite of the operations of one soul-catcher, the patient's strength still sinks, some other practitioner is usually called in for consultation. In the case of a chief the help of three or even four may be invoked, and the ceremony of catching the soul may be repeated again and again with greater elaboration of detail, and may be prolonged with brief interruptions through many hours and even days.

The operation of extracting pain is usually performed by a *Dayong*, and is applied more particularly in cases in which localised pain is a prominent feature of the disorder. The *Dayong* comes provided with a short tube, made from a plant of the wild ginger family. After inquiring of the patient the locality of his pains, he holds up the polished blade of a sword, and, gazing at it as one seeing visions, he sings a long incantation, the public joining in in a sort of chorus or refrain.

During the singing of a number of verses in this way the *Dayong* seems to become more and more distraught; and when the singing ceases he behaves in a strange manner, which strikes the attendant crowd with awe, starting suddenly and making strange clucking noises. He then produces the tube, and, pressing one end upon the skin of the part indicated by the patient as the seat of the pain, sucks strongly, and, presently withdrawing it, blows out of

R

it on to his palm a small black pellet, which moves mysteri-
ously upon his hand as he exhibits it to the patient and his
friends as the cause of the pain. If the patient has com-
plained of more than one seat of pain, the operation is
repeated. It only remains for the *Dayong* to return
gradually with violent contortions to his normal state, and
to receive his fee, which properly consists of the sword
used by him in the ceremony, and a live fowl. The whole
procedure is very well calculated to secure therapeutic
effects by suggestion. The singing and the atmosphere
of awe engendered by the *Dayong's* reputation and his
uncanny behaviour prepare the patient, the suction applied
through the tube gives him the impression that something
is being drawn through his skin, and the skilful production of the mysterious black pellet completes the
suggestive process, under the influence of which, no doubt,
many an ache or pain has suddenly disappeared. The
black pellets are, in point of fact, bits of dark beeswax
which, carried upon the finger-nails of the *Dayong*, are
surreptitiously introduced by him into his mouth as
required before being blown through the tube ; while the
mysterious movements of the pellets upon his palm are
produced by the help of short fine hairs. Thus, while
a certain amount of deception is undoubtedly present, the
general effect cannot be said to be fraudulent. After all,
Harley Street is not entirely contemptuous of suggestion.

The use of superstition is even better exhibited by
the manner in which many of the sea-coast tribes
seek to drive away epidemics. One or more rough
human images are carved from the pith of the sago-
palm and placed on a small raft, boat, or full-rigged ship,
together with rice and other food carefully prepared.
The boat is decorated with ribbons made of the leaves and
with the blossoms of the areca palm, and allowed to float
out to sea with the ebb-tide in the belief or hope that it
will carry the sickness with it.

On the other hand, precautionary or prophylactic

measures are common, especially with reference to articles of food. When certain maladies are suspected, particular kinds of food are forbidden ; and it is found that a refusal to follow the doctor's orders usually takes the form of wasting sickness with pains in the head, a chronic cough, dysentery, and spitting of blood. When a Kenyah has, even unintentionally, violated a rule of health, and incurred the penalty, he subjects himself to a process of purification. At break of day he, with other members of his family, descends to the brink of the river, bearing a chicken, a sword-blade, two frayed sticks, and a length of a spiky creeper known as *atat*. This latter is bent into the form of a ring, within which he takes his stand and awaits the appearance of the omen-bird *Isit*. When the bird appears and calls in reply, he pours out a long-winded address, charging him to convey to Bali Penyalong his prayer for recovery. He then snips off the head of the chicken, and wipes some of its blood on the frayed sticks and on the ring. This, with the chicken and the frayed sticks, is then lifted above his head by his attendants, and water is poured upon them from a bamboo, so that it drips from them on to his head. Eight times the ring is lifted up, and each time the pouring out of the water is repeated. Then, standing on the blade of the sword, he completes the rite by again addressing the omen-bird as before.

A similar rite of purification is practised by most of the other peoples. In some cases the principal feature of the rite of purification of a small child is being spat upon by the chief.

It may be broadly said that all these peoples are constantly on the alert to provide against unknown dangers ; that, having no definite theories of causation, they are apt to accept every hint of danger as due to outward influences, and to seek to avoid or to counteract these influences by every means that in any way suggests itself to their minds as possibly efficacious. Of such unknown dangers the worst is madness, which is supposed to be caused by various

evil spirits throwing themselves into mortals, devils with
red eyes which flash like lightning.

Madness, in Borneo, has one peculiar feature, probably
unknown elsewhere, that a sufferer may qualify as a
practitioner. For instance, if a woman (or more rarely a
man) is insane she is commonly urged to become a medicine woman, while admitting that she is possessed. If she
does this she herself may be healed and may at the same time
acquire the power of helping others to cast out devils.
She cannot, however, herself determine whether she can
become a medicine woman or not. She has to undergo, for
periods of eleven days, a series of tests lasting about a
month : these tests are designed partially to satisfy her
own people, partially to appease the devil. When she has
passed through these tests, she is supposed to be " in touch "
with the demons ; but, even so, she cannot infallibly
guess when a spirit has ceased to infest a person, for although an initiate can exorcise demons from her own
person, she cannot always do so from others.

The ceremonial connected with this belief is known as
Bayoh. This ceremony takes place preferably after a good
harvest, when an epidemic, supposedly due to the presence
of an evil spirit, has fallen upon the house. Offerings of
eggs and fowls to the good spirits having proved fruitless,
a day is fixed for the *bayoh*, and a room is prepared for the
reception of the powerful spirits invited to the house.
Great tassels of white shavings are hung upon the walls,
a white cloth adorned with the blossoms of the areca
palm hides the rafters, and is spread out fanwise over the
doors and among the long strips of shavings. In one
corner a hollow cone of areca blossoms and shavings spread
over a framework of rattan is suspended from a rafter ;
and a model of a ship or raft is placed just outside an open
window. To give light—for the ceremony is an evening
one—candles made of beeswax are variously disposed.
At the appointed time brass dishes are put on the floor with
rice of many colours—yellow, red, and blue—spread in

patterns of crocodiles; popcorns of maize and rice, water for washing utensils, boxes of betel ready for chewing, tobacco, and cigarettes, to appease the varied appetites of the spirits invoked. Just after sundown the neighbours troop in and settle themselves round the room. Soon the house is full of people, the boys and old men contentedly chewing and smoking, the women retiring to the darker parts of the room to gossip. People of importance are received with civility, but without any definite ceremony. Arabian incense (which is used nowadays because the native *garu* wood has too high a value for export to be consumed at home) disperses a not unpleasant smell throughout the gathering. Then the fun begins, gongs and drums are struck, and the strains of music sound through the village. At intervals of a quarter of an hour every two hours, the monotonous melody proceeds until seven the next morning, to be resumed, in all probability, the next night for another twelve hours, and perhaps maintained night after night for a whole week.

In the middle of the room, and generally to the number of three are the medicine women, personalities usually more experienced than attractive, despite the gorgeous raiment with which they conceal their aged frames and the hawk-bells which jingle as they move. At first they collect round the earthenware censers to warm their hands. They then begin to step in time with the music and wave their arms, hissing loudly through their teeth the while, and occasionally breaking into a whistle. After a time they sit down and nod in time with the music, as though engaged in training the muscles of the neck. As the music of the drums and gongs goes faster, their loosened hair flies round with their heads. The whistling is varied by a chant known as *sadong*, in an ancient language now barely understood, which consists of short sentences such as : " Why do you speak ? Why are you such a long time ? As long as it takes a *pinang* (areca) nut to become old ? The fruit of the cocoanut has had time to ripen and drop.

Come to this country below the heavens. What do you wish ? What is your desire ? I have come to heal the sick one who lies on the floor, feeble and unable to rise, thin and shrivelled like a floating log. Have pity from your heart and prevent my soul from parting from my skin and my bones from withering. My sickness is heavy on me and I cannot fight against it."

One of the women now goes to the patient, who, clad in black, sits alone on a mat, and brings her a *pinang* blossom to hold, covering her head with a cloth. The unfortunate sick person is then brought to the hollow cone of shavings and seated within it ; it is then whirled round till the white strips and shreds of palm leaves rise like a ballet dancer's skirt. Gradually she is worked up to a frenzy, while, keeping time with the music, the medicine women sway before her and wag their heads significantly. Throughout the night this weird dancing, howling, whistling, and chanting go on. Then the medicine women are whirled round in the cone, and one by one fall into a swoon, to be recovered by fanning with the *pinang* blossom. They dance about and brush against the on-lookers as though unable to control their movements, and are only kept at a distance by finding handfuls of rice flung in their faces. The point of giddiness and hysteria eventually reached can only be compared with certain stages of drunkenness.

The outsider will find it difficult to detect much method in the madness, but on more sober occasions the performers can offer intelligible explanations of their behaviour. An account given by an old medicine woman at Niah, and confirmed by the man who conducts the ceremonies at the same village, shows that the part taken by the spirits is quite as definite as the performance of the exorcisers. Attracted by the music when the *bayoh* has begun, the followers of the chief evil spirits are said to gather round the house, and to ask the chief medicine woman why she has called them. She replies, " Tell your master that I have called you because there is a person here sick." They then go back and fetch the more powerful spirit whom they serve. This demon comes up from the sea to the *jong*, a small ship or raft that stands behind the house, and finds his way up the rope ladder. He asks the *bayoh* woman, " Why have you called me, mother ? " She answers, " I have called you because there is a sick person here, whom you can help. Try whether you can help him." If the demon finds the cure beyond his powers, he says, " I cannot help you ; get someone else," and the next night another one is invoked, until the evil spirit of the patient is cast out.

If after seven nights there is no improvement, the *bayoh* is stopped and medicines are tried again, but with little hope that they will do any good. One of the *bayohs* I saw at Niah was on behalf of a slightly mad woman, who became very violent during the performance. She was said by her relations to have become mad because she had entered the Mohammedan faith (of which they disapproved), and it was explained that the Melano demons had little or no power over the evil spirits of Islam. The poor woman was consequently put into stocks in her own room, and not long afterwards recovered.

When a powerful spirit comes into one of the medicine women, she feels its presence " like a bright light," but does not see its form. If it agrees to help, she goes on with the regular *bayoh*, and soon feels confident that she is able to make the patient well. She asks for rice and other food, and a spirit made from fruit, which she consumes to gratify the demon within her. She calls upon the people to see that the viands are good, but not from any selfish motive, for apparently she is not even aware that she is eating. The demon invoked to help calls out to the evil spirit in possession of the sick person, " Go or remain in this ship while I sit here. If you do not wish to stay here you can go to your native place, in the woods or the pools of the river." The evil spirit then goes from the patient into the basket prepared for his reception, and is then induced or ordered to depart by the demon. What remains of the food set apart for the spirit is scattered along the river. The *bayoh* is stopped, and thank-offerings are floated out to sea that the exertions of the supernatural powers may not have been in vain; sometimes these gifts are taken into the forest, where the hollow cone and raft are also placed or hung from a tree by the river.

The medicine women work for a fee, the amount of which may perhaps influence the length of the *bayoh*. Sometimes the ceremony is most gorgeous. A rattan swing, covered with a beautiful cloth, is provided for the women and the patient, with a platform near at hand to receive the evil spirit. Sometimes Ula Gemilang (the God of the Sea) himself is invoked. On these occasions the expenditure is profuse. A box is placed in the middle of the room with a handsome covering. The floor is covered with cloth of gold. There are seven candles in seven brass sticks, seven betel stands, and seven men carrying spears. When the god arrives, seven people carry the umbrella over his head. If everything is not perfectly satisfactory he demands through the medicine woman whose body he has occupied some expensive gift, and if this is refused she and her attendant women may fall in a dead faint. Eventually they recover, but there is now but little hope for the patient, for Gemilang is angry, and the only hope lies in the assistance of some minor power.

Among the Ibans medicine-men (known as *manang*) are more numerous than among the Kayans; they are more strictly professional in the sense that they do but little other work, depending chiefly on what they can earn by their treatment of disease and by other ways of practising upon the superstitions of their fellows. They generally work in groups of three or four, or more in cases of serious illness, and, with the imitativeness and disregard for tradition which is characteristic of the Iban, they have developed a great variety of procedures, into most of which the element of fraud enters to a much greater extent than into the practices of the other peoples. The Iban *manang* is usually covered with a skin disease and shirks the communal hard work of the village.

A peculiar and infrequent variety of the Iban *manang* is the *manang bali*. These are men who adopt and continuously wear woman's dress and behave in all ways like women, except that they avoid as far as possible taking any part in the work of the house. They claim to have been told in dreams to adopt this mode of life; they are employed for the same purpose as the more ordinary medicine-men, and practise similar methods.

Among the Ibans it is not hard to obtain a reputation for sorcery. There are believed to be many such, who work harm in many obscure ways, especially to health; but their procedures, which probably include poisoning, are not generally known, and, like the practices of our European witches in recent times, they probably have but little existence outside the timorous imagination of the public. Such persons are disliked and shunned, though not killed as they would have been among Kayans or Kenyahs. They are not professional sorcerers, *i.e.* their help is not called in by other persons who wish to work evil on their enemies, for others do not dare to do so.

Magic is an art practised by some of the coastal Klemantans, especially the Melanos and Kadayans; but among the Kayans and Kenyahs, the Punans and the Ibans it is in a neglected and backward state. The Kayans definitely discourage all magical practices except such as aim at the public benefit. There are no recognised magicians among them other than the *Dayongs*, who perform the functions of the priest and physician rather than those of the wizard or sorcerer.

A form of wizardry, which is supposed to be transmitted in certain families from generation to generation, is known as *tepang*. The head of such a man is supposed to leave his body at night and to wander about doing harm, especially to the crops. This power is passed on to a child of the family by the mother, who touches the cut edge of the child's tongue with her spittle. At the present time in Sarawak if a man accuses another of practising *tepang*, he is liable to be sued for libel.

The most important form of magic is one occasionally resorted to among all the peoples for the purpose of bringing about the death of a personal enemy. For this it is not usual to call in a practising magician. The attacking party retires secretly to a spot at the edge of a rice-field, or of some other clearing, where he can see a large expanse of sky and yet feel sure of being unobserved. Here he sets up the *batang pra*, two poles supported horizontally some six or eight feet above the ground, their ends resting on two vertical poles. A little figure of a man or woman (according to the sex of the desired victim), carved for the purpose out of soft wood, is fixed upright in the ground beneath the *batang pra*. This is called *tegulun kalingai usa*, " The reflected image of the body." The operator makes a fire beside the *tegulun*, digs a small hole in the ground, and fills it with water coloured with ferruginous earth, to represent *Bawang Daar*, the lake of blood. Sitting before it he scans the space of sky framed by the *batang pra*, searching for some hawk upon the wing. As soon as he sees a hawk within this area, he addresses it, waving in one hand a small frayed stick, and saying, " Put fat in the mouth of So-and-so," [1] and he puts a bit of pork fat into the mouth of the *tegulun*. Then saying, " Send him to *Bawang Daar*," he immerses the *tegulun* in the pool of red water ; and taking it out again he thrusts into it a little wooden spear. After this he buries the *tegulun* in a hole in the ground, covering it with earth. (Only people who die by violence or of some much-feared disease are normally buried in this fashion.) This done he keeps shouting to the hawk to go to the left, at the same time waving his stick in that direction. If the hawk passes out

[1] Fat is always put in the mouths of heads taken in battle.

of the area of operations towards the right, he knows that his attempt will not succeed, and he desists for the time being ; if it flies out to the left he knows that his arts will prevail, and he addresses the hawk as follows :—

" O Bali Flaki, go your way, let this man (*N or M*) die ; put him in the lake of blood, O Bali Flaki ; stab him in the chest, Bali Flaki ; put pig's fat in his mouth that he may die, to-morrow ; let him be killed by a falling tree, to-morrow ; let him die from a wound ; let him die by the hand of his enemy, to-morrow ; let him be drowned, to-morrow ; let him die of a deadly disease ; let him be caught by a crocodile ; let him die of pain in the head ; let him die of pain in the chest." It will be observed that the formula calls upon the hawks to give effect to the male-volent wishes, so that the operation is not one of direct magical or sympathetic action, but rather is one by which the aid of a higher power is invoked. This feature of the process renders it one which the strongest-minded cannot pooh-pooh.

With this comprehensive curse the rite is concluded and the vengeful man returns home and secretly observes his enemy. The latter may become aware that magic is being worked against him through dreaming that fat is put into his mouth ; and as he is almost certainly aware of the hatred of his enemy, it is not unlikely that such a dream will come to him. There can be no doubt that, if a man learns that he has been made the object of a magical attempt of this sort, he, in many cases, does suffer in health ; and it is probable that in some cases such know-ledge has proved fatal. If it is discovered that a man has attempted to injure another in this way, he falls into general reprobation, and, if the case can be proved against him, heavy damages in the form of pigs, gongs, or other valuables may be awarded by the house chief.

A curse is sometimes imposed without formality, and in the heat of the moment, in the face of an enemy. Under these circumstances the curse is usually muttered indistinctly, but seems then to work upon the victim all the more powerfully. The words used are similar to those of the curse written out above.

The Ibans have a characteristic but simple curse. If a man finds that someone has deposited dirt in or about his property or premises, he takes a few burning sticks and, thrusting them into the dirt, says, " Now let them suffer the pains of dysentery."

As regards "White Magic," charms are extensively used by all the peoples, except, partially, the Kayans. In every house is at least one bundle of charms, known as *Siap aioh* by the Kenyahs, by whom more importance is attached to them than by any of the other tribes. This bundle, which is the property of the whole household or village, generally contains hair taken from the heads that hang in the gallery; a crocodile's tooth; the blades of a few knives that have been used in special ceremonies; a few crystals or pebbles of strange shapes; pig's teeth of unusual shape (both wild and domestic); a fowl's feathers (these seem to be substitutes for Bali Flaki's feathers, which they would hardly dare to touch); stone axe-heads, called the teeth of Balingo; and palm leaves that have been put to ceremonial use.

The whole bundle, blackened with the smoke and dust of years, hangs in the gallery over the principal hearth beside the heads, usually in a wide-meshed basket. It constitutes the most precious possession of the household, being of even greater value than the heads. No one, not even the chief, willingly touches or handles the *siap*. When, therefore, it becomes necessary to touch the bundle, as in a move to a new house, some old man is specially told off for the duty; he who touches it brings upon himself the risk of death, for it is highly *parit* to touch it, *i.e.* strongly against custom, and therefore dangerous. Its function seems to be to bring good fortune of all kinds to the house; without it nothing would prosper, especially in warfare.

Many individuals keep a small private bunch of *siap*, made up of various small objects, of unusual forms, but generally without any human hair. These are said to be obtained through dreams. A man dreams of a gift of value, and then, on waking, observes some peculiar object, such as a quartz crystal. He takes it and hangs it above his sleeping-place; when going to bed he addresses it, saying that he desires a dream favourable to any business he happens to have in hand. If such a dream comes to him, the thing becomes *siap*; but if his dreams are inauspicious, the object is rejected. Since no one can come in contact with another man's *siap* without risk of injury, the inconvenience occasioned by multiplication of *siap* bundles puts a limit to their number. Nevertheless a man who possesses private *siap* will carry it with him attached to the sheath of his sword; and in most houses special hooks are provided for the hanging up of swords so embellished.

There are, however, many instances of specialised *siap*. A man specially devoted to hunting with the blow-pipe will have a special blow-pipe *siap* tied to his quiver (this is especially common among Punans). He will dip this *siap* in the blood of every animal he kills, until it becomes thickly encrusted, and its virtue proportionately increased. Another special kind is one which ensures a man against hurt from fire-arms, through causing any gun aimed at him to missfire.

A curious object occasionally seen in Iban houses is the *Empugau*. This is a blackened bundle hung in a basket among the heads above the hearth. It is covered with the smoke and soot of ages, and though it is generally claimed as the property of some one man who has inherited it from his forefathers, even he knows nothing of its history and composition, and is unwilling to examine it closely. It is regarded by the Ibans as the head of some half-human monster. After careful examination of a number of specimens I discovered that the *empugau* consists of a large cocoa-nut in its husk, tricked out with a rude face mask having part of the fibrous husk combed out to look like hair. The Ibans regard it with some awe, and it seems probable that it has formerly played some part in magical procedures.

Love charms are used by most of the peoples, though the Kayans and Kenyahs are exceptions, since they prefer to rely chiefly upon the power of music and personal attractions. These charms are in almost all cases strongly odorous substances. The Iban youth strings together a necklace of strongly scented seeds known as *buah balong*. This he generally carries about with him, and, if he takes a fancy to a girl, he places it under her pillow, or endeavours to persuade her to wear it about her neck. If she accepts it, he reckons her half won.

Klemantans, among whom love charms go by the generic name *sangkil*, make use of a variety of these, one of the most common being a scented oil that they contrive to smuggle on to the garments or other personal property of the woman.

The Ibans use charms to ensure success in trapping wild animals. The trapper carries a stick, one end of which is carved to represent the human form. He uses this to measure the appropriate height for the wooden spear which springs these traps when set for animals of different heights, such as a deer or a pig.

Sir Charles Brooke, G.C.M.G., 2nd Rajah of Sarawak, who reigned
from 1868–1917.

PART VI

MORALS AND MENTALITY

Collective consciousness and responsibility—Serious offences rare—
Innate superiority of Kayans and Kenyahs—Crime and punishment
—Incest—Homicide—Suicide—Minor crimes—Modesty of Kayans
—Right and wrong—Religion and conduct—Individual great men—
Desire for peace and friendship—Laki Avit, Tama Bulan, and Tama
Kuling—Death and disease—Bornean mentality—Numerals—
Mensuration—Distances—Local topography—Physical phenomena—
Veracity—Difficulties of the *Penghulu*—General conclusion.

I HAVE said that among the Kayans the immediate
criterion of all actions and of judgments is custom, and
that the sanction of custom is generally supported by
the fear of the *toh* and of the harm they may inflict upon
the whole house. The principle of collective or communal responsibility thus recognised in face not only of
the other communities, but even of the spiritual powers,
gives each individual an interest in the good behaviour
of his fellows, and at the same time develops in him the
sense of obligation towards his community. The small
size of each polity, its clear demarcation by its residence
under a single roof, its subordination to a single chief, and
its hitherto perpetual conflict and rivalry with other
neighbouring communities of similar constitution, are
other circumstances which also make strongly· for the
development in each of its members of a strong collective
consciousness, that is to say, of a clear recognition of the
community and of his place within it and a strong sentiment of attachment to it. The attachment of each individual to such an organism is also greatly strengthened by
the fact that it is hardly possible for him to leave it, even

255

if he would. He cannot hope to maintain himself alone, or as the head of an isolated family, against the hostile forces, natural and human, that threaten him; and it is most difficult for him to gain admittance to any other community.

It is only when we consider these facts that we can understand how smoothly the internal life of the community generally runs, how rarely serious offences are committed, how few are the quarrels and cases of insubordination against the chief, and how tact and good sense can rule the house without the infliction of any punishment other than fines and compensatory payments.

Yet, when all these circumstances have been taken into account, the orderly behaviour of a Kayan community must be in part regarded as evidence of the innate superiority of character in the Kayans. For though the Ibans, Klemantans, and Muruts live under very similar conditions, they do not attain the same high level of social or moral conduct. Among the Muruts there is much drunkenness and consequent disorder, and the same is true in a less degree of the Ibans: among them and some of the Klemantan tribes quarrels within the house are of frequent occurrence, generally over land, crops, fruit trees, or other property. These quarrels are not easily composed by the chiefs, and frequently lead to the splitting up of a community, or to the migration of the whole house with the exception of one troublesome member and his family, who are left in inglorious isolation in the old building.

The higher level of conduct of the Kayans is, however, in many respects rivalled by that of the Kenyahs, and some importance must therefore be attributed to the one prominent feature of their social organisation which is peculiar to these two peoples, namely, the clearly marked stratification into three social strata between which but little intermarriage takes place. This stratification undoubtedly makes for a higher morality throughout the peoples among which it obtains; for the members of the highest class

The Miri Petroleum field, showing derricks on the top of the hill.

Tanks, workshops, and other buildings of the Sarawak Oilfields, Ltd., at the mouth of the Miri river.

Oil wells at Pujut, Miri river district.

are brought up with a keen sense of their responsibility towards the community, and their example and authority do much to maintain the standards of conduct of the middle and lower classes.

I have said that almost all offences are punished by fines only. Of the few offences which are felt to require a heavier punishment, the one most seriously regarded in the past is incest. For this offence, which is held to bring grave peril to the whole house, especially the danger of starvation through failure of the rice-crop, two punishments were in former times customary. If the guilt of the culprits was flagrant, they were taken to some open spot on the river bank at some distance from the house. There they were thrown together upon the ground and a sharpened bamboo stake was driven through their bodies, so that they remained pinned to the earth. The bamboo, taking root and growing luxuriantly on this spot, remained as a warning to all who passed by; and, needless to say, such a spot is even to-day looked on with horror by all men. The other method of punishment was to shut up the offenders in a strong wicker cage and to throw them into the river. This method was resorted to as a substitute for the former, owing to the difficulty of getting anyone to play the part of executioner and to drive in the stake, for this involved the shedding of the blood of tribesmen.

The variety of incest most commonly committed is that of a man with an adopted daughter, and (possibly on account of its frequency) is the kind which is most strongly reprobated. It is obvious also that this form of incest requires a specially strong check in any community in which the adoption of children is a common practice, since, in the absence of severe penalties, a man might be tempted to adopt female children in order to use them as concubines. Support for this view may be found in the fact that intercourse between a youth and his adopted sister is allowed and is not regarded as incest, and the relationship is not regarded as any bar to marriage.

s

The punishment of the incestuous couple does not suffice to ward off the danger brought by the crime upon the community. The household must be purified with the blood of pigs and fowls; the animals used are the property of the offenders or of their family; and in this way a fine is imposed.

When any calamity threatens or falls upon a house, especially such a rising of the river as may threaten the house or the tombs of the household, the Kayans are led to suspect that incestuous intercourse in their own or in neighbouring houses has taken place; and they look round for evidences of it, and sometimes detect a case which otherwise would have remained hidden.

All the other peoples also, except the Punans, formerly punished incest with death. Among the Ibans the most common form of incest is that between a youth and his aunt, and this is regarded at least as seriously as any other form. It must be remembered that, owing to the frequency of divorce and remarriage among this tribe, a youth may quite commonly find himself in the position of step-son to half a dozen or more divorced step-mothers, some of them perhaps of his own age, and that each of them may have several sisters, all of whom are reckoned as his aunts; he has therefore to remember his family tree, and the loppings of the same.

Kayans, as we have seen, have no scruple in shedding the blood of their enemies, but they seldom, if ever, go to war with other Kayans; and the shedding of Kayan blood by Kayans is of rare occurrence. To shed human blood in the house, even that of an enemy, is against custom. When, however, a case takes place, if two or more men have deliberately attacked another and slain him, or one has killed another by stealth, the guilty party would in former times have been made to pay very heavy compensation to relatives, the amount being graded according to the social status and wealth of the culprit; the fine might equal, in fact, the whole of his property and more besides; and he might, in order to raise the amount, have to sell himself into slavery to another, slavery being the only equivalent of imprisonment. The relatives would probably desire to kill the murderers; but the chief would generally restrain them, and would find his task rendered easier by the fact that, if they insisted on taking the murderer's life, they would forfeit their right to compensation. This would not be always true of similar cases among Ibans, among whom the fine paid to the house or chief would be heavier in proportion to the rank of the murdered man. But there are cases in which chiefs have, with the approval of the house, had a murderer put to the sword. A criminal who has paid compensation has, however, by no means set himself right with the household, but they continue to look askance at him. Cases of murder by a Kayan of a member of another house are adjudged by the chief of the guilty party.

"Running amok" is not unknown among Kayans, though it is very rare. If a man in this condition of blind fury kills anyone, he is cut down and killed, unless he is in the house; in which case he is knocked senseless with clubs, carried out of the house into the jungle, and there executed.

Suicide is strongly reprobated, and, as has been seen, the ghosts of those who die by their own hands are believed to lead a miserable and lonely existence in a distressful country, Tan Tekkan, in which they wander picking up mere scraps of food in the jungle. Nevertheless, suicides occur among Kayans of both sexes. The commonest occasion is the enforced separation of lovers, rather than the despair of the rejected. I have known of two instances of Kayan youths who, having formed attachments during a long stay in a distant house, and then, finding themselves forced to return home with their chief and unable to arrange marriage with their mistresses, have taken their lives. The method most commonly adopted is to go off alone into the jungle and there to stab a knife into the carotid artery. The body of a suicide is generally buried without ceremony on the spot where it is found. Suicides of women are rarer than those of men, desertion by a lover being the usual cause.

As regards minor crimes, it may be said that dishonesty in the form of pilfering or open robbery by violence is, in spite of obvious temptations, of rare occurrence. Fruit trees on the river bank, even at some distance from any village, are generally private property, and offer a great temptation to passing crews when their fruit is ripe; however, the rights of the proprietor are usually respected or compensation voluntarily paid. Theft within the house or village is practically unknown. Even before European government was established, Malay and Chinese traders could securely penetrate with boat-loads of goods far into the interior; and now such enterprises are regularly and frequently undertaken. Occasionally a trader establishes himself in a village for months together, driving a profitable trade in hardware, cloth and tobacco, travelling usually in a small boat with a crew of only two or three men, and being practically defenceless against any small party of the natives who might choose to rob or murder them. Such traders have in the past now and again been robbed, and sometimes even murdered, by roving bands of Ibans, but I know of no such act committed by Kayans or Kenyahs. The trader puts himself under the protection of a chief and feels that his life and property are safe.

In the matter of veracity it would not be true to say that the Kayans or any of the other peoples are always strictly truthful. In describing any event they are given to exaggeration, and their accounts are apt to be strongly biassed in their own favour. Nevertheless, deliberate lying is a thing to be ashamed of, and a man who gets himself a reputation as a liar is regarded with small favour by his fellows.

The Kayans, as I have said elsewhere, are not coarse

of speech, and both men and women are strictly modest in respect to the display of the body. Though the costume of both sexes is so scanty, the proprieties are observed. The bearing of the women is habitually modest, and though their single garment might be supposed to afford insufficient protection, they wear it with a skill that compensates for the scantiness of its dimensions; they bathe naked in the river before the house, but they slip off their aprons and glide into the water so deftly and swiftly, and on emerging they resume their garments with such skill, that the most exacting could not take offence. The same is true of most of the other tribes, with the exception of some of the men of Kenyah and Klementan communities that inhabit the central highlands; these, when hauling their boats through the rapids, will divest themselves of all clothing, or without the least embarrassment will sit naked round a fire while their waist-cloths are being dried.

It is difficult to find Kayan words that can properly be translated as Justice or Injustice; yet it is obvious that they view just conduct with approval and unjust with the reverse. The word *tekap* is nearest to our " just," but it is of more general application, and may be applied to any situation which evokes a judgment of moral approval; for example, on witnessing any breach of custom or infringement of some restriction a Kayan will say *nusi tekap* (" it is not right "); *tekap* meaning, roughly, " seemly " or " appropriate."

Specialised terms for moral qualities are, however, not lacking. The ruling of a just and wise chief would be said to be *tenang*; but this word implies less purely a moral quality than our word justice, and more an intellectual capacity : the word is especially applied to describe the quality of a political speech which meets with approval. The word *haman* means skilful or cunning, capable both physically and intellectually. A man who fights pluckily is said to be *makang*, and the same word is applied to any bold or dashing feat, such as crossing a river when it is dangerously swollen. To disregard omens is likewise *makang*; so that the word seems also to carry an implication of rashness.

Saioh means good in the sense of kindly or affable. *Jaak* is bad in the senses (1) of a poor crop, (2) an unfortunate occurrence, or (3) a sore foot, and conveys no moral flavour. Morally bad is generally expressed by the word *sala*; this is used in the same sense in Malay and may well be a recently-adopted word. In general the language seems to be very poor in terms expressive of disapproval, adverse judgments being generally expressed by putting *nusi*, the negative, before a word of positive import; thus a cowardly act or man would be denounced as *nusi makang*.

It is probably true to say that, although they thus distinguish the principal qualities of character and conduct with appropriate concrete terms, they have no abstract terms for either virtues or vices.

Religious beliefs seem to have only this much influence on the moral conduct of the Kayans, that the fear of the *Toh* serves as a constant check on the breach of salutary and essential customs; this fear does, however, at least serve to develop in the people a certain self-control and the habit of deliberation before action. The part which the more powerful spirits are supposed to play in bringing about or warding off the worse kinds of calamity remains extremely vague and indefinite; but, in the main, faithful observation of the omens, of rites, and of custom generally seems to secure the favour of the gods, and, to an extent, their protection; and so far religion makes for morality. Except, however, in such conduct as is definitely prescribed by custom and tradition, its influence seems to be negligible, and the marked high standard of the Kayans in neighbourliness, in mutual help and consideration, in honesty and forbearance, seems to be maintained without the direct support of their religious beliefs.

The high moral level attained by individuals among Kayans and Kenyahs, and less frequently Klemantans and Ibans, is best exemplified by the enlightened and public-spirited conduct of some of the principal chiefs. It might have been expected that the leading chiefs of warlike and conquering peoples like the Kayans and Kenyahs, which, until the advent of European governments, had never encountered any resistance which they could not break down by armed force, would have been wholly devoted to conquest and rapine ; and that a chief who had acquired prestige and found himself able to secure the adhesion in war of a number of other chiefs and their followers would have been inspired with a mere lust of conquest. But though some of them have shown tendencies of this kind, there have been notable exceptions who have recognised that mutual hostility and distrust, such as had always been chronic in the relations between the various tribes and villages, were an unmixed evil. Such men have used their influence tactfully and persistently to establish peaceful relations between the tribes. Unlike some savage chieftains of warrior tribes in other parts of the world, such as some of those produced by the fine Bantu race, or those who established the great confederation of the Iroquois tribes, they have not sought merely to bring about a federation of all of their own stock in order to dominate over or to exterminate all other tribes. They have rather pursued a policy of reconcilement and conciliation, aiming at establishing relations of friendship and confidence between races of a wide diversity. Some fifty years ago one such powerful Kenyah chief of the Baram district, Laki Avit, had earned a high reputation for such states-manship before the district was incorporated in the Raj of Sarawak. His policy was to bring about intermarriages between the families of the chiefs and upper-class people of the various tribes. A leading chief of the same district at a later time, Tama Bulan, spared no efforts to bring about friendly meetings between chiefs of different tribes,

for the purpose of making peace and of promoting intercourse and mutual understanding. Such peace-making
ceremonies are generally of lasting effect, the oaths taken
being respected by succeeding generations. Among the
Kenyahs of Dutch Borneo, Tama Kuling pursued a
similar enlightened and spontaneous policy.

Death, it has been said, is not recognised by savages as a
natural process, but attributed either to violence or black
magic. This is not true, at least, of the Kayans; few, if
any, deaths are ascribed by them to the efforts of sorcerers.
Natural death is recognised as inevitable in old age, and
disease is vaguely conceived as the effect of natural causes;
though as to what those natural causes are they have no
definite ideas. Their attitude of doubt is shown by their
readiness to make use of European drugs and of remedies
for external application, quinine for fever, and sulphate of
copper for the treatment of sores, being most in demand.
Again, since cholera and smallpox are the great epidemic
diseases which periodically have ravaged large areas of
Borneo, they recognise that both these diseases spread up-
stream from village to village, and that to abstain from
intercourse with all villages lower down the river and to
prevent anyone coming up-stream contributes to their
immunity. With this intention, the people living on a
tributary stream commonly fell trees across its mouth or
lower reaches so as to block it completely to the passage
of boats, or, as a less drastic measure, will stretch a rope
of rattan from bank to bank as a sign that no one may
enter. Such a sign is generally respected by the inhabitants of other parts of the river-basin. They are aware also
of the risk of infection that attends the handling of the
body of one who has died of an epidemic disease, and
attempt to minimise it by throwing a rope around the
corpse and dragging it to the graveyard, and there burying
it in a shallow grave in the earth, without touching it with
the hands.

The mentality of the Bornean is curious and attractive.

Few or no Kayans can state their age without going through some preliminary calculations, and even then their statements are apt to be vague. A Kayan or Iban mother can generally work out the age of each of her children on request; but, to do so, she puts down in a row bits of leaf or stick, one for each year, working back from the present, and recalling each year by the name of the place where the rice-crop of that year was raised. When she reaches back to the year of the birth of any one of her children, she says that the child was born about the time of this particular harvest, and by counting the pieces of stuff laid down she then arrives at the child's age.

An elderly man, likewise, can generally make no more accurate statement regarding his age than that at the time of the great eclipse of the Sun he had just begun to wear a waist-cloth; or he may say that when the great guns were heard (*i.e.* the sound of the eruption of Krakatoa in 1883) he was just beginning " to look for tobacco."

Bornean numerals are very much like those prevalent in the rest of Indonesia, although most of the tribes use very few of the numbers beyond ten. In counting any objects that cannot be held in the hand or placed in a row, the Kayan (and most of the other peoples) bends down one finger for each object enumerated, beginning with the little finger of the right hand, passing at six to that of the left hand, and from there to the big toe of the right foot, and lastly to the left foot. When the tally has been made up, he holds the toe reached until he or someone else has worked out the number; if the number was, say, seventeen, he would keep hold of the second toe of the left foot until he had counted up the number implied by that toe, either by counting or by adding together five, five, five, and two; except that when the count ends on the little toe of the left foot, he knows at once that the number is twenty. If a larger number than twenty is to be counted, as when, for example, a chief has to pay tax for each door of his house, he calls in the aid of several men, who sit before him. One of these makes the tally on his fingers and toes while the chief calls the roll of the heads of the rooms; after twenty, a second man begins on his fingers, the first continuing to hold on to all his toes. To complete the count a third or a fourth man may be used.

The door-tax for a house is two dollars for each door; but, in paying it, a chief does not count the doors and then multiply the number by two : he simply lays down two dollars for each door and pays in the lot, generally without knowing the total. If a chief were told to pay in the tax for half his doors only, he possibly would not know how to carry out the instruction. Subtraction is accomplished only in the most concrete manner, *e.g.* if a man wished to take away eight from twenty-five, he would count out twenty-five of the objects in question, or of bits of leaf or stick, then push away eight and count up the remainder.

It will thus be seen that the arithmetical operations of the Kayans are of an extremely concrete character and are practically confined to addition; those of the other tribes are similar, except that many of the Klemantans get confused over simple counting.

Tama Bulan, the Kenyah chief, obtained and learnt the use of an abacus from a Chinese trader, and used it effectively; and although his case is held to be an exception, and although the Borneans are considered to be incapable of cyphering, there seems to be no good reason to doubt that most of the peoples could be taught to use figures as readily as the average European; those children who have entered the schools seem to pick up arithmetic with a reasonable rapidity.

The Iban often deposits sums of money with Government officers, and is quite well aware of the amount paid in; but when he withdraws his deposit he generally expects to receive the identical dollars paid in.

In the matter of mensuration, the Kayans use two

principal standards of length, namely, the *buka* and the *buhak*. The former is the length of the span from finger-tip to tip of outstretched arms; the latter is the length of the span from the tip of the thumb to the tip of the first finger of the same hand. In buying a pig, for example, the price is determined by the number of *buhak* required to encircle its body just behind the forelegs. The half *buka* is also in general use, especially in measuring rattans cut for sale, the required length of which is two and a half *buka* (or fifteen feet). In order to express the half, they have adopted the Malay word *stingah*, having no word of their own.

Distances between villages are always expressed in terms of the average time taken by a boat in ascending the stream from the one to the other. Distances by land are expressed still more vaguely; for example, the distance between the heads of two streams may be expressed by saying that, if you bathed in one, your hair would still be wet when you reached the other (this means about one hour); or a longer distance, by saying that if you started at the usual time from one of the places you would reach the other when the sun was as high as the circling hawk (which means a journey of about four hours, that is, from sunrise to about 10 a.m.), or when the sun was overhead (*i.e.* at noon), or when it was declining (about 3 p.m.), or when the sun was put out (sunset), or when it was dark (a few minutes later).

In order to describe the size of a solid object such as a fish, a Kayan compares its thickness with that of some part of his body, the forearm, the calf of the leg, the thigh, head, or waist. In describing the thickness of the subcutaneous fat of a pig, he makes his calculations by finger-breadths.

Of local topography and the general features of the district an intelligent Kayan can give a fairly good general description. To do this he will map out the principal features on a smooth surface by placing pieces of stick to represent the rivers and their tributaries, and other pieces of stick or leaf to represent the hills and mountains; he will pay special attention to the relations of the sources of the various streams. In this way a Kayan chief of the Baram can construct a tolerably accurate map of the whole Baram district, putting in Brunei and *Usun Apo* and the heads of the Rejang, Batang Kayan, Tuto, Tutong, and Balait rivers. He knows that all the rivers run to the sea, though few Kayans have seen the sea or, indeed, been outside the basin of their own river, for to have been to another river, or to have seen the sea, is a just ground of pride. He does not know that Borneo is an island, though he knows that the Europeans and the Chinese come from over the sea; he will confidently assert that the sea is many times larger than his river, even ten times as large. He seems, indeed, to regard the sea as a big river of which their main river is a tributary, and foreigners as living on the banks of rivers much like his own.

The Kayans do not observe the stars and their movements for practical purposes, but they are familiar with the principal constellations, and have fanciful names for them, and relate mythical stories about the personages they are supposed to represent. The Klemantans, who seem to have paid no attention to the planets, have more such myths; but, curiously, the stars are regarded as small holes in the floor of another and brighter world, through which the roots of plants have penetrated.

The sky they regard as a dome which meets the earth on every hand, this limiting zone being spoken of as the edge of the sky; but they have no notion how far away this edge may be; they recognise that, no matter how many days one travels in any one direction, one never gets appreciably nearer to it, and conclude, therefore, that it must be very distant. They understand that the clouds are very much less distant than the sky, and that they merely float about the earth. Neither sun nor moon seems to be regarded as animated.

Two total eclipses of the sun have occurred in Borneo

in the last century. These, naturally, caused much excitement and some consternation. The second occurred during my residence in the Baram district, when the alarm of the people was largely prevented by the issue to all the chiefs of tallies foretelling the date of its incidence. Nevertheless, one woman, at least, was so much frightened by the spectacle that she ran into her house and dropped down dead.

In general, it may be said that in Borneo, as elsewhere where man has had to make provision, even for his mere animal needs, against the hardness of Nature, a speculative spirit is found, inquiring as to the causes of various phenomena. Conventional answers may be given ; but to the keener-minded and younger men there is little satisfaction in convention : they ponder over the deepest questions and, from time to time, discuss them among themselves. A common question among the Kayans is, " Why do not the dead return ? " or (perhaps), " Why are the dead only visible in dreams ? " The meeting of dead friends in dreams generally leaves the Kayan doubtful whether he has really seen his friend ; and he tries, therefore, to obtain evidence of the reality of the *revenant* by prayer and by looking for a favourable answer in the liver of a pig, the entrails of a fowl, or in the behaviour of the omen-birds. He argues that persons who have been much attached to their relatives and friends would surely return to visit them frequently if such return were at all possible.

Curiously unrelated questions, commonly put, are those as to the whereabouts of the home of Europeans, and how long is spent on the journey thither. On the other hand, Tama Bulan once raised the question of the motion of the sun, and having been told that really the earth revolves and that the sun only appears to move round it, he argued that this could hardly be, since we see the sun move every day. For a long time he said nothing more on this topic, but it continued to occupy his mind ; and after a period which definitely amounted to years, he recurred to it and announced that he now accepted the once incredible doctrine, because he had inquired concerning it of every European he had met, and all had given him the same answer.

Like all other varieties of mankind (some few savage tribes perhaps excepted), the Bornean is apt to distort the truth in his own favour, in describing from memory incidents seriously affecting his interests. When a party has allowed itself to commit some reprehensible action, such as over-hasty and excessive reprisals, a whole village, or even several villages, may conspire together more or less deliberately to " frame up " some plausible version of the affair so as to excuse or justify the act in the eyes of the Government. It is a case like this that calls for all the tact and patience of a good *Penghulu*. He will send for those immediately concerned and patiently hear out their version of the incident. If it departs so widely from the known truth that he will find reason to suspect the whole story, he will not charge the parties with untruthfulness, or attempt to extort the truth by threats or bullying (as is done sometimes in more highly civilised courts) ; instead, he keeps silence, shrugs his shoulders, and tells them to go away and think it over, and to come back again at another time with a better story. In the meantime he hears the version of some other group, who view the affair from a different angle, and thus puts himself in a position to modify the revised version of the first group. When he has in this way gathered in a variety of accounts of the incident, he finds himself in a position to construct, by a process of judicial triangulation, an approximately correct survey ; this he now lays before the party immediately concerned, who, seeing that their theory is no longer accepted, will often fill in details and supply minor corrections. Throughout this process the tactful *Penghulu* never shuts the door upon his informants or tries to pin them down to their words, or make them take them back ; rather he keeps the whole story fluid and shifting, so that,

The Residency at Claudetown, in the Baram District.

Wireless station at Kuching, the capital of Sarawak.

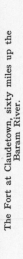

The Fort at Claudetown, sixty miles up the Baram River.

Government Dispensary at Kuching, with some Government Offices in the background.

when the true account has been constructed, the witnesses
are not made to feel that they have lost their self-respect.

It has often been attempted, sometimes in influential
quarters, to exhibit the mental life of savage peoples as
profoundly different from our own ; to assert that they act
from motives, and reach conclusions by means of mental
processes so utterly different from ours that we cannot hope
to interpret or understand their behaviour unless we can
first, by some impossible, or, at least, by some hitherto
undiscovered method, learn the nature of these mysterious
mental activities.   To apply to the savage peoples of the
interior of Borneo such a fantastic theory, I should char-
acterise a delusion natural to the anthropologist who has
studied his subject in the aloofness of a London club.
Indeed, the more intimately one becomes acquainted
with these barbaric tribes, the more fully does one realise
the close similarity of their mental processes to one's own.
Their primary impulses and emotions seem to be in all
respects like ours.   It is true that they are very unlike
the typical Civilised Man of some of the older philosophers,
whose every action proceeded from an algebraic calculation
of the pleasures and pains to be derived from alternative
lines of conduct ; but we ourselves are equally unlike that
purely mythical personage.   The Kenyah or the Iban
often acts on impulse and in ways which by no means
conduce to further his best interests or deeper purposes ;
but so do we also.   The " Practical Syllogism " of the
Kenyahs and Kayans often works out differently from ours ;
but are we entirely certain that we are always right ?

Let us now see how these divergent tribes have been
eventually brought with their own consent and with the
minimum of armed force from savagery into the category
of civilisation and good government, in which they themselves play an active part.   From the earliest days of the
history of Sarawak under its white Rajahs, the direct administration has been in the hands of the Rajah himself
assisted by the heir-apparent.   In the absence of the

Rajah, or his deputy, the charge of affairs is vested in a Committee of Administration, consisting of the senior officers of the Civil Service. The country is divided into five Divisions, each of which is presided over by a Resident assisted by an adequate staff of District Officers and others representing the various branches of the Service. The Central Administration is located at Kuching, which is the capital of Sarawak, but each Division has its own Administrative centre, at which the Resident has his head-quarters, and from which he controls the work of the District Officers within his Division.

In 1923, after a lapse of sixty years, the title of Chief Secretary was revived. His duties are to co-ordinate and supervise matters of administrative detail common to the whole Service, to submit to the Rajah the more important questions affecting the Divisions and technical departments, and to see that the decisions of the Rajah and Government Orders are carried out. The usual public services are represented by Departments—the Treasury, Lands, Surveys, Forestry, Trade, Municipal, Customs.

An Advisory Council holds its meetings in the Sarawak Government Offices at Millbank House, Westminster, where all the Agency business of the Government in England is also conducted. The first Rajah had the responsibility of introducing law and order among the various tribes, and the second Rajah carried on this work during his long reign with admirable tact and thoroughness. The present Rajah, during his period of control, has continued in the paths of his predecessors, with, if possible, more active progress and development in accordance with the demands of the time. He has reorganised the public services in co-operation with his officers and brought the administration of the territory into the forefront of efficiency. The delicacy of the task can be understood from a perusal of the preceding chapters, which show the different customs and habits of the tribes, and the former fighting characteristics of the people and the constant internal strife.

The principles according to which the Government has been conducted cannot be better expressed than in the words of the late Rajah, Sir Charles Brooke, when he said that a Government such as that of Sarawak may " start from things as we find them, putting its veto on what is dangerous or unjust, and supporting what is fair and equitable in the usages of the natives, and letting system and legislation wait on occasion." So the secret of success was found in adapting and improving all that was good in the existing usages of the natives, without indiscriminate destruction of ancient customs. When new wants were felt, the Government has examined and provided for them by measures made rather on the spot than imported from abroad ; and to ensure that these should not be contrary to native customs, care is taken to consult the people before they are put into force.

The prime duty of the Resident in his Division and the District Officer in his District is to preserve order and to punish crimes of violence. For this purpose there is a small but effective body of native soldiers and police under the charge of European officers. The military force, which is called the Sarawak Rangers, has its head-quarters in the fort at Kuching, with small detachments located at each of the principal out-stations in the country. The police are similarly stationed, but they are generally recruited from the area in which they serve. It is quite remarkable that so small a body of men should exercise control over such a large and widely scattered population, but this result has been attained only by a carefully considered policy by which the people and their chiefs are constantly kept in touch with the Administrators by sympathy and consultation. In this way the co-operation of the people has been obtained in the government of the country, and the leading chiefs and influential men have thus been harnessed into the work of progress and responsibility. It is really one of the romances of central and local administration that

T

European officers, under a wise and benign autocracy, should have by the least possible interference with the customs and even superstitions of fierce and barbaric tribes enlisted their hearty support in the work of peaceful administration and development. Law and order now generally prevail, natural resources such as minerals and petroleum are being exploited, rapid progress has been made in education and public services, and a spirit of mutual trust and good-will established amongst tribes that a generation or two ago were deadly enemies.

Such are the tribes, and such the wonderful country they inhabit. In the course of a century they have been brought into the great world movements of the time, and the country has probably passed through more rapid and beneficial changes during this period than in all the recorded and the still greater number of unrecorded centuries of their history. To me personally the quarter of a century of my life which I have given to the service of the Rajah and of the people of Sarawak is replete with memories of gratitude and pride that my lot should have been cast in such pleasant places, and that I can recall not only the happiest recollections of my association with my fellow-officers, but also of such kindly feeling towards these remarkable tribes, to whom generally and individually I am indebted for so many acts of kindness and friendship. While I hope that I have been of service to the people, it is a pleasure to record that I have learned a great deal from them and from their simple and honest ways. It is indeed true, as Pope says, that

> " All are but parts of one stupendous whole,
> Whose body Nature is, and God the soul " ;

an organism self-dependent and self-sufficing.

INDEX

PRINTED IN GREAT BRITAIN BY RICHARD CLAY & SONS, LIMITED,
BUNGAY, SUFFOLK.

CAMBODIA

GEORGE COEDÈS
Angkor

MALCOLM MacDONALD
Angkor and the Khmers*

CENTRAL ASIA

ANDRÉ GUIBAUT
Tibetan Venture

PETER FLEMING
Bayonets to Lhasa

LADY MACARTNEY
An English Lady in Chinese
Turkestan

DIANA SHIPTON
The Antique Land

C. P. SKRINE AND
PAMELA NIGHTINGALE
Macartney at Kashgar*

ALBERT VON LE COQ
Buried Treasures of Chinese
Turkestan

AITCHEN K. WU
Turkistan Tumult

CHINA

All About Shanghai: A Standard
Guide

HAROLD ACTON
Peonies and Ponies

VICKI BAUM
Shanghai '37

ERNEST BRAMAH
Kai Lung's Golden Hours*

ERNEST BRAMAH
The Wallet of Kai Lung*

ANN BRIDGE
The Ginger Griffin

CHANG HSIN-HAI
The Fabulous Concubine*

CARL CROW
Handbook for China

PETER FLEMING
The Siege at Peking

MARY HOOKER
Behind the Scenes in Peking

CORRINNE LAMB
The Chinese Festive Board

W. SOMERSET
MAUGHAM
On a Chinese Screen*

G. E. MORRISON
An Australian in China

PETER QUENNELL
Superficial Journey through
Tokyo and Peking

OSBERT SITWELL
Escape with Me! An Oriental
Sketch-book

J. A. TURNER
Kwang Tung or Five Years in
South China

HONG KONG AND MACAU

AUSTIN COATES
City of Broken Promises

AUSTIN COATES
A Macao Narrative

AUSTIN COATES
Myself a Mandarin

AUSTIN COATES
The Road

The Hong Kong Guide 1893

INDONESIA

S. TAKDIR
ALISJAHBANA
Indonesia: Social and Cultural
Revolution

DAVID ATTENBOROUGH
Zoo Quest for a Dragon*

VICKI BAUM
A Tale from Bali*

'BENGAL CIVILIAN'
Rambles in Java and the Straits
in 1852

MIGUEL COVARRUBIAS
Island of Bali*

BERYL DE ZOETE AND
WALTER SPIES
Dance and Drama in Bali

AUGUSTA DE WIT
Java: Facts and Fancies

JACQUES DUMARÇAY
Borobudur

JACQUES DUMARÇAY
The Temples of Java

ANNA FORBES
Unbeaten Tracks in Islands of the
Far East

GEOFFREY GORER
Bali and Angkor

JENNIFER LINDSAY
Javanese Gamelan

EDWIN M. LOEB
Sumatra: Its History and People

MOCHTAR LUBIS
The Outlaw and Other Stories

MOCHTAR LUBIS
Twilight in Djakarta

MADELON H. LULOFS
Coolie*

MADELON H. LULOFS
Rubber

COLIN McPHEE
A House in Bali*

ERIC MJOBERG
Forest Life and Adventures in the
Malay Archipelago

HICKMAN POWELL
The Last Paradise

E. R. SCIDMORE
Java, The Garden of the East

MICHAEL SMITHIES
Yogyakarta: Cultural Heart of
Indonesia

LADISLAO SZÉKELY
Tropic Fever: The Adventures of
a Planter in Sumatra

EDWARD C. VAN NESS
AND SHITA
PRAWIROHARDJO
Javanese Wayang Kulit

MALAYSIA

ISABELLA L. BIRD
The Golden Chersonese: Travels
in Malaya in 1879

MARGARET BROOKE
THE RANEE OF
SARAWAK
My Life in Sarawak

HENRI FAUCONNIER
The Soul of Malaya

W. R. GEDDES
Nine Dayak Nights

A. G. GLENISTER
The Birds of the Malay Peninsula,
Singapore and Penang

C. W. HARRISON
Illustrated Guide to the Federated
Malay States (1923)

BARBARA HARRISSON
Orang-Utan

TOM HARRISSON
World Within: A Borneo Story

CHARLES HOSE
The Field-Book of a Jungle-Wallah

EMILY INNES
The Chersonese with the
Gilding Off

W. SOMERSET
MAUGHAM
Ah King and Other Stories*

W. SOMERSET
MAUGHAM
The Casuarina Tree*

MARY McMINNIES
The Flying Fox*

ROBERT PAYNE
The White Rajahs of Sarawak

OWEN RUTTER
The Pirate Wind

ROBERT W. SHELFORD
A Naturalist in Borneo

CARVETH WELLS
Six Years in the Malay Jungle

SINGAPORE

RUSSELL GRENFELL
Main Fleet to Singapore

R. W. E. HARPER AND
HARRY MILLER
Singapore Mutiny

JANET LIM
Sold for Silver

G. M. REITH
Handbook to Singapore (1907)

C. E. WURTZBURG
Raffles of the Eastern Isles

THAILAND

CARL BOCK
Temples and Elephants

REGINALD CAMPBELL
Teak-Wallah

MALCOLM SMITH
A Physician at the Court of Siam

ERNEST YOUNG
The Kingdom of the Yellow Robe

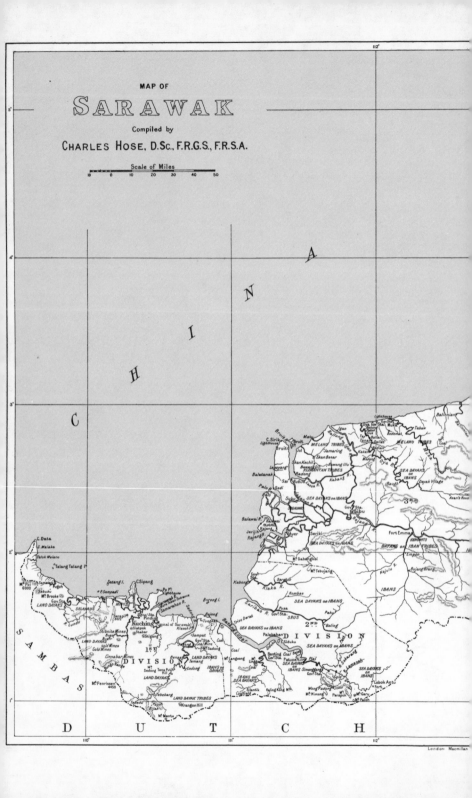

MAP OF

SARAWAK

Compiled by

CHARLES HOSE, D.Sc., F.R.G.S., F.R.S.A.

Scale of Miles